Items should be returned on or before the last date
shown below. Items not already requested by other
borrowers may be renewed in person, in writing or by
telephone. To renew, please quote the number on the
barcode label. To renew online a PIN is required.
This can be requested at your local library.
Renew online @ **www.dublincitypubliclibraries.ie**
Fines charged for overdue items will include postage
incurred in recovery. Damage to or loss of items will
be charged to the borrower.

Leabharlanna Poiblí Chathair Bhaile Átha Cliath
Dublin City Public Libraries

Dublin City
Baile Átha Cliath

Rathmines Branch Tel: 4973539
Brainse Ráth Maonas Fón: 4973539

Date Due	Date Due	Date Due

CRASH LANDING

An Inside Account of the Fall of GPA

CRASH LANDING

An Inside Account of the Fall of GPA

CHRISTOPHER BROWN ∿

Gill & Macmillan

Gill & Macmillan Ltd
Hume Avenue, Park West, Dublin 12
with associated companies throughout the world
www.gillmacmillan.ie

© Christopher P. Brown 2009
978 07171 4642 0

Index compiled by Cover to Cover
Typography design by Make Communication
Print origination by O'K Graphic Design, Dublin
Printed and bound in Great Britain by MPG Books Ltd,
Bodmin, Cornwall

This book is typeset in 12/15.5 pt Minion

The paper used in this book comes from the wood pulp
of managed forests. For every tree felled, at least one
tree is planted, thereby renewing natural resources.

A CIP catalogue record for this book is available from
the British Library.

5 4 3 2 1

For John Brown

CONTENTS

AUTHOR'S NOTE

So why this book now? Or rather, why update all the previous work for publication nearly two decades after my initial private literary scratchings in early 1990? In retrospect maybe I should have rushed the book out in the immediate aftermath of GPA's collapse, when the iron was hot. Surely that will be the first and general reaction —it would be mine. However potent reasons not to publish existed back in both November 1993 and April 1996—the two principal watershed dates—despite the attractions. In any event there were, certainly in late 1993, still significant issues to be worked out to their respective conclusions. Also, emotions were riding high—maybe too high for comfort. I certainly did not feel comfortable having the only contemporary account of the crash in my possession. Some corporate, if not personal or even official litigation was still a distinct possibility back then. Vested interests were real and possibly numerous. Too many people had too much to lose for an insider 'warts and all' exposition of the GPA story so quickly on the heels of GPA's demise. Billions of dollars were involved; enormous losses were sustained; senior downfalls occurred; careers were blighted; lives were changed. Lastly, maybe I owed GPA and my ex-colleagues some loyalty by keeping my observations of the previous years quiet at such a charged time—a loyalty overriding the considerations of those who would have welcomed the publication of information deriving from a relatively well-placed source within GPA itself. I therefore believe the overall interest has been served by the delay, as well as certain personal interests benefiting from a passage of time since the events this book relates.

Anyway, that reasoning or rationalising has maybe come at the expense of any continuing relevance or interest in the GPA debacle after such a long time. Why should the Irish or wider community have any enduring interest in porridge so cold as to verge on fossilised? Mischievously, coprolite springs to mind. Well, in defence of this volume, maybe History (with a capital 'H') demands. Secrets eventually come out; that is their nature. There lies the interest. This book presents an insider's view; no other has emerged. At the time, GPA's plight was probably the most engaging, massive corporate disaster story ever for the island, with reasonably dire consequences for well-known members of Irish society. The celtic tiger economy's first casualty of real note. The amounts involved even 15 years after are still boggling.

As always, there are enduring lessons to be gleaned from what happened. I may spell out some as we go along; the rest can be individually divined by the reader, each to his or her own. There will undoubtedly be testing times to come in the Irish and worldwide commercial aviation industry—what was achieved by GPA in the end may serve to encourage those involved next time around never to say die should they find themselves in similar mortal circumstance.

Some lessons, though, seem never to be learned, as human rapacity can hardly be overestimated. The present world economic crisis is a testament to but lightly bridled greed—both individual and threadbarely cloaked in the wider disguise of 'legitimate shareholder interests'. I cannot be alone in thinking over the last few years that the headlong progression of hedge funds and so-called synthetic finance in particular, wrapped in short-term bonus culture rather than valid security, was bound to take us sooner or late to the scene of a very nasty accident.

Whatever (and how the meaning of that word has changed in the interim), here is the tale. I hope you find it interesting, enlightening and salutary.

Christopher Brown
28 May 2009

| BACKGROUND 1975–1990

From very small beginnings in 1975, dividends began to take off ten years later as nascent commercial aircraft 'megalessor' Guinness Peat Aviation gradually acquired the wherewithal and the track record to buy and finance new airliners in numbers during the second half of the 1980s and put them out to airlines on innovative 'operating' leases.

However, back in 1975 the company comprised just a handful: Tony Ryan, Christy Ryan, Peter Ledbetter, Peter Swift, Sean Braiden, Billy Yeoman, all looked after by secretary Mary McCarthy. Operating at near shoestring levels, trying to chase down aviation deals anywhere in the world, one of the biggest problems was the sheer cost of flying. In the early days there were no preferential travel discounts, as were later arranged by Air Tara (initially the wet lease quasi-airline arm of GPA) with Aer Lingus and through that connection many other airlines for '50 per cent firm' travel—a guaranteed seat for half the normal fare in any class. Because funds were tight, 'rides' were bummed at every turn. A good GPA Christmas card might have had executives drawn standing hopefully at the end of a runway, thumbs out for Santa. From the start GPA enjoyed close links with Aer Lingus, where most of the staff had spent their earlier years in aviation. In fact, initially GPA more or less tried to pass itself off as Aer Lingus to achieve any sort of foothold with prospective airline customers. GPA would send SITAS—an industry-wide private system of telexing between airlines and at that time the quickest method of communication—requesting meetings etc. using the SITA address SNNGAEI. The tripart code breaks down as Shannon-Guinness Aviation-Aer Lingus.

The first real business was the provision of Boeing B737-200 aircraft on wet lease to Nigeria Airways. A wet lease meaning the supply of all or some of the flight crew, cabin staff, maintenance and insurance to an airline as well as the aircraft itself. By contrast, a dry lease was one where just the aircraft was supplied. A damp lease was ... well you can work that one out. In leasing parlance there could be varying degrees of dampness, depending.

The 1970s were still real fly by the seat of the pants times in most of Africa, as African State airlines began to acquire the fine skills needed to operate advanced technology jet aircraft with African flight crew members new to the task. Many developing countries were eager to replace expatriate aircrew with indigenous pilots to underline their advancing global status as represented by their respective sovereign airlines. Under the Air Tara banner, GPA provided very experienced, down-to-earth, mainly ex-Aer Lingus and ex-Air New Zealand captains on the flight deck, with Nigeria Airways providing the first officers, to fly the B737-200s on domestic and regional scheduled services. A story, probably apocryphal, which flavours the very earliest stage of training came from a GPA executive travelling on one of the leased-in aircraft from Lagos to Abuja on business. The aircraft being full of fare-paying passengers, GPA's man sat in the cockpit jump seat behind the Irish training captain, listening to him go through the pre-flight checklist and briefing. Having completed the checklist items, the captain painstakingly went through the intended progress of the flight from start-up to shutdown. He ended by very briefly explaining to the first officer, on his very first revenue-earning flight, exactly what he was expected to do throughout the entire sector. To confirm that the first officer fully understood his duties, the captain asked him to repeat them back to him. The first officer, not at all fazed by the instructions, confidently stated, 'Yes sir. I am to sit here and not touch a fucking thing.'

GPA spent several years in Nigeria training pilots and developing services, at the same time building up its business elsewhere, principally in Sri Lanka, where it played a major part in the early development of Air Lanka, the State airline.

The role of GPA was to enable an airline effectively to rent a modern aircraft for a precise period, with a relatively limited outlay of capital used as a deposit, paying the monthly rental and building up maintenance cost reserves out of revenue earned by the aircraft's operation. Rental periods varied but were mainly between one and five years. In theory there was usually a five year minimum period for new aircraft. Aircraft were expected to go out on serial leases throughout an estimated 25 year useful lifespan. It was a modern concept pioneered by GPA and its arch rival ILFC in the US and dubbed the operating lease. In those days, aircraft finance was rather unsophisticated by today's standards: generally it meant buying an aircraft, needing a 20 per cent cash deposit upfront, paying the balance, the interest and the lender's profit back over the next seven to ten years, while the aircraft was mortgaged to the lender—usually a bank. At the end of the period the aircraft would be paid for and the airline could acquire the aircraft for a nominal sum—it would then have ownership of a seven year old aircraft. This was known as a finance lease (vanilla flavour)—altogether an expensive outlay and an inflexible method for a youthful, developing airline with limited capital resources, not yet too sure of its market and prospects.

Apart from the significant financial differences between the two types of lease, there was an equally great philosophical difference between the respective lessors. Whereas a bank finance lessor would need relatively little aviation expertise as such, covering its downside risks by ensuring comfortable margins and refusing finance to untried borrowers without sufficient security for the loan, an operating lease lessor had to be less picky and much more hands on. The operating lease product could be inherently more risky at the user end—the security from each airline lessee was minimal, no fat margins for error. The user airline—the lessee—never acquired ownership. At the end of a lease it simply handed back the aircraft, whereupon the operating lessor would hope to be in a position to deliver the aircraft, without costly downtime, to its next lessee so that there would be no loss of revenue between leases. The operating lessor was itself on the hook with its own finance lenders who were financing the aircraft in the first place. A case of fleas and lesser fleas, and as we shall see, those fleas could bite.

So, it was one thing if British Airways needed an aircraft for a year on an operating lease to fill in a temporary gap in its otherwise owned fleet—the risk to the operating lessor would be negligible (as would the returns), but if a start-up, relatively undercapitalised airline wanted four brand spanking new aircraft straight off the production line for a new operation, the lessor had to have some idea of what it was getting into and keep itself abreast of its lessee's progress, competitive pressures and the market it served, throughout the lease term. This required aviation expertise of a high order on the part of the operating lessor. GPA possessed that vital expertise.

The operating lease also offered flexibility. Airlines, needing to be quick on their feet to respond to changing market situations, craved flexibility—to be able to tailor their enormously expensive fleets to demand relatively quickly, up or down, and to switch capacity and aircraft types. As a result, airlines were often prepared to pay more or accept an otherwise commercially less than perfect aircraft when conditions warranted, either to maximise their position or minimise downturns.

In an expanding commercial civil aviation industry the idea of the operating lease gradually took root, and GPA began to thrive. In the eighties, GPA became able to buy aircraft of its own—a milestone—the ability to leverage equity, acquire finance, take delivery of an aircraft and put it out on operating lease, acting as a principal. Whereas previously GPA had to stand between airlines with excess aircraft capacity and those requiring it, a matching process, adding bells and whistles as necessary to make a deal, now it could increasingly hawk its own aircraft stock. Commercial aviation is unfortunately beset by agents and intermediaries. Rarely, these can be the lubrication of the industry, but mainly tend to be the bane of existence: often corrupt, usually time wasting, hardly ever beneficial, in all shapes and sizes (and disguises), invariably attracting deep suspicion. The reason of course for all the agents is the high value nature of commercial aviation transactions. Even the smallest commission percentages can yield extraordinary returns if linked to multimillion dollar deals. Initially GPA had been of that ilk, surviving ferally, purely on its connections and wits—excellent training for what was to come.

Once GPA owned its aircraft, the scope for diversification of its services became greatly enlarged. It embarked upon trailblazing, sophisticated international financial products, mainly driven by tax considerations, as its Capital division grew and blossomed alongside the Leasing division within the organisation in Shannon.

For a while, between 1986 and mid-1992, Tony Ryan and his aircraft leasing creation, Guinness Peat Aviation, or GPA Group as it later became, were *the* Irish corporate success story. In Ireland only Tony O'Reilly, the chairman of Heinz Foods, seemed to enjoy greater personal standing.

Here was a rare homegrown, almost rags to riches saga, a self-made Tipperary entrepreneur from a lowly background leading the world from Shannon, itself a strong echo from transatlantic aviation's early glory days, in the impoverished West of Ireland.

Tony Ryan though had not settled in Shannon for sentimental reasons. To encourage local development in a depressed region, the airport and its immediate surrounds had been designated by the Irish Government as a tax-free zone. Coupled with other laws relating to the treatment of profits as tax-free dividends, it was a perfect financial climate for aircraft leasing and trading. Geographically too it suited Tony, being on Tipperary's doorstep, although accessing the outside world from Shannon could be a pain.

Tony's inspiration for setting up Guinness Peat Aviation was said to have come from his experiences as an Aer Lingus manager, tasked with leasing a B747-100 to Air Siam, now long defunct, in the early 1970s. He apparently saw the potential for shorter term aircraft leasing and, again it was said, with a borrowed $50,000 and the backing of Guinness Peat Bank, started out alone in 1975 with a select group of aviation industry stalwarts to help him.

I can still recall reading about the launch from my position within a leading British airline. Even then it had an air of quality, such was the calibre of the early few, fate's threads already spinning our paths to cross ten years later.

Eventually the figures involved in GPA's aviation business were like telephone numbers: orders for new aircraft in billions of dollars; billions more in banking facilities to pay for them; billions of public debt issued; annual revenues in the billions; net worth in excess of a billion, and so on.

From the very first, to incentivise the team, the GPA workforce was encouraged to buy shares and work tirelessly for profits to earn dividends from them, which were tax free. At that time the personal rate of income tax in Ireland was something like 58 per cent, so the benefit was significant.

Tony Ryan was a perilous individual, always goading his employees to greater efforts. The rollickings of executives, from top to bottom, were legendary, the subject of national newspaper articles. The whole country knew about the savage Monday morning meetings he used to chair in GPA House. This building was the company's headquarters—a modern, cube-shaped office block powerhouse, stuffed with modern Irish artworks, its blunt iconic outline prominent on the Shannon Airport development estate.

Thus from those modest beginnings in 1975, profits grew year on year until ten years later dividends began to rocket as GPA started to buy new aircraft in numbers in the mid-1980s and put them out on lease. GPA created a spate of dollar millionaires and multimillionaires, based on their incomes and shareholdings. Even amongst secretarial staff were some of the wealthiest people in western Ireland. However, those early joiners would never forget how hard it had been, the first ten years spent fighting for presence, for credibility—obtaining business by getting between the mouse and the cheese, as one was later to say. It had never been easy. Even as late as 1985/6 persuading Boeing to sell new aircraft to GPA had been a 'hell of a job'.

Tony Ryan eventually owned around 9 per cent of the company, having sold shares to first-rank global investors—among them the Prudential, General Electric Capital Corporation and the Long Term Credit Bank of Japan. His paper wealth at one time, during GPA's heyday, was estimated at over a quarter of a billion dollars. He received millions each year in tax-free share dividends. With dwellings in

Ireland, Ibiza, Monte Carlo and Mexico, he lived a life almost beyond the stuff of dreams.

As success arrived, GPA became awash with money. Amongst executive and management ranks it was everywhere. All the senior people and the early joiners had it. Everyone expected it. Many owed it as they leveraged for shares and yet more shares. One of the first executives borrowed money in 1976 at 21 per cent interest to buy shares and used the first seven years' dividends just to pay it off. At a time when the future of the company was by no means assured, his share loan was greater than his house loan. He was keenly aware that he had mortgaged his entire future, a huge risk. However, eventually when the boat did come in, his annual dividends easily topped $1m.

As the decade progressed through the 1980s, banks in Ireland were lending money to GPA staff members to buy shares on a non-recourse basis. In other words, if there was a default and the borrower could not repay the loan for any reason, the bank would simply take over the shares and forfeit any other means of trying to recover any outstanding balance of the loan (but not the interest, as it transpired) from the borrower. Such was the confidence of the financial community in Ireland in GPA at the time. The loans themselves were more than repaid out of the dividends, which kept climbing during the later 1980s at such a rate as to render a loan an easy burden relatively quickly.

My first experience of this was a loan arranged for me to buy 400 'A' Preference Shares for $80,000 in 1986 soon after my arrival. In later years some executives in the company, young and old, contracted bank loans way over $1 million, even for ordinary shares. The coveted 'A' Preference Shares, available only to Irish residents, rose from their original one dollar value to $650 per share at the height. Annual dividends per share eventually reached $275. Some people had thousands of them. Personal financial realities became thoroughly distorted by the scale of this largesse.

A thousand dollars? Small change. A hundred thousand? Doable. A million? Why not?

The projections, which had always been exceeded hitherto, were for more and more money coming in, unendingly into the future.

Commercial aviation was expanding everywhere, world fleets doubling and tripling in every industry long-range forecast. The larger the company became, the greater the figures and, wonderfully, the more solid and secure would the company become. It was a sure thing.

One looked at the trend of future dividends and tried to suppress a stupid grin. It was like sitting on a lottery where only you and your colleagues could win. It paid out every quarter.

Even though the tax breaks would be staged out over time, beginning in the early nineties, the introduction of tax would be compensated for by profitable growth.

It seemed impossible but it was real. The figures were there, incontrovertible. GPA had a viable business. This was no fly-by-night scheme. The company made huge profits. The staff participated. For anyone employed by GPA in an executive capacity and for the non-executive directors, it was simply the best financial opportunity in several lifetimes. It was unbelievable.

Tony Ryan put in place arguably one of the best company teams ever seen anywhere, ever. The board of GPA was studded with internationally renowned stars and captains of industry. The quality and strength in depth of the staff overall was unrivalled in their particular fields. The new trainees in their early and mid-twenties were Ireland's brightest and best, many coming from Trinity and UCD, with others attracted from success elsewhere by the prospects.

GPA was world class and getting better—the cream.

In hindsight, there was only one drawback—Tony himself. Even surrounded by such talent, he insisted on having his way in all things. GPA was 'his' company and 'his passion'.

Ultimately GPA's buck stopped at Tony's judgment.

GPA's founder, its greatest strength, was in retrospect its greatest weakness. Tony had far more chutzpah than was good for the company. Unfortunately it was generally seen as vision, drive, leadership, decisiveness, charisma and inspiration, based on GPA's track record. Even when he was demonstrably wrong, as in the case of the IPO share pricing, no one in GPA, prior to April 1993, ever stood up to him, with maybe one exception.

Tony Ryan's supergutsy ideas came to life on the back of the greatest global bull market the world had ever seen in the late 1980s, and died on the rack of the recession which followed.

All the company needed once it was on track was good management, not, as an outside celebrity board member was later to say, rocket science, to make sure that downside risks were covered. The healthy GPA that laid the fabulous golden eggs only required looking after. Instead it was treated as a *foie gras* goose and died a similar death, overstuffed, choked on assets it could not stomach.

GPA's greatest competitor, ILFC, based in Century City, Los Angeles, showed there was a right way to do it. Begun around the same time as GPA by two Hungarian Americans, it continues today as the world's longest existing, most successful aircraft leasing company, expanding intelligently with the industry, riding the downturns and earning its owners billions annually.

Despite its ultimate survival as a corporation, the GPA story is really a tragedy enacted against the backdrop of the world economic cycle.

In 1989 GPA announced a series of orders with the major aircraft and engine manufacturers for hundreds of new aircraft, on firm order and on option, worth some $15 billion in total, at that time the largest single batch of aircraft orders ever placed. To get some idea of the magnitude, expressed in 2009 dollars the orders would have been worth some $30 billion.

In the event, execution of those purchase contracts were the signatures on GPA's death warrant, the beginning of suicide by overdose. At best they were betting slips for the whole ranch—which would later be lost.

We all knew it was a huge step. Tony Ryan was insistent: GPA was headed for the stars.

Early action, if it had been taken in 1990, could have saved the day, probably, by renegotiating the orders and preparing for battle. But by then Tony was on 'Full Ahead'. The policy was to acquire available product, even fleets of used aircraft at enormous cost, each deal costing hundreds of millions of dollars, from United Airlines, from Egyptair and nearly from Gulf Air. There were no indications I could pick up that anyone seemed to see approaching disaster as a possibility.

That was when, during the first part of 1990, having been increasingly worried for some time, I started a private diary, specifically to record what I really feared would happen, knowing that if it did, the story would be worth telling. Whatever criticisms I may have to endure, at least the genuineness of my concerns at that time is proven—the diary is tangible evidence.

Earlier, in 1986, in my own particular area, I must admit I encouraged Tony to go for the new as yet uncertificated Fokker 100 jet, which I saw as a well built, Rolls Royce powered, modern technology successor to the prolific Douglas DC-9-30. Tony decided to order 50 firm and 50 option F100 aircraft to reduce the unit price and corner the market. As things turned out, only a fraction of that number were ever delivered. In respect of the F100, Juan O'Callaghan, Tony's strategic adviser at the time, was a kindly, graceful opponent. At around $16 million a copy, he said it was too expensive. He said we should stick to Boeing 737s. He was right.

But that was only part of it. GPA ordered A320s, MD-83s, B737s, widebodied aircraft, even MD-11s and other types including turboprops, in large numbers. Even if we had bought all Boeing 737s (not that we could have done, Boeing was already edgy at the numbers of its aircraft GPA had on order), it would have made no difference.

In the end it was sheer weight of numbers of aircraft being delivered and on order, because of the amount of equity and finance required to fund them, combined with the recession of the early 90s, which first prevented the public flotation in 1992 at its asking price and then effectively killed GPA in 1993, in practical terms, so far as the staff were concerned.

———

Reporting for duty in GPA in August 1985, I was immediately struck by the freewheeling attitude to travel. Instead of trying to control jaunts, everybody was positively encouraged to get out and about in the world.

Tony Ryan, prowling through an office midweek, would give short shrift to any marketeer without the best of reasons to be around.

The catch of course was that no one was expected to come back empty-handed. We had to 'bring back the bacon'. No one could hide. Tony would be there next Monday morning in Shannon acridly demanding results. To sit in one of those meetings as the responsible executive, with nothing to show, could be an excruciating experience.

The high cost of international air travel was strictly secondary to getting into the field: sitting with deals *in situ*, wherever that was. The GPA travel office at Shannon set up and co-ordinated all the travel requirements. It was an early centre of patient cheerful competence under non-stop pressure, a recurring GPA theme.

In those early middle days GPA was not so well known internationally. Neither was the operating lease concept. We had to spread both messages. Travel dominated our scene. Nothing worked like physical presence. Deals were constant but nothing like the scale of business which was to follow in a few short years.

We worked like one-armed paperhangers on speed. Life was work. As a marketeer you had to enjoy travelling or it would have been unbearable. I remember one August going twice around the world in successive weeks, west to east—the 'wrong' way round. By New York on the second lap I no longer knew where my body was in terms of its functions. I fell asleep over dinner in a restaurant in Little Italy during the main course, luckily only with a colleague. Whenever I awoke I had no idea where I was, or the time. If it was dark, I was completely disoriented.

A colleague recalled looking in his diary in 1986 and counting 200 flight sectors flown in the previous 180 days.

In general, travel just meant tiredness, but it was always countered by the excitement, the buzz, of long haul flying, of GPA. Ability to sleep soundly in an aircraft seat was the knack to survival. The era of lie flat seats I helped introduce had not yet arrived. Even now in a seat I can sleep restoratively for five minutes at a time.

In GPA I guess Jim King, Tony's shadow, was the king of travel. He was apparently impervious to jet lag and never seemed jaded whatever the journey. Both he and Tony always dressed immaculately, usually in bespoke double breasted suits, always with top pocket silk handkerchiefs overflowing showily.

When I became Shannon based in 1986 and moved my family over from Cambridge, UK, the second thing to really strike me, as we entered the community, was the importance locally of senior GPA people and the deference shown to us. Estate agents, shop staff, hotel staff, restaurants, taxi services, garages, riding stables, suppliers, all knew within a minute that you were GPA or a GPA wife and from then on nothing was too good. They all knew you had the means and you were part of the incredible ethos, the growing magic of GPA.

In the west of Ireland affluence was a rarity. The area in general was poor. Personal taxes were high, unemployment high, wages low and property values low in a sluggish market which regularly saw beautiful country homes languish for years unsold at what we regarded as ridiculously cheap prices. At this level GPA personnel were the market.

Limerick, the local city, was grey and cheerless under frequent rain clouds. In the few shops where quality items were sold, you were known by name. The only immediate comparison I can draw is Hollywood film stars shopping in Beverley Hills. O'Connell Street is a far cry from Rodeo Drive, but the attention was not.

GPA was a royal family. Above the recognition, we proceeded, secure in our cachet. I was a minor player compared to some of the others, although my title in those days as managing director and president of a newly formed GPA joint venture gave me and my wife access to the best social events. We missed far more than we attended due to the constant travelling.

More established senior staff and their wives were individually famous in the area and their names were dropped all over by non-GPA people for effect. This elite class grew larger over time and included all of what became, in my eyes, the Old Guard.

It took some getting used to.

I remember at the time discussing the phenomenon with my wife. We felt that most of the populace must probably really hate us swanning around in their faces in expensive cars, boats, light aircraft, even a flying boat. Lakeside at Lough Derg by Killaloe was the place to live in those days, usually with a house in Dublin as well. The disparity between us and the average person in Counties Clare or Limerick was so marked. We lived the life of Reilly; theirs the life of Murphy.

We were such an easily identifiable group—conspicuous consumers, high on GPA.

Later, when GPA's crystal world shattered, I could understand how much the rest of Ireland must be enjoying the crash. I am sure this longstanding groundswell of natural envy, the element of comeuppance, mixed with some feelings of loss at the downfall of an internationally successful Irish company, fuelled the intense national press coverage of GPA's problems.

Regrettably there was much arrogance in the company, especially in the upper echelons and later with some of the newly arrived young bloods.

There was certainly arrogance in the GPA manner of business, abrasive, combative, tough—Tony Ryan's house style. I remember being out for the day with my family on the *Coronado*, a luxurious yacht belonging to Rudi Bay, grand old man of Spanish aviation, cruising in the Bay of Palma. I was just about to join GPA and still thrilled with the opportunity. A fellow guest on board, a New York lawyer, told me in no uncertain terms that I was joining a 'bunch of bandits'. Coming from a Manhattan attorney that was some damnation.

In the years from 1985 to 1990, GPA grew like Topsy. It transformed from a small team into the slick Shannon machine known to every airline and financial institution in the world. The Trading Floor with its futuristic computer systems came into being; joint ventures proliferated; Capital Markets began to hum. The Technical, Finance, Corporate, Administrative, Legal, Insurance and IT divisions, the support services, all geared up. The turnover and profits took off. So did the dividends.

What follows is the diary I began when I thought it a worthwhile exercise to undertake. It is raw, full of hearsay and my musings. I have resisted the temptation to go back and clean up any of the entries. Obviously, therefore, some of my prophesies were wrong. It is written from my point of view and my point of vantage. I apologise for the inescapable egocentricity, but I was trying to give a flavour of what it was like to be on the inside, in Leasing/Marketing anyway. No one else has contributed to the account, because no one else was aware of what I was doing. Perhaps some of my surmising holds the stick by the wrong end. So be it. Often the mood is very sour and critical, but at the time that is how it was. It wasn't just me. I tried to reflect, at the time, the atmosphere, as well as what was happening. Overall, I think it is a fairly accurate account. To the extent I am mistaken, doubtless there will be many who will tell me so. All the entries were written on the days stated, or very nearly so. There are large time gaps between some entries; on the other hand the diary covers more than half of the 1990s. Hopefully it will give a little more insight to those interested, incidentally provide a window into the corporate mores and ethology of the last decade of the twentieth century and serve to some extent as a record of events. I believe there is no other.

Chapter 2

WAKING UP TOO LATE
1990–1991

Monday 30 April 1990

Last Friday was a bad day. I really felt there was no way out for GPA, ultimately. I have been having worrying thoughts for some time now—seriously worrying thoughts—but it is difficult to sort out worrying from desperate. Aviation is a high-risk industry. Worry and uncertainty are everyday feelings. The point is one of degree. I have now reached the stage where I am beginning a diary to chronicle what I believe are the final days of this company.

What will bring us down? Let me guess.

It will be a combination of events and circumstances. First, we have ordered a huge number of aircraft—too many. Some types will not be leased easily. The MD-80 series in particular concern me. These are old technology aircraft which barely meet the current noise regulations and there is only a small customer base worldwide for these aircraft.

Second, recession could well be coming, or at least enough of one to affect us. Signs from the US and elsewhere presently are starting to look ominous. Increasing interest rates on the horizon, little domestic growth, carrier profitability suffering and the steady trend towards fewer, larger airlines with whom we, so far, have very limited business. Recession will not only mean aircraft being returned to us through repossessions for lessee default, bankruptcies etc. Worse, aircraft may be held up in bankruptcy proceedings, unable to be repossessed or earn money, even if they could be otherwise leased out.

There is in our corporate financing package a covenant which restricts the number of aircraft that are allowed to be on the ground at any time. At the end of March this year people were getting very agitated as we were close to breaching this covenant! If we are in breach, effectively we are in default with our bankers. This would be a black mark against our future prospects, when everything so far has been up and up. The financial press would have a field day if they got to hear about it and our shareholders could wobble. We have been very careful to build up a blue chip circle of investors. By the same token they will be less than impressed if we fail to perform.

I am worried about our corporate debt facility, lately set up to fund our aircraft purchases. True, a huge sum of money has been raised—$2.5 billion—but the terms have been negotiated on our side by financial people with very little airline experience. Already we have seen that the financing terms produce an arduous operating lease contract, which is difficult to argue with an airline lessee to whom we are trying to lease an aircraft. It is practically onerous and virtually unchangeable. I am afraid we have also paid too little attention to the downside possibilities, because our negotiators simply did not have the experience to know what these could be. Already the near breaching of the 'aircraft on the ground' (AOG) covenant is a sign of distress which should not be ignored.

Recession will also mean that the market for aircraft will be depressed or maybe even disappear, in that the values will hold, there just will not be any buyers. This has happened before in 1982/3. For us the result will be aircraft round our necks we cannot dispose of, either by leasing or sale. We will be in default with our banks. We will still be bound to accept more new aircraft we have contracted for but cannot fund. We would have to reschedule our debts—a fraught business. I am sure we have a unanimity rule with our lenders, i.e. every bank involved in the facility has to agree to any change. This is a tough rule in practice: banks with just a tiny percentage of the facility on their books can stymie the entire set-up by refusing any course of action with which they disagree. With so many banks in the facility, 30 plus, there is plenty of room and vested interest for mischief.

Ironically, the aircraft manufacturers would be glad to see us depart the scene. The major airlines would also be glad to see us go. The former mistrust our ability to lease the number of aircraft we have ordered. Their fed-up salesmen tell me that every aircraft sold to us is an aircraft they have to sell twice as far as they are concerned—once to us and again to the airline lessee. The latter dislike the way we have tied up the manufacturers' order books for years to come, thereby forcing them to make fleet decisions far in advance of their wishes. They see us as usurping their traditional role as the principal customers of the manufacturers. I cannot blame either of them. They have their own heavy risks to cope with and do not need the extra volatility in the industry we represent.

In defence of GPA and our breed, we are supplying an innovative, excellent product—new aircraft without the need for much equity— always a problem for airlines, especially start-ups or undercapitalised carriers. Nowadays we take going on a cheap package holiday in a modern, clean aircraft completely for granted. Almost exclusively that has come about due to operating leasing. Previously, leisure carriers were in the old banger market. I mentioned Rudi Bay's yacht *Coronado* previously, this was named after the Convair 990 which bore that name. These aircraft, which resembled the Boeing 707, made up the backbone of Spantax, Rudi's airline, and he loved them. They were powered by extremely smoky GE engines and a single aircraft would fly by looking like four Sabre jets in formation. It was also reputed to be the fastest airliner of its day—able to break the sound barrier in level flight, but with 60s technology, hopeless economics and galloping obsolescence, they were the main reason Rudi began leasing our aircraft. I digress.

The trouble with GPA is that we are greedy. We rationalise our rapacity with talk of market share, discounts for bulk, critical mass etc. but the truth is we are greedy and now we have bitten off more than we can chew. People never learn.

The world civil aviation scene is moving from a very tightly regulated system to a quite loosely regulated one in terms of market entry and route licensing. In the old days a relatively few large national airlines—the 'IATA Club'—protected by monopolies and pooling arrangements, ruled the aviation world. Now, the pendulum is swinging towards a different set of large carriers, again few in number, who will rule by economic dominance in a world with few rules to restrict their activities.

The protracted transition from one extreme to the other has spawned many new carriers and has encouraged the growth of smaller established airlines. It is to these airlines that the leasing companies have overwhelmingly committed their fleets, yet these carriers are likely to be either severely diminished, wiped out or swallowed up by the mega carriers' emergence. The move towards 'megarisation' is plain and unstoppable. Such is the financial clout of these huge corporations that they can raise vast amounts of financing on very flexible terms and of course every aircraft and engine manufacturer is eating out of their hands. GPA has virtually no business with these mega carriers. American Airlines, British Airways, Lufthansa, Delta, Singapore Airlines, Air France and so on—basically they do not need us. To them we are opportunistic, whiz-kid, Johnny-come-latelies; superfluous middlemen, taking an unnecessary and large cut.

So much for the industry. What of the company itself?

Five years ago when I joined GPA by invitation, there were 40 staff in total; the last annual profit had been $12 million. Today those figures are 200 plus and $250 million. Back then the company was ruled by the iron hand and will of a very visible Tony Ryan. Decisions were easy to obtain. Lines of communication were administratively short, however long they may have been geographically. Today, Tony or rather Doctor Ryan (following the grant of an honorary doctorate) is unseen by the majority of the company. He has a beautifully decorated ground floor office suite yards from the front entrance, an inner sanctum removed from the restrained hurly burly of the rest of the building. Below Tony come those executives who have fought their way to the top of the pile.

This fighting has taken its toll on the company. No longer a place where everyone strives for the common good, it is now a place of division, camps, protégés, favour, kudos and brownie points. Perhaps growth beyond a certain, limited size always brings the same problems. Whatever, the company is not functioning as it should. People are discouraged, fed up. Start a conversation with a leasing colleague and the state of the company immediately comes up, to be followed by disparaging references to a certain individual—at whose uncomprehending feet should be laid the responsibility for most of the uncharacteristic apathy now afflicting the leasing arm of the organisation. The Leasing division is the engine room of the company and there is a fault in its current management.

It is an eye-opener. Tony Ryan has been the most generous employer I have ever come across. We all do fairly spectacularly well, some astronomically so, and yet we whinge and whine as a company just like any other. Good pay alone, it seems, is not the answer. You have to nurture staff, make them feel wanted, build them up, address their concerns, direct them. This is where we are failing and yet it seems petty to say so in the face of such generosity.

There we are—some of the constituents of the broth in which we are now well and truly immersed.

Caught by our aircraft orders, our greatest asset is our greatest liability. The paradox reminds me of shopping in Hong Kong—going broke saving money. We have overbought, overreached. I see no safety net, no plan B in sight, only go go go. When disaster happens it will be unbelievably quick—like the Falklands War—come from apparently nowhere and be irretrievable. I feel it in my bones. It is a constant burden on my mind.

I never read the daily stars. Sometimes the annual ones. Patric Walker who used to do the *Daily Mail* annual predictions was the best. Coincidentally, yesterday I read a prediction by him in the *Mail on Sunday*: 'A spectacular aspect is coming so expedite your joint financial arrangements . . .' Well, there you are, good as told. I am selling my GPA shares as soon as I can.

In terms of a simple diary entry for today, we had the Monday morning meeting in Shannon. The ex-Braniff Airlines A320s, 12 of them at present but more coming, are still around our necks, although Mexicana and America West are interested. America West are also asking us for $200 million by way of a grant because the airline does not want to go back to the market for more money at this time. If we acquiesce to this in any way we must need our brains testing. America

West, a carrier not yet ten years old, born out of deregulation in the US, is almost a No. 1 candidate for being bankrupted by competitive pressures from much larger airlines.

Aerocalifornia is, it would seem, dead on its feet. It has ten of our DC-9s, ex-Aeromexico. Here we go again, another bunch of worthless aircraft to sit on the ground beside the equally worthless ex-Braniff BAC 1-11s and bump up the number under our bank covenant. In the old days Tony would have been discernibly apoplectic at the sight, at the thought, of any AOG. Now we seem to tolerate it; there's not the urgency to get out there and stay out there until the problem's fixed. Overall in Marketing in the Leasing division we're not as afraid as we used to be of Tony angrily coming among us, implicitly threatening our individual livelihoods. Not that we should need it.

Personally, today I am trying to complete a sale of a B737-200 to Zambia Airways. I have been trying for the past week. Just don't ask me about it.

That is the entry for 30 April, the first one. They will not all be as long as this. I hope the diary will peter out as my concerns prove groundless. I believe otherwise.

Tuesday 1 May 1990

German Wings filed for bankruptcy in Germany today. Seven more MD-80 series aircraft on the market. ILFC are said to be offering MD-83 aircraft ex-British Island Airways at $112,000 per month. Our usual lease rate is around $260,000. There sure is pressure in the MD-80/82/83 market.

Aerocalifornia is looking very bad. We are considering a cash injection. It is not to my mind worth it. We cannot prop up non-viable carriers. Once again I reckon the effects of that bank financing covenant are at work as we try to prevent AOGs.

Patrick Blaney is trying, after I called him, to come over to London on Thursday or Friday to talk to us about restructuring the Leasing division. As the memo setting out the new order is supposed to be out by 4 May, his visit would seem post event. We in the London office are somewhat confused.

Thursday 3 May 1990

Met Roy Gardner, MD of Virgin Atlantic. He believes Harry Goodman, International Leisure Group and Air Europe have lost £17 million and sees only problems for them. I agree. By pure chance I also met John Jones, MD Viking International. John reckons Odyssey International, a Canadian charter carrier which collapsed last week, will go to Canada 3000. According to him, seven Canadian airlines have gone in the last year. He tells me the message he gets from his airline clients is that GPA is 'too arrogant' and difficult. Same old story.

Friday 4 May 1990

I have heard that we are actually in breach of our bank covenant. Apparently the criterion is 15 per cent of the fleet on the ground at any time, by value of the fleet. We are now operating on a 30 day waiver while we try to sort out a different covenant everyone can live with.

Today is the annual presentation by us to the Corporate Debt Facility Banks, where we update them fully on our business.

Saturday 5 May 1990

Reported this morning: Dan Air has made a £3.3 million loss this year, as against a £9 million profit last year. Heard today that Guernsey-based Havelet Leasing has gone into receivership today. They have about 15–30 aircraft.

Spoke with Peter Denison-Edson (SVP Japan and close to Maurice Foley) and heard that yesterday's bank presentation went satisfactorily. Apparently the experienced UK banks used to aerospace are not showing concern. However, a Japanese bank (name unpronounceable) spoke privately to Peter at the reception afterwards, stating that matters would have to be handled 'with kid gloves' with the Japanese banks. These banks know little of the aviation industry and a breached covenant waves a flag that all is not as it should be. Peter said we presented our current problems as a small hiccup to be expected at our level of business, not a warning of things to come. I countered saying, 'Yes, but are *we* taking it as a warning?' He became somewhat more edgy, but stated that we were. I believe there is some serious thinking going on in the higher reaches of management. I hope so.

End of another week and I am still worried. Next weekend is the GPA annual conference. It should be interesting.

Monday 7 May 1990

I and my London-based colleagues have been summoned to Shannon on this bank holiday to attend the morning meeting and also, we anticipate, to be either asked to contribute in relation to the Leasing division restructuring—no memo having surfaced—or more likely told what our new places will be in the restructuring.

At the meeting Jim King (head of leasing) is in the chair, his face red from the Bermudan sun from where he has just returned. We start on the AOGS: principally the MD-80s and the Braniff A320s. Nothing much is happening. America West is still the new hope for the A320s. The airline is trying to grow by 100 aircraft, of which our 26 A320s will be a part. The $200 million the airline is looking for is apparently at the rate of $2 million per aircraft, so this deal will cost us $52 million upfront. To be fair, we probably have it ourselves in manufacturer credits (i.e. discounts off the aircraft list price), but giving it away comes straight off our bottom line—off our dividends.

We spend the next hour going through the weekly activity report. Jim's new deputy, Patrick Blaney, come from GPA Capital, has a problem with our GPA Asia office over a Chinese deal with CATIC which is unresolved.

When it comes to receivables, the amounts owed to us by our airline customers, the total is in excess of $30 million. A large sum is owed by Brazilian carriers as a result of President Collor's overnight measures to achieve zero inflation. A side effect has been nearly zero passengers for the domestic airlines, Transbrasil and VASP. These are both very good B737 customers of ours. Their bank accounts have been frozen by the government. We have received a ministerial letter of comfort, but we are still very nervous. The present balance outstanding is already above $10 million and climbing quickly. We have had to issue formal default notices—'to make it easier for the airlines to negotiate with their own government' it is said, but this is not the only reason. We need to protect our contractual remedies.

We are owed substantial amounts by Spanish airlines operating in the charter leisure market. This is another disaster area. Already within the last year Spantax and Hispania have collapsed. Canafrica and Air Sur cannot be far behind. All customers of ours and all owing not only aircraft rental but maintenance payments, European *en route* navigational payments and airport landing charges—all huge amounts and all ultimately payable by us if we want an aircraft released from detention. It is a harsh system that encourages lazy accounting by the various authorities, as they know we will pick up the tab.

The meeting ends and we, the London contingent of three, go back to our borrowed hi-tech cubby holes on the Trading Floor to get on with our work and await the summons regarding the restructuring.

Generally during the day the rest of the marketing staff are stirred up, everyone trying to find out what the London people are doing in Shannon on a UK bank holiday. Is the London office closing down? Nobody discounts the possibility—how revealing of the general mood is that? I however believe the possibility is remote. GPA needs all its experienced people at this point and London is very convenient as an office location in its own right—much more so than Shannon in terms of the outside world.

In the event Jim King asks to see the other two, but not me. During the day I had spoken briefly to Patrick: he wanted to discuss restructuring issues with me when he could get out from under his newly acquired piles of paperwork. The two finally got their calls into Jim's office in the early evening and had the usual briefest of meetings punctuated by incoming calls. Later I learn that one got posted as No. 2 in the new region of Central & Eastern Europe and the other was asked to resign.

I spend the evening with Joe and Brid Clarkin. Almost sole topic of conversation—the state of the company and Leasing's management. We decry the changes in the company over the last couple of years. Joe effectively brought me into GPA five years ago after we met on a deal. I say to him if I was in his shoes—I would guess a several times millionaire on paper, and wealthy besides—I would sell and go. Joe is being messed about also: Jim wants him out of being MD GPA Airbus and into General Counsel Leasing. Joe is not keen and is considering the offer. As to selling up, he jokes, 'My kids would worry if they didn't see me going off to work. They tell me, "Everybody's daddy goes to work."'

Tuesday 8 May 1990

Still in Shannon. AOGs still AOG. The Fokker F100 deal for 12 aircraft with Iran is looking ill. It had been a deliverance for the GPA Mitsubishi Fokker joint venture. They cannot afford to lose it. Aerocalifornia is still looking very sick. Phil Bolger, head of the Trading Floor, has been looking over the operation, based in Baja. He reports the airline is run out of a peripatetic CEO's briefcase. Departments of the airline show enthusiasm, but little competence.

After the morning meeting I ask Jane O'Callaghan of Irish Aerospace (IAL), the GPA MD-80 joint venture, how I can help with the MD-80 AOG situation. She is dispirited. She tells me the expectation is that the four returned MD-80s from Unifly, a recently failed Italian airline, will go into a large US airline, but that is being dealt with by very senior management in GPA Group and is effectively out of IAL hands. The other good prospect is in the USSR/China, but that once again is being looked after by other very senior GPA Group staff. She feels stifled. All that is left is a small band of MD-80 airlines and the two IAL marketeers (the third is in hospital recovering from an operation) are in constant contact with all of them, to no effect. So, thank you, she says, but you cannot help us. The problem is that the very senior GPA Group staff—almost certainly Tony, Jim King and Jim Worsham in Los Angeles—are burdened (except in the case of Jim Worsham) by other pressing problems and cannot devote their full time to the matter. Meanwhile the aircraft sit there, idle and deserted in their brilliant scarlet livery on a taxiway at Shannon Airport, thrust reverser buckets sagging untidily open as the hydraulic pressure falls off. These aircraft are nearly brand new. Each has a value of some $28 million. There's already a name for them—the Red Arrows.

In the old days any AOG was a live, bright issue, Tony boiling over with ire—who were we to allow an aircraft to come back to Shannon? Today though we are big and it's someone else's problem.

I return to the Trading Floor and have a meeting with Patrick. We discuss the restructuring. It seems I am to be in charge of leasing in the Middle East and Africa region. I am surprised. With my British as against a neutral Irish passport, I will be much more at risk in the Middle East—whether on the ground or in a hijack situation. All my background is in the UK and Europe where I know many of the airlines' top people. Apart from my forays into Zambia I have no experience of Africa. I will have two others to help me. I ask Patrick to reconsider, bearing in mind these two points. He will think about it. I ask about remuneration changes. He cannot discuss that now. Nothing has been settled.

On the one hand I am glad to have control of one of only five marketing territories worldwide, but on the other I am fairly appalled at the prospect of spending so much time in Africa—the third world of the Third World. I know I have Phil Bolger to thank for my promotion, or rather recognition. I feel sure he fought my corner in the face of opposition.

Discussion with Patrick moves on to other topics. I tell him we should be unloading our aircraft at lower rates to bigger airlines, just to get them off the ground and reduce the stream of new aircraft soon coming to us. We should be trying to break into the major airlines, even if only around their edges. It is a weakness on our part not to be in this league, with the unstoppable tendency towards larger, fewer airlines. Patrick says there are little returns, because these airlines command very low lease rates. I counter saying we should be happy to unload the aircraft virtually at cost for now, the way things are shaping up. At least it takes them off our hands, the lessee credit will be good, so no prospect of the aircraft coming back prematurely and it will build relationships for the future with these companies. Patrick seems to take it in, but I feel nothing I say matters in this place, so what is the use?

Wednesday 9 May 1990

I spoke with Graham Boyd in London. An executive VP, he is virtually a founder member of GPA. He started and ran the US office and is now GPA's buyer of new aircraft. His greatest worry is the fleet of 29 ageing DC-8-71 passenger aircraft we have bought from United Airlines for conversion into freighter aircraft. He believes this deal is a huge mistake. The aircraft are too expensive for what they are, the conversion costs will be high—circa $4 million per aircraft—and they will be difficult to market, in short, a millstone around our necks. These aircraft are part of Tony's drive for 'more product'.

Thursday 10 May 1990

I give Graham my larger airlines spiel. He is not in agreement with Tony's policy to buy up available second-hand aircraft, zealously put into effect by Jim.

Friday 11 May 1990

Our company secretary Liam Barrett says we will talk to American Airlines (AMR) and TWA about large tranches of MD-80s at cost. At last. It seems to me that my talk with Patrick and maybe Graham is bearing fruit. On the other hand, I have come to regard myself as a nonentity with GPA since my opinion is never sought on anything and my London location has outcast status compared to Shannon. Therefore to think that my mini polemics may be moving upper management is gratifying; but far above that feeling is sheer relief that we appear to be finally girding up for battle. That's what it is, battle for our survival. Hardly any of us know it yet.

The overnight report from Shannon also bears the good tidings that LAV, a South American carrier, has signed a letter of intent for one of the AOG ex-Unifly aircraft.

Tomorrow is our annual conference, where we take over the auditorium of wherever and review our business. I can hardly wait to hear Tony's speech on the state of the group. A real problem these days, however, is that we allow bankers and other invitees to listen to what should be, and used to be, a private get-together. The result is sweetness and light or merely exhortations to do better, instead of hard-headed, realistic confidential debate about our situation. What is never said is that we will be lucky to survive the next 12 months unscathed and yet this should be the message to the marketeers at least.

Saturday 12 May 1990

The conference is a big nothing. Still no public announcement about who is doing what in Leasing. Jim King's speech revealed that out of ten objectives he set himself for the past year, he (or as he put it) we, achieved only four.

At one stage though I looked round and thought what other company could boast such quality in such depth in its team.

The evening barn dance at Tony's Tipperary country estate, Kilboy, was good fun.

Monday 14 May 1990

The format of the weekly activity sheets we use to scan the events and status of the marketing effort has been rearranged to show aircraft deals pending, not by product type but by geographical area divided into the various regions. Fine, except we have still not officially heard who is doing what where.

Friday 18 May 1990

I am in Manila. Peggy Vera, SVP of strategic planning at Philippine Airlines, states that the market for leasing B737-300s has softened. She needs a replacement for the aircraft that burnt out on the ground last week, but not at our prevailing rates. She also wants to go ahead with the BAC 1-11 deal, i.e. GPA to buy PAL's fleet. We need those ten old crates like a hole in the head.

Thursday 24 May 1990

Joe Clarkin, in charge of GPA Airbus, our joint venture on the A320 fleet, calls me up to tell me he has resigned from his position. He was offered the head legal job in Leasing and then it was withdrawn. He's fed up with it all. Plus he has had to leave his offices on the 3rd floor and take up residence in the warren of open plan cubicles near the Trading Floor. Owen Roberts, general manager of the F100 joint venture, is there too, having also been evicted from his suite of offices. He is still hurting inside; I can feel it.

Friday 25 May 1990

I'm in Shannon. The place is still stirred up. I hear that Owen Roberts is reported to have resigned. Further, Ed Bolton, head of GPA Inc, our US arm, may be resigning, as may Bob Greenspon, our US General Counsel. It looks like the Stamford office will close and the staff will have to commute to Manhattan. Still nothing about the restructuring. Mike Jones finds me. Unofficially he has heard he will be assigned to my area. I tell him unofficially I have heard that too. Later Patrick Blaney shows me an organisation chart. It is not yet released. He is powerless to do anything. It's all down to Jim King.

Tuesday 29 May 1990

Still no reorganisation memo. I speak to Anne Lee, once my secretary and now secretary to Owen. She sounds down; she tells me I'm lucky to be in London because the atmosphere in the Shannon office is very bad.

All the AOG aircraft are still AOG.

Maurice Foley, No. 2 in GPA after Tony, has let it be known he would like any non-Irish residents holding 'A' Preference Shares, unable to take the Irish tax breaks, to convert into ordinary shares and receive the same preferential level of dividends by way of an equivalents scheme. I fall into this category, having returned to the UK from Ireland over a year ago. I write a memo asking to sell my 'A' Preference Shares and go on to the equivalents scheme. I will only do it though as long as I can be assured that I can actually sell my newly converted ordinary shares immediately as part of the same transaction. GPA needs the 'A' prefs for new people and I want to use that leverage to sell up. I want to realise some money and safeguard myself somewhat in view of my fears. The transaction is slated to close by the end of June. I am battening down some hatches.

Thursday 31 May 1990

I speak with Graham Boyd at length about company problems. He says he told Tony last week that company morale was very low. Apparently Tony has taken it on board. We shall see. Graham is learning of the problems from all sides. He knows everything is stemming from one person's inability to manage. We also talk about the future. I reiterate my fears that the large airlines might want to freeze us out.

Friday 1 June 1990

Still nothing either on AOGs or reorganisation. I deduce from my salary slip that my base salary has gone up by £4,000 as from April.

A colleague leaves the London office today to return to our Stamford, Connecticut, office. Graham and I go out for a farewell drink with him. We spend three hours talking about the current ills of the company. It turns out Graham has been buttonholed by other very senior executives about the same subject. Always the discontent circles about one individual. Graham says he knows the problem is worse than he initially suspected and that he will talk to Tony again. We discuss an alternative management; it isn't difficult. Graham agrees with the consensus view and recites not only the personnel related situation but also the unprecedented number of AOGs. The Braniff A320s alone are costing us $6 million a month in lost profit.

Wednesday 13 June 1990

I'm in Shannon during the day, having arrived the previous evening with Owen Roberts. He is still pushing the Iran Air deal. Over the past month it has died and come back to life. The deal consists of us selling twelve F100s back to Fokker at a premium over our purchase price, so that Fokker can then sell the aircraft on to Iran. As we have such a stranglehold over Fokker's production availability, with our huge (100 unit) order, I always envisaged that a large part of the profits of the F100 joint venture would come from sales back to Fokker. Anyway, the crucial need for this deal to be done has not gone away.

Owen is hopping. He is angry that rumours of his leaving the company have surfaced, though privately he admits to me he is going.

He relates the circumstances. Apparently he met with Jim King in terms of an annual review (some people seem to get them) at the end of April. Jim made certain comments; Owen responded and the conversation thereafter escalated to the point where Owen said he would leave the company. He insists he had no such thought in his mind when he went into Jim's office.

Owen looks to have found a job. I think he is leaving at the end of August to go to his former boss from his Chemical Bank days. He will be based in London setting up an office for a relatively new Seattle-based company—Boullioun Finance or something like . . .

I am due to fly back to the UK on the 5.50 pm flight. After 5 pm, just as I am about to leave for the airport, Jim invites me into his office. He has seemed very subdued all day. There was a GPA board meeting yesterday, with no Japanese board members present, so maybe it was bumpy.

Anyway, Jim is friendly and says words to the effect that everything from my point of view is settled in terms of the Leasing division restructure, referring to my meeting with Patrick. I don't bother to tell him that nothing was settled with Patrick. Jim will tolerate nil criticism or even disagreement from subordinates, so there is no use in remonstrating. I'll speak in due course to Patrick. Jim tells me the long overdue memo will be released on Friday. Here from the horse's mouth I reckon I have a definite date.

Belatedly I dash to get on the plane. I end up just making the flight, in a middle seat with everything on my lap or round my feet, because there's no room left in the overhead bins for latecomers. I get home by 9 pm, having struggled through rather than round the M25. I have a love hate relationship with that road.

Thursday 14 June 1990

I leave the house at 6 am by road *en route* for Manchester Airport to sort out a problem in relation to a Boeing 737-200 we are delivering to Tan Sahsa, the Honduran airline. This aircraft is one of four we have had leased to Airbus Industrie for the past 15 months, and subleased by them to Indian Airlines. Everything possible has gone wrong with this

Airbus/Indian deal from beginning to end. Jim pushed it through against everybody's advice, on the laudable basis of laying foundations for more business in India. There were problems from the outset. The aircraft all needed expensive modifications to comply with Indian Airlines' requirements. These were carried out by Tramco in Seattle. The Indians were difficult to deal with contractually and technically. At Jim's behest, I went to both Delhi and Seattle with Christophe Mourey of Airbus to make it work. There were quite a few rags seriously lost on the Airbus side. Staying in the Four Seasons in Seattle dealing with Indians in person and with Airbus and Delhi by telephone kept us awake almost 24 hours a day when you work out the time differentials. At one stage we even flew one of the aircraft empty from Seattle to Las Vegas on a delivery flight (delivery in Nevada for tax reasons), just to have the captain declaim from the top of the aircraft stairs to the desert air, 'I hereby tender this aircraft for delivery.' Nobody from Indian Airlines replied because they were back in Seattle disputing that the aircraft was ready for delivery. It was. The aircraft then flew back to Seattle. Point made. And so on. After all the aircraft were delivered, nobody from GPA attended upon the Indians. By all accounts Jim blocked visits by anyone except himself, but didn't find time to go. Although the aircraft were leased on an interim basis to cover the period Airbus needed to manufacture new aircraft, the B737s were supposed to stay with the Indians for years (so the theory went), but the airline did not extend the leases. The four aircraft were due to be redelivered in April, but true to the continuing saga, none were delivered on time. All were in a terrible state. Jim has vowed never to lease another aircraft to Indian Airlines. So much for that.

Anyway, the Tan Sahsa aircraft is the last one of the four to be re-leased, thankfully, but here we are in mid-June! Eventually I am able to sort today's problem out, but only with excellent help from Jim. I get back home around midnight.

Friday 15 June 1990
No memo. No one is surprised except me, this time.

Monday 18 June 1990

My alarm goes off at 4.25 am. I catch the 7 am flight to Shannon. Tony is on the flight. I sit next to him and we talk desultorily. We're probably worried about the same things, but there's no bridge between us. Some people I can instinctively talk to; some I can't. Tony is one of them. It's a pity because he has a good sense of humour, but somehow our conversations never get there. Whatever, I couldn't begin to tell him that his company is being pissed away and everyone knows why. Neither my loyalty nor my motives would be believed and by the end of the morning I would be out on my ear. I can't afford that.

Today I find everyone I meet in the Leasing division deeply apathetic. We should all be wearing printed cards round our necks with the message, 'I don't know anything either.' It would save conversation. I hear though that Ed Bolton and Bob Greenspon have agreed terms and are still on board. Bob tells me that the way in which it was handled reached 'a new level of badness', even by GPA's low standard. At least it seems Joe is still on board.

I spend over an hour with Patrick discussing immediate business I am dealing with and a few other things. The restructuring memo will not be out for at least another week. My package and review have apparently been done and are being looked over by Jim.

I ask him how he is settling down. He still bemoans the endless paperwork. Already though he has distanced himself from Phil Bolger's job managing the day-to-day issues. Patrick is now tackling 'strategy' with Jim; Brian Hayden, managing director of Air Tara, our technical arm, has been drafted in to handle much of Phil's tasks. So now it seems we have Patrick and Jim overlapping at the top of Leasing. Hmmm.

Patrick is fizzing. Today is his last day before leaving for final practice prior to taking part in the 'Round Ireland' yacht race. He and Colm Barrington (his ex-boss and head of GPA Capital) and some friends have chartered the boat which came 4th in the recently finished Whitbread Round the World Race, together with the skeleton professional crew that came with it. It is plain he expects to win the race outright with any luck and can't stop talking about it.

I catch the evening flight back. I am sitting next to Gill Driscoll, a lawyer on a year's secondment to GPA from a City practice. At one point she asks me, out of the blue, why no one, either in the press or in financial circles or even our shareholders, has yet tumbled to the serious position GPA is in, in view of its AOGs and the poor immediate outlook for leasing new MD-80 aircraft. I am surprised at this level of awareness from a temporary member of staff, albeit a very intelligent one. I give a low key reply. I am not about to share my thoughts with her. It's strange. I had been feeling a bit more optimistic about prospects with our Chinese deal just signed and the other odd pointer, but her words bring reality flooding back again and I am deadly worried as usual.

Tuesday 26 June 1990

I have just returned to London from Geneva meeting the Algerian Minister for the Economy at Jim's request. Peter Ledbetter is in the office. A long-term GPA shareholder, Peter is seriously rich, being one of the first people into GPA back in the mid-70s. He has recently resigned to take up consultancy work for us as and when he wants to. I know he has been wrestling with the decision to resign for a long time, but it seems to me his timing is a bit too perfect. Whatever, he is here trying to sell new GPA shares to potential investors. An uphill task, he reckons.

Peter tells me our main competitor ILFC has been bought out today by AIG, a large US insurance group, for $1.3 billion. The price represents a premium on ILFC's quoted share price. I say wouldn't it be nice if we could do the same. He agrees. He sees harder times ahead and quotes the day's depressing news about the Nikkei's large falls and the coming of recession in the US.

We raise the subject of the company. Here it comes again, within a few seconds a name comes up and remains focal. Peter thinks people have been treated appallingly. We agree that 'your man' has none of Tony's capacity for instilling fear into people, nor of motivating them. Peter says that whereas previously he would have been too frightened to return from anywhere without having brought off the deal he was despatched to do, there is now really no such pressure. He says the company is becoming softer—people even want to come home for weekends!

I tell him I am worried when I see people like Juan O'Callaghan and him resigning. The news about ILFC could be a piece of the same too. We are losing ground.

Wednesday 27 June 1990

Still no restructuring memo, now two months overdue. Jim has shot off to Montreal. No chance of it appearing before next week, I hear. Patrick is back in the office from the race: one third of the way around the sail track came away from the mast, ending their hopes.

Saturday 7 July 1990

This week, taking up my new regional duties on a *de facto* basis, I spent Monday in a meeting with Uganda Airways in London, Tuesday with Air Botswana in Gabarone, Wednesday with Namib Air in Windhoek, Thursday and Friday with Zambia Airways in Lusaka, returning this morning. Some travelling salesman!

I remain despondent. ILFC is apparently sold out of aircraft through 1992. Would that we were in that happy position. Not being in it will be our undoing, I still believe.

I have heard that the placement of shares is not going too well. These are not new shares, just ordinary shares existing corporate shareholders want to dispose of. Nothing extraordinary in that; simply exercising their respective internal corporate policies. No one is selling out— merely reducing the value of their holdings due to the previous share price climb. However, placing at $650 each is not yet subscribed. If there is not a sufficient market for these shares in the limited sphere of the type of shareholders we seek, there will probably be unstoppable pressure to go public.

Already I hear we have committed to go public by next July (1991). I can hardly think of a worse time, in view of the thoughts and fears I am expressing here. Another little management touch has come to light, as against being announced. It has always been management's policy to favour share sales by employees, as against other shareholders, whenever the two were competing for buyers. Now that policy has been reversed, so that non-employee shares are now first in line. Further, it seems that with the current lack of appetite for shares, the employee shares which are presently waiting for buyers (and there are some, it now being the short option exercising season) will probably not sell. This will be a severe blow never yet experienced. There are many GPA employees, with huge loans to buy shares, relying on the dividends to service those loans. If there is no market for the shares at the present price, with high dividends, what will be the position if the dividend drops—at all? I would be very worried indeed. I know loans are not now limited recourse to the shares alone in a default situation, because I tried to borrow some money on that basis rather than sell my 'A' Preference Shares, and the banks refused.

I can see the company's point in reversing the policy: no one wants to rattle the institutional shareholders. It is the covertness of the change. We obviously have problems. GPA has been staving off a Public Offering because we did not need it. Financially, our outside shareholders were blue chip and happy. Being privately owned, we completely ignored the public stock market crashes and swings, while management had a freer hand to run the group as it saw fit. Now the system is creaking. Institutional shareholders find themselves with shareholdings which in value terms exceed their corporate limits due to GPA's success to date. Naturally they want to dispose of the excess quickly and efficiently. This is becoming difficult, as I've stated. Such is the power of our chosen shareholders, we cannot ignore their wishes. Ergo we must go public. A Public Offering for shares should ideally be when the corporation is on a high and the market has appetite. The way things are shaping up here, we shall not be able to pick our time with any real flexibility. When we go public the situation and the immediate outlook could well be horrible. What a prospect! We have missed the boat. We should have gone public just before the Braniff Airlines collapse some months back.

I have been told that the 300 options I wanted to exercise for immediate sale will almost certainly not happen. Does this mean that options are practically meaningless, that these golden handcuffs are fool's gold? Just these 300, a percentage of my holding, mean nearly $200,000 to me, and now nothing. I am stuck for the present.

At least the sale of my 'A' Preference Shares seems to be progressing, but I cannot be sure in this new climate. There has been a real sea change. How amazing only so few in the company have felt it. Hopefully no one outside the company, but it is only a matter of time, time which is rapidly running out.

Monday 8 July 1990

Up at 4.30 am to catch the 7 am to Shannon for the Monday morning meeting. I drive nearly a hundred miles from my home to Heathrow: at this early hour thank goodness for light traffic on the M25.

Patrick is in the chair; Jim has gone to Mexico. The meeting is very sharp. Patrick is crisply on top of it. He wants more focus on the AOGS and he wants more accountability as to what the regions are doing about shifting our problem aircraft. This is more like it. I get the feeling that maybe the rot has stopped. Instead of drifting, Patrick wants to have some answers and is going to kick ass if necessary. Part of me groans at the extra burdens he is laying on me as a regional head, but the major part is very relieved at the real change in attitude.

For my part I report that the Zambia Airways managing director has promised to come to London tonight for meetings tomorrow to close the aircraft sale, so that we can get our money this week. It is apparently important that the profit be brought into the first quarter's figures. Later I find out why.

Patrick announces that the restructuring memo will be out during the day. John Tierney, head of Finance, says he still has some comments on the last draft. Good grief!

After the meeting I learn the Zambian has put off his travelling until Tuesday. I am incensed because he has broken our agreement and time is short. I discuss it with Patrick. He leaves it to me but says the deal is critical. I compliment him on the morning meeting. He is pleased at the reaction, but wonders what Jim will make of it. I say Jim should be delighted someone else is doing the work.

I fly back at lunchtime wrestling with the Zambian problem. On the flight I talk with Trevor Henderson—likeable and very successful, heading our Boeing division. He believes Patrick's ambition is such that

Jim's position will be taken by him. I say that my appraisal is that Jim quickly comes to a decision as to whether a person is willing to be totally supportive and subordinate to him or not. If the latter, then watch out. Patrick will be on an endgame if he loses. Fascinating watching.

Trevor declares himself devoid of ambition and one who merely enjoys his job. Sean Donlon, Trevor believes, is also ambitious, however to me Sean nowadays doesn't seem as close to Tony as he was. Nobody makes it in GPA unless they have Tony's implicit support. Maybe Sean has somehow suffered in the competition for top spots, which is odd as he only relatively lately came to GPA as a star from outside—where he had been head of Ireland's diplomatic service. Trevor's position with Sean is somewhat odd too, both overlapping in very senior marketing positions in Leasing. Trevor will win any contest. Sean, in my opinion, will probably leave if he can find a more lucrative position. Trevor shows me a draft of the restructuring memo. More on that later.

Coming off the plane I talk to Peter Denison-Edson. He is on his way to Tokyo, where he is engaged in trying to sell GPA shares to institutional investors. It is hard going. We talk about it and I mention the problem with my options. I say there will be real upset among the staff if it becomes clear there is no market for the shares. He knows the point all too well. This indicates that Maurice Foley, No. 2 in GPA and Peter's boss, is also aware of it. Tony apparently takes the view that no employee should be selling shares and that they are 'traitors'! I think he says Tony has a list of all the employees now seeking to sell shares. Anyway, Peter seems hopeful that in the end all the shares will be sold including employee shares. Maybe he feels the company cannot afford not to sell them.

Peter goes on to say that a staple part of the presentations to the potential investors are our profit figures and forecasts. In the comparison of annual profits and quarterly profits, he says my Zambian deal is critical to bring up the first quarter's profits in line with the annual forecast. It is vital to show an amount of profit growth in the first quarter as will, if continued throughout the rest of the year, achieve the annual forecast. Of course if we fail even to reach the first quarter's target, it harms our credibility.

On the way back home to Cambridge from Heathrow, I get the message that the Zambian MD has put back his travelling again—to Thursday. I ask our travel office for a reservation for the evening flight to Lusaka. It is full; I am waitlisted. I get home, throw some clothes in my overnight bag and leave, this time for Gatwick, some 120 miles away. The flight leaves at 10 pm. I am on it.

What a day. Up at 4.30 am, I have driven 320 miles, flown to Shannon and back, put in a day's work and now take a nine hour overnight flight to Zambia to go straight into crucial meetings with the national airline's MD over a $16 million aircraft sale. This is GPA.

Tuesday 10 July 1990

I arrive in Lusaka at 8.45 am. By 10 am I am showered, shaved and in the MD's office. Are they surprised to see me. I am to spend the next month energetically trying to close this deal in London, Paris and Lusaka.

Wednesday 8 August 1990

London office. A GPA Finance department team is in town. They are meeting with our Corporate Debt Facility (CDF) bankers, trying to work out a mutually acceptable rework of the clause which has put us in default under our CDF provisions for several months now—the value of our AOGS. It needs 75 per cent agreement, by value, of all the participating banks to come up with a new agreed formula. Some are being difficult, Westpac of Australia for one, but we cannot buy out an individual bank to overcome the problem. Like a trade union, one out, all out.

I remain despondent. Nothing they say makes me feel any happier. The Gulf crisis is another blow. Talk of recession, fuelled by high oil prices, is about. At least most of our fleet is new and therefore fuel efficient, but we still have enough old 'coal burners'.

My shares are still unsold and the position is uncertain, although Liz Barry remains optimistic it will happen.

Monday 13 August 1990

The Fokker Iran deal is signed. Fingers crossed delivery happens. Getting rid of six aircraft is a big relief.

Colm Barrington's America West A320 deal isn't signed. My Zambia deal is finally expected to close tomorrow.

The MD-83s for this year are still unplaced; similarly the two Tristars and the BAC 1-11s. A few others too are still available. ILFC is sold out through 1992—we read this enviously. The reason is simple. We have overbought aircraft, in some cases new ones and in others older ones.

Patrick Blaney's reign has thrown up one feature of note—paperwork. It's everywhere. If we're not all falling over stacks of reports we're all supposed to read avidly, then we're writing them. Electronic mail seemed such a good idea, but it's a rod for our backs. Everyone has writing mania.

Still no restructuring memo. I've given up on it.

Thursday 13 September 1990

One ex-Unifly aircraft remains on a Shannon taxiway. The others are thankfully gone. One more BAC 1-11 contract has been signed with a Zairean airline, Shabair. The America West transaction trails on.

My Zambia deal is done. At the closing ceremony I was unexpectedly told to 'fuck off' by the Zambia Airways Dutch agent whose real responsibility it was to make it all happen. Maybe Zambia Airways has refused to pay his commission because he was so useless. Anyway, I have missed posting the deal for the first quarter, but no problem. It turns out the profit gap (forecast to actual) is even bigger in the second quarter!

Last Monday we had an extraordinary meeting, following the usual one. It had been mentioned by Jim the previous Monday as being run by Graham Boyd, looking for regional inputs on likely market requirements over the next five years, so that Graham could revise his new aircraft purchase plans if necessary. He requested all regions to think about the issues, prepare some presentational material and have it ready for the meeting. Come the meeting, we are all electrified, no less, when Tony Ryan walks in and sits down at the apex of the v-

shaped table set-up we have in front of the three large video screens.
Regional heads, experienced executives, become acutely concerned at
the prospect of speaking in front of and risking public humiliation in
front of the entire Trading Floor and other interested attendees by
Tony's acid tongue. In the event he is subdued, but the fear factor his
mere presence projects is palpable.

Tuesday 8 January 1991

Well, everyone knows it now. The path over the past months has been
steadily downhill. Everything has got worse. We are still doing aircraft
deals, but the outlook is grim. Today there is a very good article in the
Financial Times targeted at GPA. It is entitled 'A Business Comes Back
To Earth'.

Wednesday 16 January 1991

The UN deadline has expired in the Gulf. We all await our fate. That
sounds a bit much this far from the Gulf, but really we do not know
where all this will end.

We joke faintly about which airlines we will avoid if war breaks out
because of terrorism threats, but the threat appears all too real, if
presently unquantifiable. Time will tell. We see other corporations
banning executive travel due to the Gulf situation, e.g. IBM. We can
have no such rule; air travel is our life blood. Will any of us get caught
up in anything? It is a sobering (and private) thought.

At a meeting yesterday in Shannon, individual aircraft for 1991
delivery were being allocated to particular regions, to make individuals
responsible for shifting them—serious stuff. During the meeting
Michael Lillis, newly arrived ex-Irish Ambassador to the UN at Geneva,
now in charge of the South America region, seemed to suggest a
moratorium on travel because of the Gulf crisis. He was heard in
stunned silence. I can only think that Jim kept quiet because of
Michael's newness. If any of the rest of us had voiced such an opinion,
we would have been considered certifiable, by GPA standards.

At the meeting, held to focus attention on the large number of
aircraft to be disposed of in 1991—this year—each of us regional

marketing heads has been given a lump of aircraft to shift. Towards the end of it Jim asks if anyone of the dozen or so senior people there believes there will not be a war. Everyone, it turns out, expects a war. So how long, he asks, will it last? Ray Tighe of GPA Jetprop reckons about a fortnight. Jim Worsham, head of GPA Asia, believes two years. Some spread of opinion! Jim King persists—what will be the damaging aspects to our business of a war? It seems to come down to two main concerns: higher fuel prices mean higher airline costs and fewer passengers; and terrorist activity will impact passenger carrying. That's bad enough, but there's more that we in the Leasing division do not mention: low investor confidence will diminish securitisation prospects and world depression caused by war will further deplete the already reeling banks' appetite for financing aircraft.

A deeply depressing outlook. Everything seems to be coming together. That's how it was with Laker Airways, one of my former existences, where we had acute anticompetitive pressures, economic recession, falling aircraft values, weak sterling revenues but dollar costs, and unco-operative lenders etc. That's how it is generally with aircraft accidents also—a fatal combination which is the killer, not any individual cause. I can see a repeating pattern here, stoking my existing fears.

Bob Greenspon, general counsel to the Leasing division, an American, wants a meeting. I follow him into his large office—I used to have one just like it down the hall in bygone days. He wants me to tell him about skiing at Zermatt. I do. He goes on and opens the subject of the company's prospects. I have known Bob a longish time, having instructed him six or seven years ago when I was with Britannia Airways and he was in US private practice. Joe Clarkin had recommended him, as he was an expert on airline Chapter 11 bankruptcy proceedings, at a time when Britannia wanted to lease a Boeing 737 to a shaky US carrier.

It turns out, Bob, a pessimist by nature, is very alive to GPA's predicament. I don't know when he came by his feelings. Lately I guess, but he, like me, sees it in terms of survival over the next few years. If we can weather the next two to three years we could be a very viable business. Sure Bob, sure. I've been wrestling with this knowledge for a year now. I wonder in retrospect whether he was disappointed at my lack of reaction and my simple agreement with him.

It is like GPA is an upward staircase: behind us are treads, in front of us there is one visible tread, then a cover over the rest of the stairs so that it is impossible to know whether there is anything there. Shades of Schrodinger.

Thursday 17 January 1991

War starts in the Gulf. Today it is all good news. We're sceptical in London but pleased.

Wednesday 23 January 1991

I am in Johannesburg seeing various airlines—Trek Airways, Air Cape, Comair, Safair, South African Airways (SAA) and Air Swazi Cargo. In the evening a pleasant surprise. A colleague, Paddy O'Meara, arrives in from upcountry Lubumbashi in Zaire. He has had a hair-raising time signing the contract with Shabair for the BAC 1-11. Our evening meal in the Carlton's exclusive club restaurant serves as a therapeutic debriefing for him. I question him closely on one aspect of this trip—bribing an official—in case I have to do it.

Thursday 24 January 1991

Still in Johannesburg. Trevor Henderson has arrived to see Trek Airways with me. In conversation afterwards talking about GPA, he believes we should be clearing our decks of aircraft, unloading them, not going for full returns. He says we should have been doing it earlier. Too bloody true. What have I been saying for nearly a year now? He is full of admiration for the strategy of ILFC, especially its sale to the huge US insurance group some months ago. He reckons we have been months behind in awakening to the situation. We sure have.

Monday 17 June 1991

I have signed the Trek/Flitestar deal, our first deal in South Africa. Everyone is very pleased. Four A320s into a new scheduled services domestic airline promised a *gelike spielefeld* (level playing field) by the SA Government in terms of competition with SAA. However, this deal is minor in the overall scheme of things.

Brian Foley in GPA Capital has a buyer for my 'A' Preference Shares. Excellent. Maybe now I can convert them for ordinary shares and sell immediately.

Monday 16 September 1991

I finally receive a cheque for my shares. I am over the moon. Even if everything goes wrong, today at least I feel something tangible has been gained.

Chapter 3 ∾

| THE IPO 1992

Monday 27 April 1992

We are in the tumult of working up to the Initial Public Offering (IPO). Well, I am not, but many in GPA Group are completely engaged in the exercise which overhangs everything presently.

Maurice Foley, Tony's second in command and head of Corporate, leads the team with Tony right there. We are finally going public at the insistence of our shareholders who need to be able to dispose of their shares in a publicly listed market. We also need to raise more finance, much more, to pay for our burgeoning aircraft fleet. We intend leveraging further borrowings against the money to be raised by selling shares in the flotation—in the IPO. We hope to obtain another $2.5 billion from the shares to be floated. I must say that as a shareholder and option holder, I too will be greatly relieved to have a ready market for my holdings, price being almost secondary.

The importance of the IPO puts everything else into the shade. It looms over us, a huge presence dominating conversation and our thoughts. We all project ourselves forward to mid-June. Everybody expects good times coming. I hope so.

GPA has put together comprehensive road shows, 'Dog and Pony Shows' as Tony calls them, to impress would-be investors and their advisers. There has been and continues to be enormous effort expended in bringing the GPA story to the investment world. We have advisers for everything—hot and cold running experts. Merrill Lynch, Goldman Sachs and Salomon Brothers act for us in the US; Schroder Wagg and BZW in the UK, with Hambro Magan in another advisory capacity. Over them, Nomura in Tokyo is the global co-ordinator—

their first shot at this type of event. There has been criticism over our using a rookie co-ordinator for a flotation of this size, but I can imagine we might have been under some benign pressure to use the Japanese, to introduce them into the big time via our deal. Also they may have been the cheapest, to win first-time business.

GPA will be one of the greatest flotations ever with some $850 million worth of shares on offer. Everything is being done to present the company in its best light. I try to suppress my horrors about the future, to believe in the IPO. I want so much to sell my shares.

Members of my family and friends come up to me and ask whether they should invest in GPA shares. To their great surprise I tell them all that I will not be buying and I would not recommend they buy either, unless they have some money they would not mind losing. Jenny Brown, our London office manager also asks my opinion. I give her the same message. I have previously advised her against taking on a share loan, not long ago, when shares were on sale to employees at a high price. She is puzzled, given what is going on all around her, but I think she will take the advice. I hope so. She is one of the best.

Monday 1 June 1992

IPO fever reigns. Large numbers of people have laboured mightily and brought out the flotation prospectus, which is an advertisement for the company, despite the caveats. Otherwise, what is its point?

However, there are some worrying signs. Quite a few companies are into large share offerings around this time. The huge Wellcome pharmaceuticals flotation will follow ours closely. There is a fair amount of press speculation about the attractiveness of shares coming on to the market, the number of them and the capacity of the market to absorb all the flotations successfully. Whatever, as a company we remain optimistic. Nigel Wilson, our new director, brought in towards the end of last year to understudy Maurice prior to Maurice's planned retirement and therefore a big wheel in the flotation exercise, tells me the signs are good. I hope so.

Unfortunately, we have been involved in well-publicised wrangling with our market setters over the GPA share price for the flotation. Tony is well above the figure he is being strongly advised to go for. He is being aggressive as usual, holding out for the higher figure. Of course it means our holdings are worth more this way, but will it also result in the market thinking that GPA shares are too highly priced and adversely affect the IPO? Tony ploughs on, ever ultra-bullish about the future prospects for GPA. This is his company, his call. This is where the buck has always stopped.

GPA has a habit of over-gilding the lily. We do it often on our deals. Instead of being content with a transaction, we constantly try to improve it for ourselves by niggling away at relatively minor things after the deal has been agreed. This invariably irritates the customer so that, come delivery of the aircraft, the relationship is already damaged by our carryings on. We often seem to see only the little picture. I detect the same sort of thinking behind the share price argument—GPA always pushing for that bit more. A smidge too far.

Disturbingly, British Aerospace has just bombed in its public share offering. It has had a very small take-up of the 500 million or so shares on sale. Were it not for its underwriters, KitKat Aitken, having to purchase the unsold shares, it would have been very serious. As it is, I guess BAE is just embarrassed. Will we have similar problems? Being part of the aerospace industry it is a bit close to home. The aviation world scene is non too rosy right now.

Tuesday 16 June 1992

I have been rather remiss in not keeping up with events on a daily basis, but GPA has been much in the national and international news over our imminent IPO. Why diarise when so much is available on the record?

I am in Harare, Zimbabwe, awaiting a crunch meeting with Affretair, the country's national cargo airline. I am trying to finalise a lease of a DC-8-71 superstretch freighter, one of the newly converted ex-United Airlines aircraft. I have been trying to do this deal for the past 18 months. The airline is known as 'WYMO' in Shannon. Jim King announced at one Monday morning meeting that this deal had taken too long; it would never happen; I should drop it and anyone mentioning the name of the airline would have to 'wash your mouth

out'—hence WYMO. Encouraging or what? Anyway, deals are so scarce
in impoverished Africa, I could not let it go, unbelievably frustrating as
it was. I had also been promised a Zimbabwe government guarantee to
support the transaction. Tenacious by nature when I want to be, I
would not stop until I knew for sure the thing was dead. I had seen
everybody from the Zimbabwean Minister of Transport down. Like the
earlier one in Zambia, the engine of this deal was only firing on the
spark of my determination.

Wednesday 17 June 1992

Hullabaloo. Today GPA is going public. The high sounding
International Initial Public Offering has been soaking up our resources
and our funds for months now. Our Corporate division has been
having field days. Our expert new director Nigel Wilson, with previous
experience of share flotation, has been in the thick of it. Maurice and
Tony seem to be masterminding as usual. The press coverage is mighty.
We have all sorts of fancy advisers—all well-known names—the biggest
swinging dicks and masters of the universe in the business, from Wall
Street to Lombard Street, you name it, all co-ordinated by first timers
Nomura. Corporate lawyers abound. What a beano! What fees!
Millions and millions.

It is to be a simultaneous offering in the stock markets of London,
New York, Tokyo and Dublin. All, we are assured, is going well. We all
know that basically it is not the best time to go to the market because
of problems in the aviation world generally, but GPA's flotation seems
to be on course. There is intense media interest. Irish newspapers carry
stories about how much GPA executives stand to make personally from
the sale. Millions and millions.

The amount of shares being offered has even increased slightly in
the last couple of weeks due to the forecast demand. Better and better.
Whenever I have been in Shannon recently I could feel the increasing
fervour generated by the coming IPO—people coming up to me asking
whether I will be taking advantage of the share sale to buy shares at the
slightly advantageous staff price; asking how much debt I was taking
on, as if the act of major indebtedness was an important factor; as if the

more there were taking on significant share debt commitments, the safer the position must be. I could empathise with their concern. Many were way beyond their financial depth by any normal yardstick, and so were relying on the progress reports, GPA's history and the general optimism to calm their natural fears, having hazarded their financial futures. As you may surmise, I have kept fairly quiet; boat-rocking is hardly in fashion. However, whenever anyone inside or outside the company has directly asked my advice on buying shares in the IPO, I have invariably advised against.

At the same time, whilst my own current holding of different categories of shares and options is relatively modest, even at the mooted take-up price on offer, my existing holdings will be liquid at last and of real value, so I am anticipating a windfall. I have been learning to fly a helicopter, now 80 per cent through the PPL course, with about seven nerve-wracking solo hours flown. I hold fond hopes of buying an R22. I can keep it at home; there is an old barn for a hangar. Perfect. We have the builders coming in too. My wife will enjoy watching long-planned improvements come to life.

All over GPA I expect it is the same. We are at the moment of realising our real reward for all the hard work and killing schedules of the past years. It is exciting.

My worries over GPA's survival are all still there, but they are damped down against the immediate expectation of the IPO. If only I can liquidate my holdings, all will be well. Our advisers and top management say it is all on course. I have to believe them—they have been doing nothing else for months but prepare for this day. Maybe we can weather the gathered storm after all. I have everything crossed, fingers, legs, you name it, hoping it will all go well.

I have been very busy so far on this momentous day. It is now afternoon. I am overjoyed. This morning the Affretair deal has actually been signed at long last. WYMO has come through—on Flotation Day. In great good mood I call my secretary Bernadette in the London office to pass on my welcome piece of news and learn the latest on the flotation.

I am met with a hushed voice. I enquire why the whisper?

'The offer has been pulled.'

'What do you mean, pulled?'

'It's off. It's not going ahead.'

We talk some more. I am stunned. The full implications are not yet clear. Obviously though it is a serious blow. Okay, I reason initially, I guess we just go back to being a private company and come back to the market if, as and when the time is more propitious. Or is it now going to go all wrong? Has the very thing I feared now hit us and will all my earlier fears be proved right? I am very depressed there in my sunny hotel room in the Harare Sheraton, worried and lacking in information. I start calling Shannon extensions to see if I can find out what is going on.

It turns out that the IPO was not underwritten. At this point words fail me. The story is that although there were enough private investors to make the IPO happen, there were not enough institutional investors prepared to pay the price GPA was demanding for its shares in the overall circumstances. The IPO was shelved because of fears (read best legal advice) that to have proceeded in those circumstances would have been 'unfair' to private investors. So there you are. After all the hoo-hah the international investment community has voted on our share price valuation and our industry situation with its feet and stayed away. Over to you, Tony.

Thursday 18 June and for the next few days

The media worldwide declare open season on GPA. The Irish press are particularly cruel; they represent a large sector of the Irish public. Fed up with hearing about GPA's successes and the affluence of its share-owning executives, they now gloat over this very public misfortune. We can all spell *schadenfreude* now.

I cancel my helicopter lesson for Saturday. I don't know why. I say I am stuck overseas. I just haven't the heart.

The following week is the GPA annual conference. Instead of an intense bout of self-congratulation and the infusion of fresh energy into the prodigious aircraft placement task we have ahead of us, it will be a time for explanation.

Trying to be objective, I suppose my worries, from a viability standpoint, have not really increased as a result of the failure of the IPO. Things were already tough. This is just a setback, I tell myself.

I start gathering my things for a trip to North and South Yemen.

Chapter 4

OPERATION REBOUND
1992–1993

Sunday 9 August 1992

Everything is much, much worse. Where do I begin to bring you up to date with what's happened.

External confidence in GPA appears to have collapsed. We cannot raise a cent. We cannot securitise an aircraft. We have a huge hole in our finances and cannot take future deliveries.

Thursday 29 October 1992

Things are worse again. Yesterday there was a special board meeting to discuss a recovery plan. Today I am working from home because the London office is full. Tony Ryan is in, also Maurice Foley, Jim King, John Tierney and Nigel Wilson. My secretary tells me the mood is gloomy.

Sunday 8 November 1992

The Sunday Times Business section has an unforgettable headline, 'Cash Starved GPA Close To Collapse'. I am not writing too much because it is all there in the media. If I was in charge of an airline, I would no longer do business with us. I wonder if it is worth going over to Shannon, but I go.

Monday 9 November 1992

The morning meeting goes very calmly. I am amazed. It is as if nothing had appeared in the papers.

Friday 13 November 1992

Jim, Maurice and PJ Mara, our eponymous public relations adviser, have spent all week trying to undo the damage of last Sunday's coverage. Mailshots have been done for all our customers to reassure them. No deals have dropped off the Trading Floor screens as a result of the articles. I am very surprised.

Thursday 26 November 1992

I am in Johannesburg trying to lease B767s or MD-11s into Flitestar.

I learned yesterday that Craig Coleman, head of GPA Capital in our New York office, died at an America West board meeting. He was 38. America West is in Chapter 11 bankruptcy and has been on the brink of total collapse virtually continuously now for months. Huge cash injections from GPA in tens of millions have helped it totter this far. Of course the upcoming IPO meant we had to give the impression everything was fine: America West collapsing would have been curtains for the IPO.

The London office is crammed every day with Shannon people including Maurice, John Tierney and often Tony, in endless negotiations with our bankers and advisers. What a depressing jamboree! When not travelling I now tend to work at home.

The situation is pretty awful. No dividends will be paid in the foreseeable future. At a recent state of the company meeting, Tony said that bonuses will be earned by people who have significantly contributed to the company during this period. Amount unspecified. Some carrot, but he is as much in the dark as the rest of us. Presumably he is fairly desperate to keep key members of the team together. No dividends for me means a 75 per cent drop in earnings. I cannot afford my present lifestyle on my basic salary. Already I have sold assets— beloved Porsche convertible and family Range Rover. I have two basic needs apart from food—the mortgage and school fees. I cannot pay both. My wife and I discuss renting out the house as a possible alternative to selling it during such a recessed period at a considerable loss. Thank goodness I am able to supplement my outgoings with the proceeds from my previous 'A' Preference Share sale.

Just about everyone in GPA must be suffering similarly. Many must have it far, far worse—I shudder to think about the position of all those with substantial share loans.

GPA is negotiating rescheduling its current Corporate Credit Facility (CCF) with its some 100 plus banks. Many people say it will succeed and bounce back, because the alternative—450 odd aircraft out on lease suddenly in the banks' lap—is too much for them to contemplate. If it is successful, then maybe my shares and options will still be worth something, so maybe I should hang on. My GPA holdings today are practically worthless. I cannot see their value returning, but for the moment I wait and see.

I believe the odds are against GPA coming out of this mess. I think that as our creditors dive deeper into the financial details of GPA they might find, in common with other bust leasing companies before us, that we have booked as profit money not yet earned. For example, ordering substantial numbers of aircraft, GPA has negotiated hefty discounts—'credit memorandums'—from aircraft and engine manufacturers. Now we are in the middle of scaling back our $12 billion forward order book by well over half. Discount levels are tied to GPA taking all the aircraft contracted for, paid upon delivery. We have received millions of dollars this way. They have been booked as revenue received. Now that we have more than halved the number of aircraft coming, a proportion of the discounts received will be repayable. How much is in there?

Again, for example, GPA is currently holding some half a billion dollars representing lease deposits and maintenance reserves paid by current lessees. At the end of a lease, the lessee expects to receive back his deposit in full. Additionally, as qualifying maintenance is carried out on the aircraft, each lessee expects to draw down money standing in his respective maintenance reserve fund to cover the work. In the lease contract it states briefly that deposits and reserves will be 'commingled' with GPA moneys. When GPA says today that it has $510 million in cash for all purposes to bolster confidence in our liquidity, $500 million of it is really the airlines' maintenance money we are holding. At some stage that money will need to be available to pay for the aircraft maintenance for which it is being accumulated. Still, at the moment we can use the money for cash because we have reserved the right in our aircraft lease agreements to appropriate it, i.e. commingle it with general moneys, but should we? What is the directors' position on this one? Might they essentially be held to be defrauding our lessees by so doing?

Again, for example, Mike Dolan and his team in GPA Capital, the financial services arm of GPA, have been feted for the past few years for various ingenious financial schemes, selling aircraft into special purpose funds at a profit, usually as a tax shelter for the investors in the funds. These schemes rely for their credibility upon GPA carrying out remarketing of aircraft as they come off lease and have to find a new home, and upon GPA guaranteeing the future residual values of aircraft, i.e. the rate of return to investors. Sometimes GPA has bought mezzanine, junk equity positions to reassure investors. A lot of money has been pumped into these schemes, of which there are many. The upfront profit has been taken, what remains is a stack of cards. For the past few years most of GPA's profit has come from GPA Capital's activities. Today it contributes nothing. Investor confidence has collapsed.

Following the disaster of the June IPO, when no one looked at the downside, just about nothing has gone right, except that things could have gone a lot worse.

The immediate response to the failed IPO from senior management was that several interdependent issues had to be resolved. Just how interdependent these issues have become was not foreseen. At that time all seemed possible, it had to. This was the list:

- AOGs had to be reduced
- Existing shareholders had to commit an extra $300 million in equity
- ALPS 2 had to be completed
- The level of future aircraft orders had to be halved to $5.5 billion

Top management teams were set up on each issue. These consisted of the same people who had previously looked after the same things, with one exception. Jim King was taken out of the Leasing division altogether, which he had headed.

Jim was given twin tasks and promoted to vice chairman. He was to spearhead the job of reducing aircraft orders together with Graham Boyd, who had latterly been responsible, under Tony's direction, for buying them in the first place. Also Jim was to have overall public relations responsibility. Jim had been in PR in an earlier existence. Assisting him in this would be PJ Mara, a sort of Irish Bernard Ingham but more pleasant, who had been drafted in to advise on the IPO PR (pre-IPO), but who seems to have been sucked into the GPA nightmare ever since.

Maurice Foley, an extremely astute man in the mould of cerebral chief executives, as against those like Tony who achieve chief status by drive and force of personality, had been responsible for the IPO overall. In the wake of the IPO 'debacle' (Tony's word), Maurice was stripped of his chief executiveship and Tony reassumed the mantle. No press release was produced. The newspapers reported the change, which must have been humiliating for arguably the best executive in GPA bar none. An unnamed 'spokesman' for GPA was reported as saying that GPA needed more aggression in the post following the failed IPO, hence Tony's return. Maurice had been shown, if not thrown, to the wolves. It was a dirty trick and one which did not do the company any good. It so happened that I was on good terms with a very senior banker, a friendship which had sprung up whilst I had been chief executive of a GPA joint venture. I had lunch with him. It became clear that GPA's banks favoured Maurice and that Tony was the most vulnerable to being asked to go. Anyway, that was a couple of months ago. Things are worse now. Maurice is back in the middle of it, still No. 2 and leading what is now officially termed Operation Rebound. At least we have not lost our penchant for pompous titles.

At the beginning of this week the first official debt rescheduling meeting was held with all the banks in the CCF. The fund is well over $2 billion. Given our present circumstances we were asking for a moratorium for 1993 and 1994 on capital repayments. The banks are now considering. When I call back in I ask the mood of those talking to the banks. The reply is usually 'gloomy'. I can just imagine. It is generally the same feeling at any company just before the end. The main plank of hope appears to be that we are too big to go down. The banks and the manufacturers need us too much. I am completely unconvinced by this argument.

The rescheduling task is vast, given the number of parties to be persuaded to help out. My experience is that although willing to help, everybody involved has to help to the same degree, otherwise it will not work. Also the underlying financial position has to be sound. We are hostage therefore to any creditor being difficult for whatever reason and to there not being any landmines or black holes in our financial position. As you know from the foregoing, I believe GPA Capital may have left us with some of the latter. As to the former, we are already locked in combat with McDonnell Douglas Corporation (MDC) over rescheduling future aircraft deliveries.

We have made a real balls-up over the MDC situation. We have ordered too many, over 20, widebodied MD-11 aircraft. These come out at over $100 million each. As passenger aircraft they are lulus. Grown out of the DC-10-30, the MD-11 has failed to live up to the performance claims of MDC both as to range and fuel economy—to the extent that significant buyers have cancelled orders and ordered alternative equipment, e.g. Singapore Airlines, now going for the Airbus A340-300. The MD-11 programme has been torpedoed. MDC has improvements in the pipeline but these are in the future and will involve lengthy downtime to retrofit existing aircraft. Also it will be costly. There are so many competing aircraft in the same or similar category that airlines have generally decided they do not need the aggravation and the aircraft has bombed. We have been negligently slow off the mark in attending to this situation. Furthermore, we have bought at least some of these aircraft (before Graham's time) without any performance guarantees. This is a basic requirement. Any airline employee, I can say with 12 years' airline experience, in charge of buying a new aircraft, who failed to have critical performance guarantees included, would be routinely fired. We have naively relied on MDC saying they would provide suitable guarantees as and when our airline customers came along. In other words, 'trust us'. On a sub-performing aircraft at $100 million a throw? Yeah right!

Sunday 30 November 1992

Graham Boyd and I met up, as we often do on a Sunday night during Aer Lingus's winter schedule where no early Monday morning flight operates from Heathrow to Shannon. We have both come over for the Monday morning meeting. Graham has been very senior in GPA since long before I arrived, having started up the Americas office in Stamford, Connecticut, in the early 80s. Apart from Peter Swift (now retired) Graham is the only other Englishman who has been really valued and has financially thrived at GPA. He has never joined the corporate rat race in the way that Jim, Colm and Patrick have. At the same time I always got the impression that he enjoyed a special relationship with Tony who, I felt, respected Graham's judgment and used him as a counterbalance to people like Jim, when Tony wanted a more independent, thoughtful view or advice. I always find Graham to be incisive, with a deceptively friendly manner that can freeze over. I get on well with him whilst being wary of the traps he can lay in conversation. He actually left GPA about two years ago but came back into the fold after several months.

Graham is close to Tony. His modest office is even next door to the sanctum, so I try to express my ideas to Graham hoping some of them might emerge somewhere interesting. He always listens closely and sometimes I recognise something we've talked about happening.

Anyway, he tells me we have two serious problems on hand with the delivery of two new aircraft, his neck of the woods. One is a De Havilland Dash 8, a 50 seat turboprop which will cost us the best part of $12 million. The other is an MD-11 costing $110 million. In each case the problem is the same: we cannot finance their purchase.

The Dash 8 is buyable. GPA has the cash, but we cannot break ranks as regards other creditors and pay De Havilland in full. The MD-11 is going into a joint venture called Aerocitra, run by GPA with Garuda, the Indonesian State airline. The MD-11 cannot be funded out of GPA's resources. We are now locked in struggles with MDC, complaining that the aircraft is not up to specified performance levels. This is a valid argument but should have been raised way back years ago when the fact of the MD-11's underperformance became known. Now, after we have taken delivery of several of the aircraft, probably accepting larger discounts to shut us up, we cannot successfully raise objections. Nevertheless this is what is happening. Because we cannot find the means to pay for the aircraft, MDC is apparently threatening to sue us.

The week before, an edict from Patrick went round, although it never reached the London office, forbidding any contact with MDC due to these problems. This is difficult as we need to be in contact with MDC on a daily basis. I am currently trying to lease an MD-11 into South Africa, so I talk to MDC almost every day. I called Shannon for some elucidation. I was told the prohibition did not affect people like myself trying to do leasing business. At present I don't know where I am. I may sign a deal only to find there is no longer any aircraft available. Actually, I do believe that will be the case.

Monday 1 December 1992

The morning marketing meeting passed uneventfully enough. We have repossessed some 14 aircraft from VASP, only to find they have been changing engines around wholesale and robbing parts. So far we have carried out five engine changes to try to match aircraft up with their engines. The cost to us of this mis-maintenance will be in the region of $20 million. The fleet is now being remarketed by us. Needless to say VASP owed GPA millions before we finally pulled the plug on them. We are sueing: good thing we issued the default notices. Apart from VASP, we have several large creditors, one of which is LAM, the State airline of Mozambique. This was a deal done before I took over Africa, but it's a monkey on my back now. They owe us $4 million. However, they do not have the money to pay. The basic truth is they could not afford our aircraft in the first place, especially the widebody B767, but Trevor Henderson was under real pressure to place Boeings.

In a sensible world we should not be doing new aircraft business with these badly managed, underfunded, low revenue, low traffic, shaky Third World carriers. It is asking for trouble. ILFC avoids all but the best of them. GPA, driven by the weight of new aircraft orders placed at Tony's insistence, has to do business wherever it can. The justification is that with such a wide customer base, one or two failures is a statistic which can be coped with and the returns are better. The reality is that GPA is overloaded with far too many 'flake' airlines, with too many of our aircraft. The risks of high chronic indebtedness to GPA and lessee bankruptcy are high. The cost is high also in time and resources nursing them along, in lost opportunity cost, in late payment, in repossession. In aviation the saying is 'be in at the cradle, never the grave'. GPA has too many graveyard customers whilst ILFC baby snatches.

Wednesday 30 December 1992

I am in the office debt collecting. My unhappy trio of ADC (Nigeria), Affretair and LAM between them owe us over $6 million. When I can get hold of them, struggling with their hopeless telephone systems, I courteously wrestle, threaten and cajole them into improving our year end position.

ILFC has just announced a $4 billion order for new aircraft. Ruefully we discuss it. They have got it right. They brilliantly manage their fortunes, buying in a down period, and now have cheap good aircraft; cheap financing via AIG; weakened opposition (us); excellent relations with the manufacturers and stocked shelves for boom time when it comes around in a year or so. For all our arrogant crowing of the past, GPA cuts a sorry figure nowadays. In social company, on the few occasions I indulge, I hate saying who I work for. Those who know treat you like a cancer patient. Walking dead.

Tuesday 12 January 1993

Still here. Margaret Clandillon, a lawyer in GPA Capital in Dublin, who joined GPA not long after me, spells out in her usual breezy, forthright style that the Leasing division is the only one making money, but even that revenue is not covering the cost of GPA's monthly overheads. Presently we are not viable. Furthermore, the rules which the banks have applied to future securitisations mean there will be no more.

Without a steady stream of aircraft sales we will make no money.

There is to be a company briefing next Monday for the staff. Everyone is exceedingly nervous, but will anything meaningful be said? I suspect not. No one will want to make waves if it means being made redundant.

Last week I was in Johannesburg with our South African customer. They are having a difficult time through no fault of their own. They have $4 million lodged with us in cash deposits. Could they have some of it back during this difficult period and repay us later when things return to normal? Otherwise there is a real possibility that we could get the four A320s back early. I really want to help them out. The deposit is in the books of GPA Airbus, our Airbus joint venture company where our partners are Airbus, Pacific West Airlines (PWA) and Banque Paribas. I call Fionnuala Sheehan in Treasury: she holds the purse strings of the joint venture companies. It is like lifting the lid and looking into hell, speaking to her. Fionnuala is a nice person, very bright, friendly, competent. She is firefighting to conserve cash. Her situation seems little short of desperate. There is no money for my customer— GPA Airbus has no money. On top of new A320s destined for InterEuropean that cannot be financed, there is the collapsing Canadian Airlines problem. PWA is effectively Canadian Airlines. They have told GPA they can pay no more rentals until at least July 1993. They have a bunch of our aircraft. It is another body blow.

Bad deals are elsewhere coming home to roost. Most were struck in the boom end of the 80s, when even with a full order book, Tony felt we had to get in as much extra 'product' as possible to swell the coffers. To appease this voracious appetite, Jim drove the traders and himself into some crazy deals—which most of us realised were crazy even then. Usually they were scrappy, difficult deals, generally concluded amidst much ire.

We bought the entire 29 strong DC-8-71 fleet of United Airlines. Built in 1968, they had been re-engined with new technology CFM-56 engines. Our idea was to convert all of them to freighters. In retrospect, United must have seen it as a heaven sent deal. They got a long and useful life out of the fleet and then sold it in one go for more than it had ever cost to acquire. The price we paid was about $18 million per aircraft. The conversion cost is about $4 million per aircraft. Some expensive deal. These aircraft have hung around our necks, been a pain in our side, a drain on our resources and agony on the back pocket ever since the deliveries began.

As previously mentioned, we bought and put into Indian Airlines for a limited term four B737s, on an interim basis, pending new A320 aircraft direct from Airbus. The whole deal was fraught with problems—very expensive with no return.

We bought a sizeable part of Egyptair's fleet, several widebody A300s and B737s—again paying literally hundreds of millions. The whole deal was full of holes. The negotiations were protracted; the Egyptians did not pay us the deposit for aircraft leased back. Come delivery of the aircraft, they were not in a deliverable condition. Indeed on subsequent heavy maintenance inspection ('D' check) at Lufthansa Technik facility, I heard one of them had structural issues although it had come from public service. We still have some of the A300s round our necks. Even if there was a market for them at present, their worth would be around $20 million each—we bought them at $35 million each. We are now rejecting the last two A300s. Apart from not wanting them, we cannot finance them.

We even tried to buy a pack of old Tristars from Gulf Air in Bahrain: luckily that deal did not materialise.

And so on.

Our future order book is now not even in tatters. However, we still have some aircraft we have to buy, for example two MD-83s—at our special price of $28 million a copy. Unfortunately, the manufacturer, in today's climate, is selling sister ships, new, to anyone, for $24 million. We can finance doodly squat at present. This financing problem is hellish and ongoing. Our bankers will not lend us any more money, yet we need some. We are between a rock and a hard place.

Graham had a conversation with Tony last week. He declined to go into detail but said Tony's demeanour was 'rueful'. Graham is looking to get out. He wants no part of GPA's future, if there is one.

Personal financial situations continue to be dire for a good number of staff. The company has said it cannot help employees with outstanding share loans, which they cannot repay in the absence of dividends on their shares.

No matter that my own remuneration has been somewhat decimated by recent events, I am one of the few really lucky ones. I have no share debt.

We have now repossessed all our VASP aircraft back from Brazil. Of course bits are missing and the aircraft are in a state. Just as bad, it turns out the deal involved the aircraft being leased in on a fixed interest rate. This means that if the lease terminates early, there are usually so-called unwinding or broken funding costs, as the fixed funding is for a stated period. Generally one would only grant fixed rate funding to a lessee of sufficiently good credit rating, so that the lessor could be confident of the lessee airliner going the full distance of the lease without problems. VASP and Transbrasil have been competing with each other, and to some extent VARIG and TAM in the volatile Brazilian domestic market. We have been supplying aircraft to both airlines, glorying in the number of aircraft involved. Trevor and Michael Barry had a fine old time some years back stuffing B737s into Brazil. Now VASP has gone as far as we are concerned and Transbrasil does not look great. Whatever, we took the risk of giving fixed rate funding and the risk has matured. Cost to GPA—$13.5 million on 14 aircraft. Total other VASP indebtedness to GPA—in excess of $25 million. The extra maintenance cost on our ex-VASP aircraft is now approaching $30 million.

The stable door has now shut; the horse is over the horizon. No more fixed funding is to be offered except to cast iron lessees. Are there such animals?

Actually, no fixed funding will be another serious blow to our marketing ability, especially in competition with ILFC who specialise in it to good lessees whom they specifically target. Lessees like being offered fixed rate funding, as against floating, if the rate is good. It means they can predetermine lease rental costs over the entire lease term. ILFC has the cream at the top of the milk bottle. We have the skim.

Friday 29 January 1993
Last week we had a marketing quarterly seminar. One of the

presentations was from Patrick, explaining to us the deals that have been reached with Boeing and Airbus to get us out of future aircraft commitments. We can barely take in what Patrick rattles out at us. Even Patrick says the Airbus deal 'sucks'. Apparently the Airbus meeting with Pierson, the head of Airbus, was hairy. Graham confirms it. Pierson blew his top when he realised GPA effectively wanted to cancel most of its future orders. Boeing have been extremely co-operative in the circumstances—they are some company—but even here it will be expensive.

Patrick makes a great point in both cases about how we have managed to hang on to future options at GPA base prices and so could bounce back into the new aircraft game. It sounds like naivety of a high order to me. First, our base prices were negotiated at the height of an order boom, so they will be at a corresponding peak. Secondly, I do not believe (a gut feeling) that our prices were that good. Certainly I have not been impressed as a marketeer with our ability to undercut other lessors in terms of rental rates. Thirdly, the large credit memorandums which came attached to large aircraft orders have disappeared as we have cancelled the qualifying aircraft. Actually this part is even worse, as it appears we have already in some instances received discounts at too high a rate on aircraft already delivered, where the manufacturers will seek a claw-back. In some other cases we have received discounts in advance of delivery and spent them.

Whatever, our decks are clearing in terms of future firm aircraft. Already we can see the outline of the rump organisation GPA will inevitably become, even if it survives. Now, as the ejecta from the eruption which followed the failed IPO settles, we can make out the shattered caldera of GPA which is left behind. Like some corporate Krakatoa, the echoes go round the world while the site of the explosion is left a smoking ruin.

Next, the company's senior strategist gives a presentation. He is identified with top management and has developed the required brusque 'don't bother me, I'm out of your league' manner to go with it, although in fairness this might be a form of shyness. A boffin who has become part of Tony's entourage—especially during the pre-IPO period—his job is essentially to forecast aircraft demand. He has series of charts covering every related criterion. Central to the fleet build-up, he has appeared with his slides at every roadshow. Now, his figures of yesteryear, bolstered by Tony's gutsy approach, are completely shot. No problem, he has some new ones for us. *Mea culpa*? Not a bit of it. I can hardly bear to listen. I feel I want to get up and walk out. Am I being too harsh? It just seems to me that having seen your predictions collapse, a period of silence might be in order. He doesn't appear to realise that his credibility might be an issue.

In the evening there is another of the now regular GPA staff briefings on the progress or otherwise of the company post IPO. It is ironic that GPA, which has always been so lax in personnel matters, is taking this degree of concern now. Truly they, i.e. top management, must want something or are feeling guilty about the situation they have brought about. Already we, the staff, can discern that Tony and Maurice, who run these meetings, are being selective with the truth. After the last one where Maurice stated unequivocally that redundancies had not been discussed, I learned almost immediately afterwards from an excellent source that they had. There is now a feeling in the company of them and us, never before apparent, between those who brought us disaster and those who will probably have to suffer it most.

Anyway, this one is worse, in terms of the state of the company. Gently, Maurice leads us through each meeting by the hand, gradually deeper into infernal financial regions with which he must now be thoroughly conversant. Many of the staff sit like skiing beginners looking at their first terrifying slope, knowing they have to go down it.

The meeting room is in the Southern Hotel at Shannon Airport. At one end is a raised dais with a table along which sit, facing the packed audience, all but one of the GPA executive directors present—Tony, Maurice, Jim, Colm Barrington and John Tierney. The other director is Nigel Wilson. He is sitting next to me, buried in the middle of the large room. He wanted to sit next to someone who 'wasn't going to be stroppy'. He refuses to sit with the other directors when I point out he is the missing one.

Nigel is a relative newcomer. Even now he has only been with GPA for just over a year. He is English, from the North East, like myself. He was crucially involved with the IPO. He drew wide amazement when he joined GPA out of nowhere and straight on to the GPA main board. He had to be *Wunderkind*. It has not turned out well. And, to cap it all, he has no share debt.

Tony obviously loathes him. Nigel has failed Tony. Nigel's role in Operation Rebound, the rallying name for our survival effort, is minimal. He is helping Mike Dolan raise junk equity—the equity equivalent of junk bonds—higher rate of equity return for a higher risk investment. It is not the mainstream effort to acquire new capital funding that is being undertaken by Maurice and Peter Denison-Edson.

Maurice moves away from the table to the lectern at the side where he will deliver his talk. He is being videoed for the benefit of overseas staff. Nigel squirms and sinks in his seat as Maurice goes through the horrors of the past few months. Unbelievably, Maurice presents our present position as a mighty achievement on his part and that of his valiant team, in view of the overall situation following the collapsed IPO. It is breathtaking in its sheer neck to listen to the same people who have led the company to the brink of perdition expecting us to be grateful for their expertise in so far handling the situation so expertly. I am dumbfounded sitting there.

Maurice outlines the position with the aircraft manufacturers, skipping round the appalling state of our relations with MDC, where a multimillion dollar lawsuit beckons. He talks about the financial restructuring plans, the proposed new equity hopes. He then spells out the interdependence of everything. This is always the killer in corporate rescheduling. I have been here before in my life, but most of the staff will have no understanding of the practical complexities this entails. He tells us that 'we have control of our own destiny', the company is being run by the management. It really is risible. Is he really fooled into thinking this way or does he seek only to reassure us? Pinocchio's song, 'I can dance and I can sing, there are no strings on me', irresistibly comes into my head.

However, Maurice continues, with all these lifesaving reducing measures the company will have to be 'redesigned'. Aha! Redundancies—what everyone has really come to hear about. Sadly there will be some, he tells us, details unknown; it is being worked on. Pre-meeting rumours say March; Maurice says two months. Same thing.

Tony takes the stand next. He starts off by harking back to the 'shocking' collapse of the IPO. He has obviously rationalised the entire failure of GPA as stemming from the unsuccessful public flotation. This diary knows the IPO crash is only symptomatic of the real illness caused by Tony's overreaching. As he speaks of the IPO, his pale eyes bore into Nigel next to me. Nigel's body language displays inner torment. He covers his face with one hand, already low in the seat as Tony impales him on his gimlet gaze.

When the redundancies occur, to satiate directorial consciences, there will probably have to be a high level reject to show pain at all levels. I feel this board casualty, this scapegoat who will unfairly carry the can for the other longer serving executive board members, is sitting next to me. I can almost feel his predicament. Nigel is in a leprous, belled situation and he will suffer the death of a thousand cuts before going. Of all of them up on the dais, Nigel the outcast is the only one I feel sorry for.

Tony gives an inspirational speech. Any redundancies, he declares, will be sensitively dealt with. People will be relocated in the aviation industry and when GPA regains its health they will be welcomed 'back into the fold'. Later as we compare notes, I find nobody believes this. At the time though it sounds good. Also, says Tony, there will be a $40 per share bonus as of now. We are truly delighted. Again, later, we realise that the greatest recipients of this largesse should be—you guessed it— the architects of our downfall, the executive board members led by Tony. $40 a share currently means $16,000 to me. For Tony the figure will be astronomic, assuming the directors are included. I have the feeling that if they are excluded that would have been specifically mentioned. Also there will be a revamping of the remuneration packages of those who are left, a further bonus in June—presupposing we are still here—and the overnight allowances are being increased retrospectively. At $112 these had not been changed, except to reduce their coverage, since I joined in 1985.

Tony must be really worried that we are all going to leave him. He needs the staff so he can represent to the banks that he still has the best team in the world to run the operation. Aircraft numbering 450 plus out on lease takes some running.

I am suddenly reminded of something. I remembered going in GPA's executive jet with Tony to Fokker headquarters in Amsterdam on one occasion back in 1987. Things were not going too well with the GPA/ Fokker/Mitsubishi joint venture I was running at the time, trying to lease a large number of 100 seat Fokker 100 jets the world by and large did not want (and still doesn't). Tony wanted to grab that meeting by the throat with some bright news and going over in the aircraft asked me what I could give him by way of ammunition. I had none, to my shame. I could just imagine Tony approaching this staff meeting in exactly the same way. He needed some gold to throw before the masses, to keep us happy, to deflect negativism.

Two days later we got a staff memo round from Tony confirming the giveaways. It starts: 'I was very encouraged by the resilience and spirit that was evident at our briefing last Monday evening' i.e. he knows we're all angry and scared, but nobody showed it.

This week I have been in Madrid for a couple of days. I return to find Colm Barrington making the headlines in his court battle with the Bank of Ireland over his outstanding share loan. The bank's Shannon Airport branch manager, whom we have all known for years, makes the unwise but true statement in court that GPA shares are unsaleable and of no value. This utterance is starting to reverberate publicly. It has also put the spotlight on the financial problems being suffered by many of the GPA executives, the corollary being that these problems could somehow prejudice the restructuring efforts. It is reported today in an Irish business magazine that Tony, with 9.6 million 'valueless' shares has a Merrill Lynch company loan of $35 million repayable in 1994. The Bank of Ireland has stated that they do not believe Colm has the means to cover his obligations. There must be other very senior people in the same position. Will this story continue to run and hurt us?

Incredibly, we are still doing leasing business. Letters of Intent continue to be signed. It just shows what faith people have in covenants of quiet enjoyment and that we still have some stature in the eyes of some airline operators.

I have just heard that MDC has unilaterally cancelled the two MD-11 aircraft due for delivery to GPA in 1993. Hardly an extra problem; we couldn't take them anyway.

There are obviously going to be huge write-offs this financial year in respect of all this pain we are having to take. A senior management figure for whom I have nil respect breathes into my ear, '$800 million.' That is most of our net worth.

Sunday 31 January 1993

I am with Graham again, propping up the bar at the Shannon Shamrock in Bunratty, just down the road from Shannon. It has become a weekly event we both sort of look forward to, discussing the present situation.

On the aircraft coming over, the Irish papers have been full of the aftermath of Colm's court case. Human interest has taken over, with the coverage of the supposed financial plight of the other GPA directors and executives. It is now a given that all GPA employee shareholders have bought their shares via loans. A list of the major shareholders is printed. For shareholder read debtor. There are photographs of the houses belonging to Tony, Maurice, Jim, Colm, etc. There is even an article on how the ex-Taoiseach, a GPA board member, is going to weather his personal financial storm. Tony's Merrill Lynch loan is re-aired, along with his allegedly worthless shares.

Graham's view is that only now will it really sink into these people the predicament they are in. He expects to see a real change in the morale of the senior people around him. I find this difficult to believe, as I have had so few illusions since last July, immediately following the pulled IPO. I feel for all the non-board member executives who have poured so much of their lives into GPA over the past years, ending up with nothing at best. Those who do not have non-recourse loans may have to work to pay off their loans for the rest of their lives—a horrific thought. Already at one lunchtime in the GPA dining room one of our colleagues on the Trading Floor, half in jest, raised the subject of assuming a new identity.

There was a fistfight between two marketing executives in the Shannon office last week. I can hardly believe it. One needed immediate medical treatment. It seems they have some domestic problems, but it is a sign of the times. Little to lose now, and under severe pressure.

Graham reminisced over his pint. He has been around GPA since the start. He decried the silly deals done under Jim's stewardship of the Leasing division at Tony's urgent behest. He believes he was taken out of the executive committee, which at that time gave transaction approval to deals, because of his perceived negativity. He even had endorsed on his annual review a criticism that he had not done a specific deal, one which he had never believed in and which now in hindsight would only have added to the misery.

Sunday 14 February 1993

En route Shannon. Peter Denison-Edson is on the flight. We discuss the progress of raising new equity from existing corporate shareholders. He is warily hopeful. He says any injection will be subject to management changes. He laughs. There is no senior management above Phil Bolger who have not been discredited by the events of the last year. We both know that short of a shareholders' or banks' blitzkrieg, there is no real prospect that the major management figures, the old guard, will ever change.

Later on, back at the Shannon Shamrock, Graham confirms the company is being run by the banks. He was at a meeting during the week with Pratt & Whitney, the engine manufacturers, trying to sort out contract commitments for engines and discount levels, which was run by Anne Lane from American Citibank—already well known for having told Tony to 'can the crap' at an earlier meeting.

Tuesday 16 February 1993

Nigel Wilson has resigned. A full GPA executive board member. The first to go. What did I say? Did he fall or was he pushed? The memo to all from Tony said that as the Corporate department is going to be disbanded in the 'redesign' of the company, as MD of Corporate, Nigel had tendered his resignation and Tony had accepted it 'with regret'. Hardly convincing as the memo goes on to say that other personnel in the department would be reassigned duties. I suspect that if Jim, Colm or John had been in the same post, they too would have been reassigned. Unfortunately, Nigel is a newcomer, has not hit it off with Tony, is a convenient fall guy etc. I recall his obvious inner turmoil at the last company briefing session for staff, when he sat next to me head in hands for the most part, speared by Tony's glare.

I am sorry for Nigel, but this has been coming plain as a pikestaff for some time now.

Meanwhile we the staff of GPA wait for the imminent management and company reshuffle. Rumours vary between 30–50 per cent redundancies. The memo is expected this week. I cannot say the waiting is pleasant, especially as the people I am talking to every day— Niall Greene, now MD of Leasing, and Phil Bolger will already know our fates. Are they being friendly because I am secure in my position, inasmuch as GPA can be called secure, or is it out of sympathy, knowing I am for the chop?

I am going to Zimbabwe tonight to escape. I will be trying to collect outstanding rentals from Affretair, one of my least favourite airlines, then on to Johannesburg.

In Johannesburg I speak to my only customer in RSA, a model lessee, which is seriously contemplating going out of business due to the anti-competitive antics of State-owned SAA, despite assurances by the Department of Transport. If it does, four A320s just 18 months old will be returned to GPA Airbus.

The joint venture company, GPA Airbus, is now in the course of being bought out by GPA. It is in terrible financial straits. What a rosy future this JV once had back in 1987. One of the venture partners, Canadian Airlines, which itself has a chunk of the venture's A320s, has stopped paying rental on them. It now says it will start to pay again in May. Who knows? Originally a smallish, well run, longstanding western

Canadian airline based in Calgary, Pacific Western grew rapidly using money received from GPA from the sale and leaseback of a fleet of Boeing 737-200 aircraft to become the large deregulation airline known as Canadian Airlines. Like us, their management must be going through hell.

The expression 'deregulation airline' is really a curse. None has survived, unless operating under Chapter 11 of the US Bankruptcy Code can be called survival. Canadian is now akin to that other millstone of ours—America West. Aviation is a hard business where only the best survive, and I mean the best managed. GPA is no exception.

Sunday 21 February 1993

At Heathrow, waiting for the flight to Shannon, I call Nigel to offer my sympathy. There is nothing to say except that maybe it is a blessing in disguise. If GPA goes bust in a few months anyway, better out now.

On the aircraft I sit next to one of the younger marketing executives. I always kid him about being a Warren Beatty lookalike. He is under 30 and single. GPA must have been a dream job for him. He has a great personality, but unfortunately the dream has gone sour. He has unpaid GPA share loans, both with the sympathetic Allied Irish Banks and the unhelpful Bank of Ireland. 'Big bucks', he says sadly. I am sorry. I do not pry further.

These loans, often contracted by our employees long after I started this diary, I fear will soon start to destroy some lives. The amounts involved are usually stratospheric by ordinary standards. I marvel at my young colleague's ability to discuss it rationally at all. Tony is right to praise their resilience. I read an article in *The Times* today by Libby Purves in which she coins a phrase I can identify with—'the Nouveau Ruined'.

Monday 22 February 1993

At the morning meeting nothing much is happening on the marketing screens, but Niall Greene in the chair says we have put away a tidy number of aircraft this month—some 20 odd. The accent is all on receivables: getting back money owed to us. The total is still enormous, over $60 million, and that is with several major debtors taken out of the total, e.g. VASP, Canadian Airlines and America West. I am doing little else than trying to extract payment from my group of old lags, while a so-called task force has been set up to chivvy all our wayward customers. Every one of our African customer airlines is behind on aircraft rental and maintenance payments except Flitestar in South Africa and Kenya Airways in Nairobi.

During the morning I hear that MDC has filed suit against us in the US courts. There is concern as to what this will do to the restructuring process. Though the banks had apparently agreed to consider finalising the rescheduling of debts, even though the MDC problem had not been settled, this agreement did not take into account an actual lawsuit being commenced. At least this is what I glean. We are counter-claiming. Luckily the media has not yet picked up on this public fact.

I take the lunchtime flight back to London. I want to get back to the London office to meet the financial director of a Nigerian airline customer. Next to me on the flight is Phil Bolger. He is on his way to Stockholm to see Solitair, a special purpose company set up through the activities of Mike Dolan back in the heady days of the late 80s and 1990, when GPA Capital and Mike in particular were making money hand over fist. Mike was an innovator with the Midas touch. I fancy even Tony was a bit staggered by what Mike seemed to be achieving profit wise. Mike was well looked after, but he never seemed to become part of the old guard.

I ask Phil when we might see the promised reshuffle/redundancy memo. He has the final draft with him. It is coming out this afternoon. He hands it to me with a weary look and says it is a personal disaster for him.

It is not a memo about redundancies, or even a redesign of the company. It is yet another meaningless reshuffle of the old guard and their principal henchpersons. Really quite unbelievable. It is like some bizarre game of musical chairs, where the music stops every so often but no chairs are removed. The players of this game—the old guard— are impervious to real change. They are secure in their own cocoon. The team that has brought us the GPA crash is still there. The rest is window dressing. Nigel's departure does not count. He never joined the old guard. He has had something meaningful happen: he has had to go. The real perpetrators stay. Phil likens it to rearranging deckchairs on the Titanic.

Colm Barrington and John Tierney are to be joint chief executives under Tony as executive chairman. Joint anything at the top is nearly always a recipe for trouble in companies. Well, now we have it. Maurice is stated to be Tony's deputy but seems to have little to do. Everyone agrees he is in the wilderness. Plainly, Maurice and Nigel have shouldered most of Tony's blame for the IPO catastrophe. Various familiar names are there as senior management.

Jim continues as vice chairman. His role—PR and some specific marketing accounts seems already a pointer back to the small team outlook of yesteryear. GPA is imploding like the collapsing shell of a spent supernova.

On the Leasing side, there is a new, odd development. Richard O'Toole is to come in and run receivables, contract administration and technical matters. He will be under Phil, who heads Leasing under Colm.

Niall Greene gets no mention, neither does Brian Hayden, MD of Air Tara and now presumably under O'Toole. Brian is a brilliant person to have in the company. He does not need or deserve a newcomer to oversee his department. The inclusion of O'Toole in the Leasing set-up is inexplicable.

The memo, which is from Tony, ends with mention being made of another exercise nearing fruition, the big R issue. Meanwhile Tony signs off, again praising the staff's resilient attitude during these dark days.

Phil and I talk a bit about the memo. He has had no input. He was not even consulted about O'Toole's appointment. Knowing Phil as I do, it seems incredible his advice would not be sought: except of course if it was deliberately not sought.

Tuesday 23 February 1993

The memo has been badly received everywhere. Nobody cares any more about another useless reshuffle of the favoured few who have led us all into this mess. The only important part of the memo are the closing remarks. The staff awaits the big one, the redundancy memo. Who goes and who stays? This is the only issue of importance. The uncertainty is a huge strain on everybody. The consensus is that it is typical that the only ones who know their future are the reshuffled ones—those who had most to do with our current condition. The irony is lost on nobody.

There is a feeling that the redundancy memo should have come first, so that the senior management could then have been chosen to reign over what is left. Instead, the chiefs have been reselected before their troops have been identified. There is much resentment. Many seem to favour an upper management clean-out, but no one dares to speak out and risk Tony's wrath and the inevitable immediate marching orders.

Phil is thoroughly disgusted with the memo. He gives the new set-up two months at most. On the flight we talk a bit more. At one stage I say we ought to enlist our non-executive deputy chairman John Harvey Jones as chief executive—let him run the company. He is supposed to be the expert. It should also help our credibility with the banks etc. The suggestion seems to take Phil aback. He appears to file the notion away for further consideration. I am always amazed no one has had the idea long ago, given the popular *Troubleshooter* TV series where JHJ specifically goes around advising stricken companies on their resurrection. Possibly JHJ would refuse an offer anyway. Perhaps GPA is too much like the Augean stables.

The memo also refers to a set of company business principles which are to be our future guide. These are to be published soon.

Friday 26 February 1993

I have spent the last two days working from home. Once again the London office has been full of Operation Rebounders, with not a desk free. Today though I get back to my office: Friday, when most people are repositioning themselves to be back home in Shannon for the weekend. I see the business principles document. It looks as if it has been written, not for the company but for the banks, telling them how we will run our business in future—like a schoolboy writing a report for his master, saying that in future he will be good. I am uninspired. It turns out that yes, it was part of the documentation put to the banks as part of the restructuring.

I ask one of John Tierney's lieutenants how the restructuring is going. I get a slow, careful smile as he says the various banks' credit committees are trawling through our paperwork and we will know more in a few weeks.

Niall Greene appears in the London office for a meeting. He is a political animal—in its literal sense. He is a leading socialist light in Ireland. He had been with GPA for a long time, but left to pursue his political career, then rejoined back in the mid-80s. He is competent, organised and will listen. He can be tough, but he is very kind. I like him. He works well with Phil running the Leasing Marketing department.

It turns out Niall is also very upset about the memo. I can believe it. He is MD of Leasing and neither he nor Brian Hayden get a mention as senior management of the division. He is particularly irritated by the installation of O'Toole. The memo states that seamless management is an objective. Niall believes, and I agree with him, that his and Phil's efforts had achieved a measure of that. He reiterates the amount of hard work that has been put in over the past months. The implication is, for what? Putting in a newcomer is making seams and divisions where there were none. Again, Niall makes the point that neither he nor Phil were consulted about the changes in their own department. He calls the memo senseless and shakes his head.

After he leaves for the airport, I reflect. I realise that actually the only thing worse than the failure of the IPO would have been its success. If we were now a publicly listed company in London, New York, Tokyo and Dublin, we would have raised a lot more money—billions more—and with it we would have continued to buy the aircraft we had ordered. In the current recession they would mainly be on the ground. Our financial state would be far more parlous than it is now. Paradoxically, maybe the IPO failure has been a favour. Of course Tony could never dare say that. Tony has really blown it. Presumably he is still around because he built the company up from nothing, therefore no one wants to ask him to go. Either they feel he can do it all over again, or it would be like separating a mother from her baby. I do not know the answer. I do know that nothing Tony has touched since about the time I joined GPA has gone right in the fullness of time—either within GPA or outside it.

Generally I have never seen aviation at such a low ebb worldwide than at present. If it were not for China waking up, there would be deeper gloom everywhere. China is going to be some power come the next few decades.

I hear that GPA Group has now acquired GPA Airbus from the other three joint venture partners for the princely sum of $1 each.

I coax a fax out of the Airbus camp to send to Flitestar, indicating financial help. We have no money; who are we to help? The only worse thing will be to get the four A320s back. To avoid that we will forgo immediate rentals if absolutely necessary and, I suppose, if the banks will allow it.

Monday 8 March 1993

One of my West African customers is having its insurance cancelled this week if $500,000 is not paid to its brokers. Will they make it? I hope so. They spend their time operating on the edge, in every sense. Sometimes I am surprised there is not a crash a day in Africa. The managing director of this particular airline once gave me a tour of his airline base at Lagos Airport. I wish he hadn't.

Rereading some of this, I am struck by my criticisms, while offering nothing constructive. As it is impossible, repeat impossible, for me to transmit my views to anyone meaningful without being held to be talking out of place, maybe I should set down here what I would do now if I was running GPA.

1. I would immediately tell the staff where they stand. Redundancies are necessary: they should begin to be implemented. Key senior (not top management) people should be talked to and assured, so that they do not start to look afield. We need to be smaller and leaner, functioning as in the days when I joined. The layers of

management and meetings should be cut out. We should all be Indians, with just the necessary chiefs. We need a reborn mentality.

2. I would have an audit of our entire fleet, in terms of what aircraft will be coming back off lease needing to be re-leased over the next five years and what depleted stand of new aircraft deliveries remain to be delivered. We need to see the totality of the task facing us over the five year rebuilding period now. Everyone staying needs to have a copy of it.

3. We should come out of our ultra swish New York offices and move to more modest accommodation. When times were good, the present offices used to embarrass marketing executives bringing customers in because of the opulence. Goodness knows what people think now we are effectively penniless.

4. We must sell aircraft, the older ones.

5. Tony must be non-executive.

6. Maurice should not be in a position to run the company on his say so alone, not even as someone's deputy.

7. Colm Barrington should leave. Patrick Blaney to be responsible for the Capital division.

8. Jim King should not be managing. He is a first-class communicator, excellent on his own. He is not a boss.

9. Phil Bolger and Niall Greene should be in charge of GPA Leasing. Liam Barrett to be in charge of all administration.

10. Operation Rebound needs to be completely overhauled. It is impossible to know how it is achieving and the signs from certain areas of it are very disturbing.

Monday 15 March 1993

Last Friday, Maurice circulated a Project Rebound update. Presumably written with the best spin available, it is a depressing document. It is divided into the main issues confronting us: banks, aircraft manufacturers, new equity and liquidity.

As for the banks it seems so far so good, but everything is conditional on the rest of the house of cards. Plus, because of the time slippage, we are having to seek further waivers in respect of the various covenants in the loan documentation we are currently breaching.

Maurice states that we have reached 'definitive' agreements with Boeing, Airbus and Fokker. This is not true. We still of course have the MDC lawsuit to deal with. He praises the 'remarkable' job done by Jim, Patrick and their unnamed colleagues in this regard. One of those colleagues is heartily sick of the undeserved superlatives handed out as usual by one member of the 'in crowd' to other members. In reality, we had to accept what the manufacturers were prepared to put up with. Even Patrick described the Airbus deal as one which sucked.

So far as new equity goes, the banks are looking to us to acquire $200 million in fresh equity to make the restructuring a runner. Our existing shareholders will not subscribe for all of this—how much they put up will be an eye opener—so we need new investors. Even at $1 each, there seems to be little enthusiasm for GPA shares. GPA is going to need all its guardian angels working in shifts to achieve this within the short timescale available.

Furthermore, the new issue will be very dilutive of existing shares. In other words, if shareholders, including staff shareholders, do not take up the new shares on offer, their existing holdings will be diminished due to the conditions attaching to the new shares.

The liquidity issue has another major problem looming. Innovatively, GPA began raising debt in the US by selling commercial paper—bonds—with a fixed rate of return. It has been decided and agreed by the banks that this chunk of GPA debt should not be restructured—that we should not default on payments as these are publicly traded notes. Maurice tells us we cannot raise money from aircraft sales at present to generate large slugs of cash, therefore we shall require 'fallback strategies' to generate the liquidity GPA will need to pay the 'significant' repayments that will fall due from May 1993.

Upon reading the memo, my initial thought is we shall be out of business at the end of May.

Today I learn that a deal we have been trying to do with the General Electric Credit Corporation (GECC), selling them half a billion dollars worth of our aircraft, has folded. Tony and Colm were in New York last week trying to save it, without success.

At the morning meeting today, our receivables were up to $73 million—$28 million to one carrier alone—and not Canadian Airlines, America West or VASP either. They owe us other tens of millions. Some of the airlines are long-term basket cases.

Remember Aerocalifornia? They permanently owe us around $3 million. LAP, the national airline of Paraguay owes us $2 million, with another $2.5 million on the way. They have been using their long range DC-10-30 aircraft from us on short hops. This is ruinous to engine maintenance costs and now the engines require overhaul way before time. The airline has virtually no money to accomplish this vital work.

Compass Airlines, a recent Australian carrier, went bust not long after start-up. It operated a fleet of Airbus A300-600 aircraft on lease. These new, large aircraft had to be returned with great pain to their lessors. Luckily we were not among them. End of Compass? Oh no. Reborn, with $4 million in equity from GPA and four of our MD-83 aircraft (three brand new) on lease, they try again. Six months later (last week in fact) they have just gone bust again and their chief executive has been arrested for fraud. We have lost our money, we have the aircraft back on our hands and we will have to pay a further $2 million to the Australian Civil Aviation Authority to lift a restraining lien on the aircraft in respect of unpaid landing fees. Additionally, each aircraft will require a maintenance check to put them on to another register. Cost? About another $1 million.

Air Ukraine, another new carrier which has been in business about six months, already owes us $1.3 million, operating two new Boeing aircraft. Already we are talking about repossession.

TAESA, a newish Mexican airline, is pumped full of our aircraft. To me it seems like a financial accident waiting to happen. Plus, they don't look after the aircraft. They already owe us $2 million.

So it goes, on and on. Why do we do this? Why do we put expensive aircraft into rotten airlines? Why do we have such a bad receivables problem? There is only one answer. We have so many aircraft being delivered to us, we had to grab at any deal to get them off the ground and into service. We have a Transaction Approval committee which vets every deal, with fancy paperwork as a strict requirement, but it is worthless. Why? Because the dialogue essentially goes as follows. 'This is a terrible deal. Are there any alternatives? No, we take the deal or the aircraft stay(s) on the ground. Approved.'

This has been the practical effect of Tony's personal vision of buying as many aircraft as possible. He has bet the GPA ranch—and lost. The supporting expertise from his senior colleagues, who he will say were with him every step of the way in all his decisions, was sycophantic hogwash, for whatever the occasion demanded, based on fear of Tony and personal greed.

We had a laudable but laughable Receivables Policy circulated lately—probably more impractical foolery given to the banks to show them how we intend to clean up our act. It detailed action to be taken, on an escalating basis, day by day, following a lessee missing a rental payment, culminating in repossession of aircraft about 14 days later. Total cloud cuckoo land! Its accompanying memo asked for comments. I told them they needed a Lessees Policy instead. So far no signs of implementing the new policy. I should think not. We would be inundated with repossessed aircraft within three weeks. Madness!

Anyway, the target for receivables by the end of this month, an important reporting point for the banks etc. is $45 million. We will never get near it.

Canadian Airlines came up at the meeting. They are in dire trouble. They have stopped paying us aircraft rents etc. and do not intend to restart until later in the year. The executive responsible, Sean Donlon, recited the things they have to do to survive. It sounded almost identical to the list of issues GPA has to resolve satisfactorily for our own survival. Asked whether he thought the airline would come through, Sean thought not. I wondered if anyone else saw the immediate comparison. I could imagine other meetings saying the same things about us. We would be outraged to be so apparently casually written off.

More people are leaving. About 25 or so now. The email on our computer screens keeps giving us details of leaving parties in local hostelries. It reminds me of one of my African contacts in their Transport Ministry, who is able to gauge the growing seriousness of the

Aids epidemic in Zimbabwe by the increasing number of requests he gets from employees to attend funerals. I hope we don't have a leaving epidemic.

Criticism of the top leadership is now widespread. 'Floundering' is a word often heard. Treatment of the staff is a sore point. We wait for the end of March, for the redundancies. The wait is crippling. If a test of courage is indeed grace under pressure, there is surely bravery here. Tony seems rarely in Shannon.

I, like many others, feel the company is a goner, and sooner rather than later. The only exception to this would be if the banks stepped in before it is too late, replaced key sections of the management and ran the company using funds as necessary to keep us going. In this eventuality, most of the top management would have to go. Maurice and John Tierney would maybe stay as the banks' representatives, as they appear to have the confidence of the banks and staff. No one else above Phil Bolger and Niall Greene has, apart from Patrick. The soul of the company would change completely. It could only be for the best. Tony is a really special person. He founded the company and drove it forward. His remuneration philosophy is the best I have ever encountered, but that's it. He has driven us over a cliff even I saw coming early in 1990—three years ago.

Where the heck is John Harvey Jones in all this? What was the use of his ever joining GPA's board? I am very disappointed.

Thursday 1 April 1993

Deeper and deeper. We have had another update from Maurice. We are losing the new equity battle. Last week our investment rating was again downgraded to, I think, triple c. This means that anyone investing in us needs their head examined.

Without fresh investment, or enough of it, we have not enough cash to pay the upcoming medium-term notes dividends. What cash we have—and it looks sizeable at over half a billion dollars—is nearly all lessees' deposits and maintenance reserves for the aircraft, i.e. untouchable, or should be.

I hear from another source what I already suspect: our bank

negotiating team is weak. Not only that, but the effort is not being managed. Everyone is so stretched. In cases of default, banks change teams completely. We should do it too. As it is, we have the people who have dealt with the banks all along continuing to do so. In view of what has happened they are, somewhat naturally, too deferential and find it hard to say no to the banks' demands. It cannot be easy.

People are leaving the company in numbers. It is proving another bone of contention. There has been no company redesign memo round yet. By now you should not be surprised at this, notwithstanding the earlier commitment to have it out by the end of March. Anyway, people cannot yet plan their futures because first, they do not know whether or not they will be made redundant, and second, no one knows the level of remuneration if they are not made redundant. A further twist—there is supposed to be a voluntary redundancy package. Those who have left have received according to the terms of this package. However, if the company does not want certain people to leave, when they ask for the package, it is refused. It is a selective scheme. This makes it even harder to plan ahead. Simple prudence would suggest that people look round for an alternative job. However, they cannot be sure they will have access to the voluntary redundancy package—a hugely important part of the equation for some people—if they ask to leave.

I guess the catch-22 could go like this. If you are stupid the company doesn't want you and you can take the redundancy package and leave the company. Because you would have to be stupid to want to stay in the company, by asking to leave you are doing what any sensible person would do, therefore you are not stupid and so you cannot leave and take the package.

It's not strictly true, but it's fun to think of it that way. Whatever, the company is up to its old tricks of screwing its friends and favouring its enemies. If you are no good you can go and take the package; if you are any good you can go, but no package. Unfortunately neither is there anything else on offer yet. No wonder the executive staff are terminally peed off, excuse me. Everyone is at the end of their financial tether. It has been nearly a year on emergency rations.

The Dublin office is to close. There is a date fixed. Some people have already left from there and have received their redundancy package. These are people the company did not mind losing. Those not seeking to leave however are apparently needed, because they have been told they will not be paid redundancy on closure—they should move to Shannon on the other side of the country. Unfair and illogical. Probably completely unsustainable in court, if challenged.

So here we are, less every day, beavering away. No one has any faith in the board of directors. No one seems to have much faith in our survival prospects. Everyone is fed up with the uncertainty. The staff have no spokesman and knowledge is not achievable on an individual basis. Unless the company wants to get rid of you, you cannot get the redundancy package. Remembering Bob Greenspon's phrase, is this another level of badness? By the way, Bob left a while ago, post IPO, to return to private law practice in New York. We still use him.

I hear $17 million has been set aside for the closure of the Dublin and New York offices and redundancies. No one knows how this sum is made up, other, presumably, than those who fabricated it.

The year end loss figure is climbing. It is now nearing $900 million. I am told the important thing is to keep the figure below the psychologically important figure of $1 billion!

Just back from Paris, today I am in the London office. The atmosphere is mentally exhausting. The pervading sense is of the company's woes. Tony, Maurice and John are all here with various minions closeted away in meetings. I cannot escape it. I swap gossip with some of the other visitors. Everyone is down.

Sunday 4 April 1993

As usual Graham and I are in the bar of the Shannon Shamrock Hotel. Later tonight, because gales have delayed our flight from London. We discuss ways ahead for the company. Graham thinks Maurice and Tony should go. He reckons he will have a coffee with Tony in the morning and rehearse a few of his thoughts. There are few people in the company with this access to Tony.

We discuss the GE alternative—GE buying out GPA for a song. I believe it would be great for the company, but what a contrast to the way ILFC sold out to AIG. Graham tells me that Tony had told him of an exchange he had with Gary Wendt, head of GECC. Says Tony of the terms offered by Wendt, 'You're raping me.' Wendt replied, 'But Tony, you're naked.' Wendt used to be a director of GPA in the past, when GECC was a shareholder, and he was not all that popular by all accounts. How the wheels go round.

There is to be a board meeting on Tuesday. This could be quite momentous as it is the time for the board to go to the banks with the $200 million new equity, a *sine qua non* for the restructuring. The equity has not been raised. Will the banks allow us to soldier on to mid-May, when the first slice of public debt interest has to be paid, to see if we can muster funds to pay it somehow? Will the banks insist on some kind of debt for equity swap, whereby they will meet the interest payment in return for equity in GPA? Or will the banks say we have failed to meet the conditions of the restructuring—already extended beyond its original expiry date—and put in receivers? I believe they will let us soldier on, as long as cash is not being dissipated and revenue is coming in.

Chapter 5

OPERATION REBOUND 2
1993

Monday 5 April 1993

What a day!

After the morning meeting, Joe Clarkin drops by the office I am using for the day. He fills me in on events. Last Friday it seems a memo was sent to Tony and, I later learn, all the other GPA directors, executive and non-executive, by Phil and Patrick, complaining about the management of the company and setting out their own plans for the future management.

In the GPA culture the courage of this act cannot be underestimated. Is this a coup, a mutiny or a *cri de coeur*? Without seeing the memo it is impossible to tell.

Further, a meeting was held on Sunday night at Phil's home, attended by Patrick and some of the senior Shannon-based marketing and capital people.

The memo is apparently due to be discussed at today's chairman's top management meeting.

Next I speak to Liam Barrett, a senior corporate manager, who used to be GPA Group company secretary. He acts as secretary to the chairman's meeting. He confirms it is on the agenda, just added that morning, as discussion of a survival strategy. Liam is disparaging of top management. He has built up, openly but on the side, a successful commercial property business. If GPA fails, he will be fine financially. Liam is an individual of high quality. He has not participated in the ambitious rat racing tactics of some of the senior people, yet it is hard to think of anybody who has come out of GPA better than him, quietly making himself solid all the while. He promises to keep me updated.

Down I go to Graham. I cannot log on to the computer as a Shannon visitor because the link with the London office is down, so there is little I can achieve workwise until it is fixed. Graham says he saw Phil earlier in the morning and told him he intended seeing Tony for a chat. 'Too late' was Phil's reply. The bomb has already been dropped, says Graham. He recalled being with Tony last Friday in Hartford, Connecticut, at Pratt & Whitney, the engine manufacturers. It was an important meeting with lunch and had been set up for over a month. Tony left the room to take a call from Shannon. He was gone for about 15 minutes and after he returned he hardly said a word. Graham believed that was when he learned of the memo. It is obviously dynamite.

I speak to Peter Denison-Edson. He is in Maurice's camp. He will be at the meeting. Peter believes there are several possible buyers for GPA. They are waiting for the right time to make final moves, i.e. until GPA has nowhere else to go. Regarding the memo from Phil and Patrick, Peter believes it is just a question of poor communication. The rest of us do not know all the things Maurice and his team are doing, it's not that they are doing it badly. Well, I say the popular conception is that the race for new equity is being lost and Maurice's last Operation Rebound report said as much.

Peter tells me that some $125 million of new equity is around, $70 odd million in Japan. Much of it is conditional—upon others contributing. I raise the prospect of using some of it to prepay the looming public debt dividend by adopting Margaret Clandillon's idea of paying before the cut-off date, at a dividend pro rata the actual value of the bonds to their face value, so that we would not need the full $200 million. Peter is silent. He knows nothing of this and I can read from his facial expression the scale of the exercise to begin to accomplish such an objective. I am left with the impression that there are bricks laid in the new equity wall, but it is not yet the full wall and if the other bricks do not arrive, the existing wall will be dismantled and the bricks removed.

MD-83—March 1990, one of the returned early Unifly Express 'Red Arrows' parked on a Shannon Airport taxiway. (© *F. Goodman*)

B737-200A—Coming in over the threshold at Mumbai in the livery of one of GPA's least favourite customers—Indian Airlines. (© *Vivek Manvi, Mumbai, India*)

DC-9-30—About to depart Los Angeles. Sickly AeroCalifornia effectively used GPA as a rolling $3m overdraft facility. (© *Aris A. Pappas*)

Fokker F100—Coming into Brussels. Portugalia was GPA Fokker's first lessee, thanks to Ron Franken's efforts. (© Rainer Bexten)

B737-300—Taking off from Kuala Lumpur on its way back to Manila. Philippine Airlines was for some time our biggest customer and one of my favourites to visit, deal with and fly with. (© JKSC)

A300-200—Ready to depart Málaga. Eventually we were so desperate to market this type we offered TransAer power by the hour—they paid only for the aircraft for the hours they actually flew, as against a monthly rental. (© *Stefan Gruenig, Thun*)

B767-200ER—Henderson's Flying Folly. Here, stopping off at Dublin on its delivery flight to Maputo, the aircraft Linhas Aereas de Mocambique struggled to afford—making me spend many days debt collecting in Maputo. (© *F. Goodman*)

De Havilland Canada (Bombardier) DHC-8-200—the Dash 8, one of our turboprop types. This one is a manufacturer's demonstrator leaving Dorval, Montreal. (© F. Camirand)

DC-8-71F—Here seen awaiting runway clearance for take-off at Gatwick, the infamous WYMO aircraft. Affretair used it mainly to transport, overnight, chilled fresh-cut flowers to Europe from Zimbabwe. (© *Wingnut*)

DC-10-30—Pictured lining up for take-off at Manchester, Miami bound. Laker Airways' second coming. Sadly, it didn't last long. (© *Andreas Heilmann* (www.haj-spotter.de))

MD-11—About to head out over the bay at Kai Tak, Hong Kong, a Garuda Indonesian Airlines (Aerocitra) aircraft. Cathay Pacific L-1011 Tristars in the background. (© *Andrew Hunt*)

A320-200—April 1993, parked at Durban, one of four leased to Flitestar, my favourite customer. I wish they were flying today—they should be. (© *Sven Pipjorke*)

B747-100—GPA's transatlantic bus service, courtesy of Aer Lingus. Daily between Shannon and New York JFK. Here rolling for take-off from Dublin, probably en route Shannon. (© *F. Goodman*)

It is this old, old problem. I met it firsthand with Laker Airways and have seen it operating many times since. All lenders, suppliers and creditors want to help. Yet help will only be offered if every other party involved helps to the same extent, pro rata. This seemingly cast iron requirement that pain is to be borne equally is the hardest to negotiate around and ultimately causes more collapses as time and money run out. Meetings become endless, activity more frantic, the all-important confidence that it will be resolved begins to evaporate. Nothing short of a white knight (who may turn out to be a very dirty black knight) will save the day.

Peter tries to convince me that there are white knights around, canny ones, waiting only for the right moment to swoop, i.e. when the damsel can not only be carried off to great acclaim but abused in the public interest as well. Next he spoils it by naming a couple of contenders. GECC we all know about, but American Airlines? I heard that Tony had gone to see the legendary Bob Crandall, head of this huge carrier. My reaction had been one of disbelief at Tony even starting to think that AMR would be remotely interested in buying GPA—American Airlines, in the midst of the worst US airline recession ever, awash in vast oceans of red ink with enormous continuing losses, locked in battle with savage competitors, cancelling orders, grounding fleets, having its credit rating reduced. Whatever could it want with buying GPA? What could possibly be the advantage? Their aircraft are cheaper than ours. Downsides from buying GPA could be prolific. What would AMR gain? I tell Peter it would be like the ancient mariner bidding for his albatross.

Peter looks perplexed, kindly. He has done more than his fair share at GPA. An ex-UK Foreign Service diplomat, if there is such a thing, we will not fail because his Japanese responsibilities have not come up to the mark. He has thrived at GPA, where Tony appears to like and value him—last time I looked. I leave Peter, interested to have seen the world more from his perspective.

Trying to confirm all the flying rumours, I see Trevor Henderson. He professes ignorance and asks me what I know. Dutifully I trot out everything I have learned during the morning. He confirms it all and marvels at the way supposedly secret information disseminates so quickly. Trevor had been invited to Phil's Sunday home meeting but had not attended due to not feeling well.

By this time news has spread via the grapevine, and Leasing is agog at events.

Graham and I deduce three possible outcomes: Phil and Patrick resign, or they carry the day; other heads roll and real change ensues; or there will be a compromise between both sides. I expect the last. So does Graham. Tony needs to be able to present to the banks that he has his marketing team intact. The banks are relying on it. It is the only area where revenue is being produced.

I visit Niall, he says the next 24 hours may be very 'bloody', but doesn't have time to elaborate as the phone rings. I leave him to it.

I had heard from Joe earlier in the day that one of the ideas in the memo was for the company to escape its public debt obligations by entering into a pre-planned receivership, with the aim of escaping from it when propitious. With everyone I see (except Niall where there is not time) I argue against this step. I quote from my Laker experience, where no matter how much support you think you have, once a receiver is called in, confidence vanishes. Our customers would clamour for their deposits, for the safety of aircraft maintenance reserves, our trade creditors would demand payment and our assets would be impounded. We would have no credit, no standing. People would look on us as goners. It would be a devastatingly quick nightmare, unlike anything expected, no matter how carefully planned. Events would run away with us. I argue that GPA keeping the outward semblance of solvency and viability is the key to survival.

But what can I do? I am a mote in GPA's existence. Nothing I say could be valuable, else why am I not higher up the ladder? QED. It is frustrating. All I can do is talk to people who have rights of audience and hope some of it rubs off.

I take the late afternoon flight back to London. On the way out I pass Phil's office. He is back from the chairman's meeting. Still alive then. I pop my head in and wish him luck with whatever is going on. He feigns surprise and asks what do I mean. Nothing is going on. 'Okay,' I say, 'I wish you luck with whatever is not going on.' At that he gives a wide if furtive grin and nods at me. I leave.

Ten minutes later in the Gold Circle lounge at the airport I call Liam to find out what went on. It turns out little was said, but there were two private meetings at least between Tony and the two protagonists. Liam felt a crisis had been precipitated for the board meeting tomorrow.

Tuesday 6 April 1993

Up at 6 am and off to the London office. Colin Hayes is in residence negotiating a protracted deal involving seven B737-400s to THY, Turkey's national airline, a deal we need to do as it will clean us out of new -400s for the year. Unfortunately we are having problems financing the aircraft. Boeing is providing the finance, otherwise we would be scuppered, with no chance of raising some $200 million plus any other way.

Waiting for the Turks to arrive, Colin comes into my office and we start discussing the events of the past few days. Apparently the memo criticises top management by name: Tony for mistakes up to the IPO, Maurice for mistakes around the IPO, and all of them for bad decisions and poor management post IPO.

I venture that I still believe a compromise will be reached, but that Colm is maybe in the weakest position. He has been looked upon as heir apparent for some time, vying with Jim, and has acted out the part with unbridled self-confidence and large cigars—*à la* Tony. He is not firmly in the Tony/Maurice bracket; neither is he allied with Phil and Patrick—clearly, since they bypassed him in writing the memo. Perhaps he will go.

It is like guessing the outcome of a horse race. The runners all have form—we judge it against the course, the distance and the going.

Much will depend on how the banks, their lawyers and advisers view all this when they hear of it—if they have not already done so. Will it be seen as healthy young management initiatives, the second generation coming through so to speak, or will the perception be of a company riven by internecine strife?

I think the banks like Maurice: steady, cerebral, fluent. John also because they know where they stand with him, as in no problems. Tony can be an ill-tempered maverick with flawed judgment, but he did build the company up from nothing. The banks probably do not know Phil and Patrick so well. I guess they will want to know whether the two enjoy popular support within the Leasing division, because the banks are supposed to regard the competence of the marketing team as being of paramount importance.

Quite a quandary. Exciting really. By the end of today we might have some resignations. Maybe the old guard will have some skids put under it. I hope above all that Phil remains. He is a linchpin in the organisation. Surely Tony recognises this. Sadly, I also think the board is filled with Tony sycophants and it will be like the morning meetings of olden days—Tony bullying his way through. It will be whatever Tony wants, I suspect.

4 pm update. The board meeting is over. No one has been fired. That smacks of a compromise. Apparently all the non-executive directors met separately with Tony prior to the board meeting. They have now all returned from whence they came, except John Harvey Jones, who is holed up in the building somewhere. Meetings have been going on in Patrick's department all day.

5 pm update. John Harvey Jones chaired a meeting this afternoon with all the old guard, plus Tony, Phil, Patrick and senior management of both Leasing and Capital. Various alternatives were discussed, but nothing definitive has emerged and the meeting broke up. Now Phil and Patrick have gone into a smaller, closed session with Tony and maybe some others. Liam is keeping me informed as he promised to. He believes that a crunching meeting may now be going on behind Tony's door on maybe more personnel-based matters.

Graham has just called me from Shannon. He corroborates Liam's account. Plus Graham was actually in the room at the John Harvey Jones meeting. Graham describes the meeting as a bit of a non-event— a discussion of options and matters regarding the run-up period to the public debt repayment; nothing more. JHJ seemed on top of the issues. Graham says the entire board is more in touch with events than he had thought. He surmises it's because the directors are beginning to feel their responsibilities *qua* directors starting to bite. He expects the second, smaller meeting may produce more results.

I call Niall. He seems bullish. Things are positive, nothing to be alarmed about. I state my concern for Phil. He says nothing to be concerned about. He sums up the support: 'There are a lot of us.'

As Jenny Brown here in London remarks: 'It is the first time in 18 years that anyone has stood up to Tony Ryan.'

Another colleague in Shannon returns a call. The latest vibe going around Shannon is that there will be a staff briefing tomorrow at 5.30 pm to announce management changes. 'New or old guard?' I ask. 'Old.'

Wednesday 7 April 1993

I am working at home today. During the morning my secretary sends me a fax. It is from Tony to everyone. Patrick has been made chief operating officer and has been 'co-opted' on to the board of GPA Group. Patrick is now in charge of Operation Rebound under Tony's direct authority. Maurice, John and Colm retain their positions and functions, except as regards Operation Rebound. There is no mention of Phil, who in my opinion is one of the best.

The situation at the top of the company is now decidedly crowded. Today's memo said that Maurice would stay as Tony's deputy until the end of his contract in March 1994. Maurice has been day to day in charge of Operation Rebound. He will now, still deputy chairman, be working for Patrick. Colm, also working flat out on Rebound and still chief executive, will be working under Patrick as far as that is concerned. John Tierney will stay as head of the Finance department, but all his work since the IPO has been with the banks on Rebound. Again he will be working to Patrick's order. Quite a shake-up. There will be some bruised egos tonight.

It seems Tony has given in to the Phil/Patrick *putsch*, Patrick having revealed the vital senior marketing support for their cause. Tony needs to represent to the banks that the marketing team is intact and behind him. He had to accommodate Patrick and Phil. Also Tony, for himself, needed to stay on top and to reassure the banks that the company was not falling apart at the seams by keeping on existing top personnel apparently intact. Beneath this façade, however, there is no doubt that a fundamental change has occurred and the power has shifted. The banks will soon find this out, as will the press.

Maurice is out in all but person. John will be finance director, looking after the purse strings as previously. I don't know about Colm. Jim King's present duties sorting out manufacturers' issues have kept him somewhat off centre stage, although he has been deeply involved in all the meetings of the past 48 hours. As always, Jim will defer to Tony. Graham has recently described Jim's efforts and demeanour as excellent.

I expect now that Patrick and Phil, as winners, will select the staff who will continue with GPA for the future. We shall see. After all the excitement of the past few days, we are all still waiting for the big 'R' memo.

Friday 8 April 1993

I am still working at home. Speaking to Liam, the general reaction back in Shannon is not that Patrick's elevation is a shot in the arm for the company, but rather another symptom of distress. I am rather surprised. Everyone is depressed. Liam believes nothing will save the company other than a takeover by GECC. Our top executives seem to be indulging in a pointless greasy pole-climbing competition.

Following the recent downgrading of our credit rating, GPA 1998 bonds are now trading at 35 per cent of their face value. I can remember John's quietly triumphant expression when our newly acquired investment rating first enabled us to access the public debt markets just a couple of years ago. Hours of effort and disrupted lives had gone into achieving that rating. It was seen as another example of the opening opportunities for GPA to raise the huge sums it was always going to need to satisfy the financial burdens of Tony's grandiose and badly timed policies.

I feel sorry for the ultimately wasted time spent building up our careers, the damaging lifestyle (rationalised in our own minds as temporary) suffered to gain the fruits of life GPA was going to bring us in a solid, long-lasting way—hard cash. Almost no one is going to come out of GPA with anything, and many will come out financially distressed.

Apparently Tony has been rescheduling his private $35 million share loan with Merrill Lynch, due for repayment in 1994. It is difficult to see where Tony will get that sort of money, even if a GECC sale goes through.

Tuesday 13 April 1993

During the morning, in Shannon, I see a senior colleague in the Finance department on a routine matter. It is the first time we have spoken in a long while—I don't get up to the Finance floor of the building that often, maybe not since the IPO. He is long-term angry. In his opinion all the executive directors should have been fired long since. Whereas previously, working somewhat behind the lines, he had been content to be carried along by the general euphoria and had bought shares at the top of the market in consequence, since the collapsed IPO he has delved into reality. He is appalled at the sheer bad decisions taken by the directors and some of the awful marketing deals struck in the time when Jim was head of Leasing. He is equally bitter about the lack of progress in restructuring the company, but is hopeful that the emergence of Patrick at the head of Project Rebound will improve the situation.

We are all in the hands of a group of people in whom we have little or no confidence. Where is John Harvey Jones? He should be in here pitching, restoring confidence, giving us some direction. Otherwise what was the point of having him on the board? He certainly has neither prevented catastrophe by seeing it up ahead, nor has he helped steer us out of trouble once it became apparent.

After my experiences with a previous airline, which had none, I used to think that non-executive directors were the answer: that their wise counsel would prevail at board meetings to curb any excesses of executive management. Now I realise that in general their grasp of the company's business and business environment is so shallow; they are so far outside the normal communication lines, they are unable to read situations or potential situations with any real understanding. Theirs is a reactive wisdom, sometimes helpful, sometimes useless. No non-executive on our board saw the problems ahead, or if they did no one did anything about it—like resigning or trying to change the company's (Tony's) strategy. All of them were taken in by the glib roadshow presentations of the old guard, supported by our in-house strategist's forecasts. An ex-taoiseach, an ex-chancellor of the British Exchequer, an EEC Commissioner for Trade, a supreme captain of British industry with an unrivalled reputation for management—all of them, all taken in, all gulled, all essentially sleepwalking.

Sunday 18 April 1993

In the Aer Lingus lounge I meet Peter Ledbetter, by coincidence, on his way back to Dublin from tennis in Portugal. He asks me how things are. I tell him. He looks grim. I am sure he knows at least as much as I do. After all, he is holding a very large number of shares. His future must be very bound up with the fortunes of GPA. It is so awful this collapse. The nearest comparison is the calamity which has overtaken many of the Lloyds Names, losing everything when they must have thought they were set up for life. It is getting hackneyed, but the John Lennon line about life being something that happens to you when you are busy making other plans can be very apposite.

Monday 19 April 1993

I am told that last Friday terms have been agreed with GECC for our takeover. Today GECC is having a board meeting to decide whether to make an offer. Apparently the terms are a steal for GECC, involving its purchase of our aircraft equity at a less than knockdown price. After two years GECC have the option to acquire the whole company, again at a bargain basement price. It may be the only game in town.

Talking with Graham later, he says if GECC takes over, bang go our shares and maybe our jobs, as GECC rationalises the GPA operation with its own, smaller Polaris aircraft leasing company. Graham recalls that the chairman of GE itself, Jack Welch, is known as 'Neutron Bomb Jack', because after he arrives, the building still stands but the people have gone.

Tonight there is to be another state of the nation talk. Unfortunately I will have to miss it. I am going to New York tomorrow and have to return to England later this afternoon to make the flight. Tony and Patrick will be speaking, with some input from John Tierney. It will be a shame to miss the expressions of Maurice and Colm especially, as Patrick takes stock after the boardroom coup. On the plane back to London, Peter Denison-Edson, who clearly knows the whole script, gives me a whispered potted rundown—a lot of anodyne waffle meant to calm people's fears that things are not settled but progress is being made. Tony will apparently finish with his now customary giveaway. This time it will be an advance redundancy payment, or something, nobody yet knows, including Tony. The details of what it is and how it will be paid are still being mulled over. The idea is to avoid tax, but no one yet knows how to do it. Still, if it is to be a lump sum payment, we will be all ears.

Monday 26 April 1993

In Shannon. Back in the Finance department speaking to Diarmuid Hyde about the advance redundancy payment, as there is complete confusion following Tony's foggy explanation at the state of the company meeting last Monday evening.

The original idea had been an unwritten voluntary redundancy scheme to pay three months' salary plus the equivalent of one month's salary for every year of service. Next, as the numbers of people wishing to take advantage of the scheme swelled (our staff numbers have already gone down from 311 to 270), the scheme was withdrawn, to be replaced by the advance redundancy method, to be paid to all as an inducement to stay. Calculation of the amount would not change, except that there would be an overall cap of seven months' pay. Now, Diarmuid explains, the latest is that whatever the calculation, it must be halved, i.e. a maximum of 3.5 months' salary. In addition, to receive it we must sign a letter binding us to the company for 12 months. I ask Diarmuid, joking, if we can also have a letter from the company guaranteeing that it will stay in business for the next 12 months.

We are supposed to get our cheques this Friday. There is also supposed to be a bonus payment coming at the end of June. I have not started to hold my breath for this one yet.

Tuesday 27 April 1993

The noose is tightening. It could all be over in days now. Coming back from Shannon yesterday, sitting next to Phil on the aircraft, he showed me a weekly round-up from Patrick on Operation Rebound.

The survival alternatives seem to be three: GRAPE, Eaglet or Plan B.

GRAPE stands for GE Rape, so-called because of the terms of the prospective takeover. Apparently the GE board has approved the plan to take over GPA. I do not know whether a formal offer has now been made, but Patrick's report makes clear that if GPA accepts any such offer, GECC expects GPA to desist from further efforts to rescue itself.

Eaglet is the brainchild of John Sharman of Spectrum Capital, a financial services—or rather financial engineering—company. Spectrum is involved in major deals. John has put together financing structures for British Airways—the cream of aviation financing. He used to work for GPA in the past before I joined up, but left because of working style incompatibilities, I believe, though without any rancour that I could detect. GPA and John have crossed paths repeatedly since. When I was in notional charge of GPA Fokker, Spectrum was assisting us to find finance for our aircraft. At that stage Peter Sokell was the partner involved. Peter later left Spectrum to head up the Aerospace division with Citibank. Citibank is the major lender to GPA in the CCF and Peter has been centrally involved in the restructuring.

Anyway, John is a powerhouse of structural and financial creativity. Ideas whirl out of him. Eaglet is one such. It is an alternative structure for GPA and there is a necessarily small team working on it. I am only guessing, but I think that maybe Peter saw the GPA restructuring coming apart, with existing investors refusing to stump up more equity and new investors staying away, and contacted John to see if there was an alternative. Or maybe it was the other way round and John took the initiative—it would be like him.

Plan B is examinership, the Irish equivalent of the US Chapter 11 procedure, a sort of cross between that and administration as practised in England.

All of these options are being worked on, together with the presently overwhelming problem of how to pay the bondholders. We have now hired Donaldson, Lufkin & Jenrette in New York, experts apparently in dealing with bondholders in these situations, where we are trying to defer or otherwise hold at bay almost immediately due payments. Our bonds are currently trading at 22 cents on the dollar. New York market bond traders are already being reported in the press as saying we are heading for examinership.

The other looming issue is the delay in restructuring, via the new $200 million equity, with the CCF banks. Because of the failure to obtain the equity requirement, we have been living on waivers from the banks in respect of the continuing breaches of the CCF loan documentation and on extensions of the time allowed to come up with the equity. Now I understand the final drop dead date is 7 May, Friday week. After that, absent any other alternative, examinership is on the cards. The banks do not want to see us pay money to bondholders out of cash reserves, which are nearly all refundable lessee deposits and spoken-for aircraft maintenance reserves anyway.

These two make up the May/June liquidity crisis. It seems that the next ten days will be decisive. Not long to go.

Patrick's report ends with a sentence to the effect that in the available timescale, maybe GRAPE is the only way out.

This week all the celebrity Rebounders seem to be furiously active in New York, with the exception of Maurice who is in London.

I recognise this final phase—everyone involved rushing around in chain meetings trying desperately to save the ship. It will go on right up to the last instant, with pleas to make just one more phone call to some crazily impossible benefactor, who could pluck the company out of its predicament. It never works. By that stage anyone not already on the scene is not interested.

Last Sunday, when Graham and I were discussing the GE situation with a New York-based colleague, Graham reckoned that GECC would effectively shut GPA down and move the whole operation to GECC's home in Connecticut. I am not so pessimistic. I believe GECC could run GPA separately, slimmed down admittedly, for a couple of years while it made up its mind whether to exercise its option and complete the ingestion. In a wait and see period it would make more sense to see how GPA could function as a unit, rather than make far-reaching changes within the GECC organisation to accommodate GPA, later to regret them. The truth is we do not know. It is very unsettling.

On the leasing front we continue to do business. We have even had some records broken. During the last financial year just ended, we delivered 203 aircraft. In the circumstances this is a truly amazing feat. The vast majority of aircraft went into Asia, particularly China, which is going to be the largest market for years to come.

A couple of weeks ago we delivered 14 aircraft in one week. It seems incredible we can convince airlines to deal with us as normal. My own customers seem remarkably relaxed about the GPA situation. People would rather trust that all is going well, if possible. That is a valuable thing to realise and file away. It also underlines my prior point about the fundamental mistake of going into a temporary, planned receivership.

I continue to travel constantly. Last week in New York, the week before in Kenya, just before Easter in South Africa, next week in Nigeria. I feel we in marketing are like civilians in wartime, who find comfort in carrying on with the simple domestic tasks of life when faced with the imminent prospect of death. I guess the truth is our successful leasing activities underpin the efforts of the Operation Rebound negotiators to convince the convincees, now legion, that the company is now long-term viable beneath the cash crisis.

I speak to a senior secretary. She is tens of thousands of dollars in share debt. She believes the lender has limited recourse, so her home should be safe. She hopes to get away with paying eighteen months' interest on the loan and giving up all her now worthless shares to the bank. Apparently the bank has heard about the so-called advance redundancy payment and seems ready to pounce on it. She has been warned by a colleague to pay the cheque in somewhere else.

I am so fortunate not to have share debt. It is bad enough trying to sort out what happens next in life during this time, without being worried stiff about enormous unresolved personal problems. Again I am bowled over by her stoicism. She has her health, she says, so the situation may be desperate but not serious—an old Irishism.

Tuesday 4 May 1993

Last Sunday's headline in the *Sunday Times* was 'Wholesale Slaughter Expected At GPA'. The bankers and bondholders are pushing for the heads of the old guard—Tony, Maurice, Jim, Colm and John. The paper says they did not have many decisions to make last year: when to float, at what price and later when to talk to the banks. They got them all wrong.

The article also cites the next layer of management as having done a great job of successfully keeping the core leasing business going in the worst of times. This is Patrick, Phil (in particular, in my book), Niall and Brian Hayden. These four stand to come out well. Good.

Some other senior heads are well down, however, in please don't see me mode.

The story has started off another flurry of press speculation, particularly in Ireland. One newspaper has got wind of the Blaney/Bolger coup, after a fashion, but not yet to the extent that Patrick is now on the board.

There is a board meeting today to be held at 5 pm at Schroders, where there are better facilities than in the London office, where I am currently back at my desk. How many people have said to me today that they would like to be a fly on the wall at the meeting. John Redmond will be: he is the minute taker. Because of the squeeze in the office, he asks if he can sit at my conference table for a while to go through the board papers. 'Lawyers are parasites,' he exclaims minutes later, going through a long opinion on directors' responsibilities. John exhibits the same symptoms as the rest of us—fed up, apprehensive, indebted, thoroughly unsettled. He does not believe that much will happen at the meeting, but concedes that it might.

We lunch together. I show him a copy of an article in the *Daily Telegraph* from last Thursday that I saw on an aircraft flying back from Africa. The article is an interview with John Harvey Jones, publicising his new book. In it he advocates that anyone in a company that looks as if it is going 'over the weir' should leave before it does so, i.e. if you are bright, you will do this. He shows great timing. Just as GPA is desperately trying to keep its personnel together, our deputy chairman is in the national press advising us to get out while the going's good, even if it means relinquishing redundancy payments. Great or what?

Talking of which: the advance redundancy scheme has sort of been resolved, to the extent that cheques are supposed to be issued today to each according to his/her length of service, the maximum payment being the equivalent of 3.5 months' salary. Having been with the company for almost eight years, I qualify for the maximum. Will the cheque ever clear? In return we have to sign a letter, so far unseen, binding us to stay with the company until the end of 1993, assuming we last that long. At this stage I will sign virtually anything, except in blood, to get hold of the cash. The whole scheme is rather ramshackle, but that is fine by me as long as the funds flow. I am sure Mr Harvey Jones would also approve.

So we all wait. By tomorrow things may have changed. Maybe even the board may decide tonight upon pre-emptive action—to go for immediate examinership as the banks close in, so that when we arrive for work tomorrow there will be notices posted up and a memo for the staff. That happened to me before, 11 years ago.

My own hope is that we get GRAPEd. I believe GECC would run us in quarantine while they decide whether to buy, rather than risk contaminating their own organisation, until our stand-alone viability factor is known.

The non-executive directors must by now be extremely sensitive to the potential for bad personal press, as part of the fallout of a failed GPA especially seeing the increasing number of media jibes at John Harvey Jones, our resident troubleshooter, the quintessence of the man in the glass house. Ex-UK Chancellor Nigel Lawson can hardly take any more knocks to his ruined reputation. Garret FitzGerald is being seen as naïve—a great epitaph for a politician. EEC Commissioner Peter Sutherland is about to become GATTman and hardly needs this send-off.

Assuming none of them wishes to become mired in the slough of

GPA, perhaps the GRAPE alternative could offer them a way to extricate themselves with little more than broken dreams and a financial hiding. They could sell it as a successful outcome—the future of the company has been assured, access to funds assured, jobs assured, banks are happy, blah, blah. Ah well, it will be interesting, whatever. Speculation in this diary is only interesting to see if it actually transpires in that way. We wait.

Last week in Nairobi (Nigeria is now next week), doing a deal to keep some B737s in Kenya Airways, I fell to ruminating about facets of GPA, passing the time in my hotel room. Whatever GPA started out as, it developed into a money factory. GPA eventually churned out money. For the early joiners the rewards were fantastic, based on the shares they had acquired for relative buttons during the first decade. In the year of the aborted IPO, dividends per 'A' Preference Share were projected to be some $375. My holding was quite modest. Jim, for example, is supposed to hold some 3,000 such shares, potentially yielding $1,125,000 in the same year—this before his salary. There would almost certainly be ordinary share dividend as well. It all added up to a lot of money, most of it tax free. Many senior people enjoyed remuneration on that scale and had done so for several years. Graham used to liken the quarterly dividend to winning the football pools every three months.

Some time ago one Irish newspaper wrote about GPA executives living like Irish princes—it was true. GPA was royalty around Limerick and certain parts of Dublin. You were known everywhere and it was taken for granted you were wealthy, overworked and had Tony constantly on your back. Generally the populace was suffering financial hardship. GPA people with their enormous tax-free dividends were like visitors from another planet.

Tony in particular was rolling in it. The prosperity appeared so permanent. It could only expand, it seemed. The gravy train acquired a momentum of its own. If only they had known it would stop so abruptly, something could have been planned. As it was, the money supply dried up virtually overnight and caught almost everyone massively on the hop. Lavish lifestyles, huge debts to service—it all required arterial amounts of cash. The scene is now one of devastation. The lucky ones are those who have emerged just breaking even. Twelve months ago such an eventuality would have been generally held an unthinkable catastrophe. Casualties run from top to bottom in the company and extend to outsiders—ex-employees, non-executive directors, retirees.

Doing the rounds in GPA now is the following. What is the difference between dinosaurs and GPA divis? Dinosaurs are more likely to return.

Wednesday 5 May 1993

Press speculation is mounting. Messrs Blaney and Bolger were seen going into yesterday's board meeting and now their names are being bandied about as the young turks coming up to replace the old guard. Details of the month old coup are now starting to be printed.

The London office is crammed today. All the executive directors are here. I have ended up sitting on the metaphorical tea chest to do my business. Colm has a chair in the tiny hallway where we park visitors awaiting meetings. There is a fizz of tension in the air. We, the London-based staff here, feel that something is about to happen. Meetings are being set up for the afternoon at Schroders with Sharman. There is a palpable atmosphere of increasing pressure.

Our bank debt is trading at 65 cents on the dollar, our bonds at 18 cents. $45 million is due to the banks on 7 May if no further waiver is issued by them. The best part of $200 million is due to the bondholders on 18 May, if no deferral or other fix is worked out beforehand. There is due to be a meeting with the main bondholders on 13 May. The old guard is taking a beating in the City pages because the bondholder problem has not been addressed much much earlier. To be fair to the directors, however, they were hoping the restructuring with the $200 million new equity would have been in place by now to repay the bondholders in full. Because that has flopped, the bondholder issue has suddenly rocketed into view as time ticks away.

Time is ever the problem. In insolvency, time always defeats efforts to save companies or individuals, inasmuch as it runs out. Deadlines are eventually not kept, payments are missed, things fail to happen on schedule. The real answer, as John Redmond uncharacteristically put it yesterday, is that the company is 'fucked'.

We are now at that unlovely stage where time is fast running out on a number of fronts. The banks keep us going on waivers of myriad covenant breaches, but their patience is wearing thin as no cure appears. The bondholders are raging because we have not attended to them until the last minute. The shareholders will not put in any more equity, and as everything sickens, their appetite must be progressively disappearing altogether. There are growing calls for the top management's heads. There seems only one way out—GECC.

Hopefully, GRAPE has been progressed to the point where we can grab it as a last lifesaving straw. My fear is that the management of Rebound is now so busy dashing around, it somehow contrives to miss the one available solution—but surely not. I could also guess that Tony does not favour the GECC option because it does not get him off the 1994 hook he is on with Merrill Lynch. Maybe if GECC could take Tony privately to one side and look after him in this respect, the GECC deal would be taken up. Maybe Tony has asked his board last night for a few more days until, say, Friday to see what else can be done before going back to GECC. Maybe, maybe, maybe. We know nothing.

The one bright spot this morning was listening to PJ Mara bawling out a reporter from the *Irish Times* over the telephone. PJ's accent grew aurally broader as the effing and blinding grew in intensity. He was complaining about the reporter having telephoned a range of people after midnight following the board meeting. He even got the hack to telephone Schroders to apologise. Unheard of. Immediately after the call PJ was in good spirits, asking if we had heard the shenanigans. When I pointed out that the reporter was only doing his job, PJ laughed. 'I know, but it does them good to shout every now and again.'

I have just learned some more about the GRAPE deal. Suddenly it does sound like violation. In a nutshell, they get a special purpose GECC company to buy our best aircraft at a steal price and we manage that fleet. We are left with our non-best aircraft and the remainder of the debt that the steal price has not retired, i.e. possibly a lot. After four years if what's left of GPA has managed to survive its debt burden and the rotten aircraft, GECC has an option to acquire 80 per cent of GPA. No wonder they call it rape, but what else is there?

A colleague over working on Rebound tells me that a new mood of realism has infected the directors. They now want to talk to the banks on the basis that nothing will turn out for the best and that there will be just a company leasing existing aircraft, earning say $300–$400 million per year positive cash flow, with no forward aircraft commitments, and how do we work with that so far as a restructuring is concerned? He says forward soundings have indicated that the banks would talk on that basis. It sounds daft to me. There are over a hundred banks now involved. Those positive cash flow figures come nowhere near what is needed to repay our debts. What about the bondholders? Would they go along with such a scheme? Unless there really is some reason the banks see an advantage in our not going into examinership, that must be where we are headed, if there is no other doable alternative and the GECC deal is really not worth going for, even at the end of a long day's dying. On the other hand, maybe the directors have decided to play hardball, prepared to face down the debtors, as in—play along with us and we might all get out alive somehow; collapse us and risk having a fleet of expensive, difficult, wasting assets on your hands and lose your shirts (not to mention your jobs). Plus, nobody will be better at preserving and maximising the fleet than GPA itself. Look at what the engine room management and the marketing team have achieved over the last year, against all the odds. Could such a ploy work?

Sunday 9 May 1993

The newspapers are full of us in the Business sections. Although biting, I liked Jeff Randall's piece in the *Sunday Times* best of all: '$3 billion to zippo in 12 months.' However, Jack Hertsch's (senior analyst with NY bond traders Whitmans) article in the *Sunday Tribune* was the most positive, giving a blueprint for survival which could be adopted by all sides, if they were in a mood to, as a basis for a pragmatic accord.

Monday 10 May 1993

What a day! Again. For a start I am in Shannon instead of Abuja,

Nigeria. Phil called in all available marketing people for a marketing meeting. I am only too happy to postpone a trip to Abuja.

At the meeting Phil reads an agenda nobody has seen. It consists of three items: confidentiality; Rebound 2 (this seems to be a revised title following Patrick and Phil's arrival on the rescue scene); and Plan B.

Confidentiality turns out to be another stricture to remain silent in the face of press enquiries. Apparently journalists have been ringing up our staffers, pretending to be lessees, trying to winkle out information. Phil reminds us that only Maurice, PJ and Jim have the right to speak to the press. For anyone else it is 'a P45 offence'. They are worried someone is leaking information because of the accuracy of the reporting in some papers. They even believe it is someone inside GPA House, not one of our advisers.

Next follows a report on Rebound 2. There is a GPA board meeting tomorrow and a meeting with the banks. The latter have given us a further conditional waiver until Wednesday (they are getting shorter) and are requiring the board to reach a decision on one of two alternatives at the board meeting. These are to place extra aircraft into the security pool so as to provide an excess of collateral for the banks, or to adopt the Bermuda Bank structure (which apparently we do not want to do). According to Phil, the board can choose one or reject both and call the banks' bluff.

On Wednesday there is a meeting with the (unsecured) bondholders in New York, to try to negotiate a moratorium. This will entail a complete moratorium, including both secured (banks) and unsecured creditors. Under it we would pay head lessors and bank interest, but nothing else for a period until we can reinstate payments.

We are due to pay the bondholders on 17 May. Actually one bondholder—Harris—we were due to pay last Friday, but we have a waiver until 16 May. The banks do not want us to reduce our cash holdings by paying the bondholders. If we do not pay and a default is called, we will have to seek protection from the Irish court and go into examinership. In addition to the $60 million due to the bondholders in May, there is an additional $170 million due in June.

Phil adds we are still trying to raise fresh equity, and the GRAPE talks continue.

We also have an Arab gentleman on the scene as a possible white knight. He owns 10 per cent of Citibank. Talks have been going on over the weekend and he has two banks doing a 'due diligence' exercise on us. In my experience Arabs are usually timewasters who will do nothing without a bank guarantee, which is of course unavailable.

Apparently we need some $250–$500 million to stabilise us and enable us to go forward.

Niall takes up the story, to tell us about Plan B. Firstly he reinforces Phil's words on secrecy. Five or six weeks ago a study was set up into examinership and preparations were begun in case it became necessary. O'Toole was in charge—so that's what he has been doing. Niall explains to us what examinership entails: it is a four month period in which GPA can seek protection from its creditors. At the end of it, or during it if possible, the company can emerge, having worked out an agreed deal with all its creditors and carry on. We even have an examiner lined up. Niall declines to name him. He tells us that court protection is virtually certain.

As Niall continues, it becomes clear to me that if we ever enter examinership, that will be the end. I sit there listening, thinking about the loss of lessee confidence, loss of industry confidence we will suffer if we turn to the court to hide from our creditors. Events will spin out of our control. Such are the gaps between our secured lenders (138 banks), the unsecured bondholders, principally in the US, and the luckless shareholders, I cannot believe we could practically agree a wraparound fix in four months.

O'Toole tells us we have a liquidity problem mainly, as the assets should cover the secured lenders. The aim of examinership is to sort out the bondholders.

There is discussion following Niall's exposition. I join it trying to make my point. We turn to a list of lessees, going through it one by one, each executive responsible stating whether in the case of examinership, that lessee would continue to pay their aircraft rentals and maintenance payments. We end up with 64 per cent paying, 17 per cent with a high risk of withholding payments and 19 per cent somewhere in the middle. Niall makes the point that $102 million in revenue flows into

GPA each month from these payments. In examinership especially this flow has to be maintained. We are to explain the position fully to our lessees, but they must keep on paying at all costs, on pain of swift repossession of aircraft. We shall be ruthless—not a word I usually associate with Niall.

Eventually the meeting breaks up. The atmosphere is tense, depressed. Small impromptu discussions start and end between us marketing people when we get back to our part of the building from the Trading Floor.

A small crowd gathers in one office. It is a group of marketing executives with unpaid share loans. They are speaking to a lawyer from A&L Goodbody, who is being paid by the company to advise them how to deal with their share loan banks. It turns out he is not very helpful. His attitude seems to have hardened. Apparently he was not told about the advance redundancy payouts, so that when he next had a meeting with the banks, pushing his clients' line, the banks confronted him with these payments and he had been professionally embarrassed. He tells them what the banks are offering and pretty much take it or leave it. Those with full recourse loans can get out if they pay 30 per cent of the principal and interest now outstanding; non-recourse borrowers for between 15–20 per cent. Also the advice is that the banks can charge interest *ad infinitum* on the loans, even with non-recourse loans.

As an outsider, it seems very good to me that the banks will write off so much. However, I can understand that 20 per cent of $200,000 is still $40,000—a lot of money. Some of the loans are very much larger than that. Looking back, GPA was fantasyland. Money took on a false value because there was so much of it. $40,000 was hardly anything. Now we are all back to earth.

In the evening I am invited out by Phil and Niall for dinner with some other out-of-towners. We start at Phil's house, a wholly renovated, typically Irish, stone house in 12 acres. It looks out across the Shannon River, over a mile wide at this point, downstream from Killaloe. Money has obviously been poured into the renovation and this is the second house Phil has renovated. But Phil has handed back his company BMW 525 for an older Audi 100 to save on tax. Things have really changed. His wife Sandra wistfully discusses flying Robinson helicopters with me. Her lessons have ceased. I am pretty wistful too.

Dinner is at Goosers in Killaloe. Of course we talk about the state of the company, a little too loudly for my liking. There are eight of us and other people in the restaurant. I am sitting next to Niall and over my John Dory I reiterate my fears about examinership. I feel the company has not taken all the possibilities of what it will mean into consideration. I believe this is through ignorance. I get the impression that the management still thinks it will be able to manipulate events even in examinership. I try to say to Niall that things will happen around us and we will have minimal capacity to control anything.

Wednesday 12 May 1993

I fly to Harare to do battle once again with Affretair. Liam Barrett, who has been looking after the collection side of things on the Affretair lease since early in the year, is leaving the company. He is buying a business—a castle—six miles from Blarney, by the water, catering to the tourist trade and locals out of season. It looks beautiful. Knowing Liam I am sure he will do well. I will miss him.

Thursday 13 May 1993

In Harare I learn we have issued a press release saying we are going to go with the GECC plan. The release is very upbeat, far too confident and I would have thought too early. To make GECC work, both banks and shareholders have to inject more funds. Nobody seems to want to do that. Anyway, I am lifted by the news and recall that it was in Harare I first heard about the IPO flop.

Monday 17 May 1993

What a day! Yet again. The weekend press coverage has been widespread and bloody, especially the Irish press which seems to be relishing the GPA saga. There is a double page spread entitled 'Countdown to Catastrophe' and another full pager headlined 'The A-z Of What Went Wrong At GPA'. The GECC deal is castigated as not being our saviour and by no means done. Every UK and Irish quality paper carries a story. Generally they say the old guard are for the chop and the younger middle managers are pushing through. Except that Colm continues to be tipped for stardom.

I am in Shannon, of course, for the Monday morning meeting. Phil takes it, with Niall as No. 2. We go through the marketing priorities, the technical priorities, the week's aircraft deliveries, the overdue receivables list—on which our old recidivists perennially appear— Transbrasil, LAM, Hawaiian, Oasis, Garuda and good ol' Aerocalifornia, still hanging in there at $3 million owed. The debts of America West, Canadian Airlines and VASP are so astronomic they have been taken off the list. Even so the figure is $68 million.

Next, as usual, comes the run-through of the marketing task for the rest of 1993, all the airline targets ranked 1, 2 and 3. This ranking goes from 'should be certain deal' to 'almost total flake' in 3—like the old line about the full gamut from A to B.

The meeting started at 8.30 am. After 90 minutes the meeting ends—but not quite. Niall waves papers saying we are on 'red alert' for examinership today! He circulates a list, stating which lessees we are each responsible for, in terms of immediate personal contact, to ensure they keep paying.

The mood is very jumpy after the meeting. Knots of marketing people keep forming back in our area as conversations occur. Everybody speaks to everyone else, fairly much, for the rest of the morning. Little work is being done as we wait for a decision.

There is to be a board meeting this afternoon. It seems 99 per cent certain that examinership will be the result. I say to Michael Barry that I believe we will not emerge from it. The best that could happen in examinership would be that GECC comes back to retrieve us or that maybe a management buyout or carve-out could be a future prospect after examinership has given way to the appointment of an administrator/receiver.

I call my secretary Bernie in the London office. She sounds weary. She has been working in the office over the weekend. Today it is packed with not even enough chairs to sit on. Everyone is there—the GPA directors, Nomura, Schroders, Citibank, Wolfensohns, and back-up staff. Chaos. The board meeting is for 2 pm at Schroders. Bernie says the feeling is frantic and panicky.

I take the lunchtime flight to Heathrow, intending to go to the office for a while before heading back out to Heathrow for Johannesburg. Practising normality on the knife's edge. The flight to London is two hours delayed due to ATC computer failure at West Drayton. On the aircraft I find myself next to Gerry Power. He has relatively recently left GPA under a quasi cloud, but is back as a consultant, earning more than his previous basic (which we are all now stuck on). Also, because of the circumstances of his leaving, he was able to get the complete redundancy package. To a wicked Irish grin I tell him the devil looks after his own.

Gerry always was a centre of information, always knew the latest scandal. He used to be Tony's PA. He tells me that on the fateful Friday when Patrick and Phil wrote their *putsch* memo, on learning of it Tony immediately fired them both. I guess he must have done it from the Pratt meeting, where he was with Graham. The meeting of the senior marketing people the following Sunday with Phil and Patrick was to gain their support, so that the two were able to walk into the office on Monday with the all-important marketing team leaders behind them, to be reinstated, which they duly were.

Reflecting on this piece of news, it seemed to me typical of Tony, a violent knee-jerk reaction to any opposition—fire them. The threat of this instant total retaliation lies at the heart of why GPA is in its present difficulties. Nobody was ever prepared to stand up to Tony and say he was wrong. Five minutes later you would be out on the street. Except maybe one and he gracefully and wisely bowed out—our former chief strategist Juan O'Callaghan. He sold his shares at the top and left. The Six Million Dollar Juan, they call him.

Tony apparently called Phil and Patrick traitors. They were the antithesis of that. It also shows how removed Tony has become from the day to day situation in 'his' company that he could have so woefully misjudged. He felt that by firing them he could put the lid on it and leave him and the old guard still in undisputed control.

Gerry went on to say that in his opinion if the GECC deal goes ahead, because it has been brokered by Tony and Colm, there will be no place for Phil or Patrick. I do not accept this—absolutely certainly not in the case of Phil. He has leadership and personal qualities that carry the entire marketing department with him.

I finally arrive at the London office in Pall Mall at 4.30 pm. It is now quiet. I find one of John Tierney's team sitting looking wan and worn out in the open plan back office. I say to him, 'I hear we are about to go into examinership.' He says I hear wrong. The board will vote for the GECC option. I am so pleased to hear it. I say that therefore the banks and shareholders will put up the money the GRAPE option requires. He nods. Apparently enough assurances have come in to make this possible.

I feel as if on the scaffold, with the noose tight and the hood on, there has been a reprieve. I leave for South Africa.

Tuesday 18 May 1993

Another day, another press release. The GECC news has broken. Again. Bernie faxes me a copy to my room at the Carlton Court in the centre of Johannesburg.

Also the so-called Bermuda Bank structure has been forced on us by the banks. This directs the lease and other revenues flowing from aircraft forming part of their security, so-called pool aircraft, to pass through a bank account in Bermuda. In the event of examinership, the banks can thereby control the flow of funds related to their secured assets. It's a cut-through mechanism. No big deal, I would have thought, in our present straits. Our lessees get new payment instructions accordingly: none of them seems to jib at it.

I get ready to leave for Mozambique.

Monday 24 May 1993

Shannon. Feeling rather deflated. A team is in New York discussing and negotiating a separate GECC/GPA management company to run the fleet. Which fleet? Whatever, it will be some time before anything happens, we are told. We will hang on. If any of us have to go, we reason that we may get more in severance pay with GECC in the frame than otherwise.

Jim and Graham will be in Hartford later in the week, seeing Pratt & Whitney who are demanding $40 million off us in previously paid engine discounts we do not now qualify for and which we have spent. To repay, even if we could, would be an undue preference against the other creditors, so we should not pay. Pratt see us going into the arms of their greatest competitor—General Electric. Why should they make it easy for us? It will take all of Jim's charm.

The MDC suit continues.

Thursday 3 June 1993

Mike Dolan and Fionnuala Sheehan are leaving the company. I can never see Mike poor. He has made a lot of money from GPA and still has most of it. Fionnuala wants to see more of her family—a reason that is becoming the late twentieth-century version of taking the stewardship of the Manor of the Chiltern Hundreds.

Although the mood in marketing is sort of post orgasmic tristis, or just post coital, strokes continue in the upper echelons of GPA, where the who fucks who game continues.

Meetings in connection with the make-up of the new GECC/GPA management company are still going on in New York. Michael Lillis has emerged as a senior player in the new order, being heavily engaged in the negotiations, representing the GPA staff interest. He will be hungry to do the best deal as he is financially challenged, share debt wise. Michael is revisiting his diplomatic skills here. He is obviously highly regarded by Phil and Patrick, who will have cast him in this role.

Colm has written to all staff a fairly impenetrable memo, which is supposed to update us on the GECC negotiations. It is full of weasel words and begs far more questions than it answers. We are no wiser, except that if all goes well the bottom line seems to be we shall end up as a GECC subsidiary. At least that is what I have been telling my customers. However, there are several rushing rivers to be crossed before we reach that supposed upland savannah: like animals on their migration, not all of us will make it.

The timescale is for GPA shareholder consent to the GECC deal during August. Consent will entail another $150 million of shareholder money being pumped in. Due diligence studies by the experts are ongoing, to prepare the way for those consents. As Maurice has stated in the press, all this is proving very, very expensive and GPA must pay. There have been so many due diligence studies on GPA over the past few years, it reminds me of what they say about London tap water—every pint you drink has been through somebody seven times before.

If all the consents can be obtained and moneys put down, it is expected the new regime will begin on or about 1 October. The uncertainty will continue up till then. There is plenty of it about at the moment, from top to bottom.

The situation at the top is interesting. Tony figured in yesterday's haul of press cuttings as saying that GPA is his passion and his life. He was yesterday in Stamford, Connecticut, trying to persuade Gary Wendt of GECC that not only should this life be allowed to continue, but could it please be in an executive capacity.

Apparently, if Tony returns victorious, executively speaking, Patrick, at least, will be out on his ear faster than a wink. Also old guard member Jim King will stay and find a favoured role. Other old guardees will also probably find a gentle and maybe rewarding end to their days.

The odds in favour of Tony staying as chief executive of GPA or, more importantly, becoming CEO of the new management company were yesterday put at 66 to 1 against. Yesterday was Derby Day.

If Tony does not come back with the promise of control, others also will go. Jim for one. Maurice is due to retire soon anyway and John Tierney can be expected to leave as soon as it is decent. That will leave Colm, Patrick and Phil at the top of the heap.

Colm was implicitly criticised by Patrick and Phil in their famous coup memo for not providing leadership and failing to stop the rot in Operation Rebound. Colm and Patrick may not prove a happy mix. Both are fanatically ambitious for the top slot. Colm has a wider power base and seems universally liked by outsiders as being the acceptable (i.e. genial) face of GPA. I guess insiders prefer him too. Also Phil and Patrick may be incompatible, despite their teaming up on the memo. There seems no real warmth between the two. Unless there can be a separate, clearly defined role for Patrick on the financial side in the new set-up and as long as he can accept the status he is given, I do not see him remaining. He appears to be on a loser whatever happens to Tony. Even as a retiree, Tony will probably do his utmost to get rid of Patrick, if he feels that Patrick has jeopardised his 'passion' in any way. The word is that Patrick is doing his damnedest to see that Tony goes.

The struggle is separating the company into at least two camps, old and new. Even our company secretary and chief counsel is finding himself fobbed off when requesting copies of documents from the new guard dealing with Rebound 2 and the GECC talks, in his secretarial capacity, presumably because he is identified with the camp of the old guard.

What a collection! Even as the GPA ship struggles with its GECC salvage tug to clear the fatal reefs of this financial lee shore, the senior officers are at each other's throats as to who shall command the vessel afterwards on behalf of the salvager.

Last Monday there was a get-together in marketing to discuss the GPA and GECC fleets and customer lists. It seems like a case of Jack Sprat and his wife—between us we should lick the platter clean. They are strong in the US generally, fairly thin elsewhere, but their customers are usually very good credits. We are weak in the US but strong elsewhere and our lessees are usually weak credits. Their aircraft tend to be old; ours tend to be new. They have some 400 aircraft on their books, via Polaris, GECC's aircraft leasing company; we have some 475. All round it seems a very good match. If things pan out for the best, GPA and Polaris could unite behind GE's credit rating and be an enormous long-term power in the aviation market, far larger than ILFC with its parent AIG, but along the same lines. GECC could have done one of the deals of the century here. It all depends on how it works out.

The point is though that GPA will be dead. Not in vain—its molecules, as it were, would be perpetuated in the new corporation. But from the point of view of this diary and the reason it was begun, the end would have been reached. My prediction that GPA was finished, made back in April 1990, unfortunately vindicated.

Friday 4 June 1993

Apparently Tony came back 'bouncy' from Stamford. Will he, won't he? Stay or go?

Patrick's position is marginal. I hear Tony wrote him a memo recently asking him what the hell was happening. Patrick replied in writing, saying he had not the time to keep writing reports. Besides, things were happening so quickly, reports were being overtaken by events. Patrick, allegedly, went on to say he had seen a press release by the GPA board standing by the present management. Patrick stated, in capital letters, that he found such a statement of support incredible in relation to a management that had contrived to lose $1 billion of the company's net worth in one year. This was a direct insult aimed at Tony.

Interesting to see whether he can come back from that, so far as Tony is concerned. Maybe Tony should take the view that any thrusting company needs bright, brave, disrespectful younger executives. Tony was never one for misplaced respect himself.

Tuesday 15 June 1993

Most of the GPA senior people are in Stamford talking to GECC, or in San Francisco talking to Polaris—Colm, Patrick, Phil, Niall, Brian Hayden etc. Yesterday in Shannon at the morning meeting, before flying out, Niall said GPA is 'subsumed' in discussions with GECC. Last week in Shannon, this week in the States. There is supposed to be a report on structures, functions and resources available for GECC management by the end of this week. Small subcommittees have been set up with both GPA and GECC people to look into the different elements which will go into the final report. These groups are headed up by various GPA persons, among whom the names of Maurice and John are absent.

Somehow a colleague contrived to glimpse a document that purportedly set out the GECC, Polaris and GPA marketing teams as numbering 65, accompanied by the forecast that only 45 would be needed for the new management company. GECC seems to be going straightaway for a merging of all resources, so that there will be redundancies, even on the marketing side, where some people had believed themselves to be relatively secure.

Everyone, naturally, is trying to work out how the split will be made and whether they will make the cut into the next round. Me included.

Last Thursday, Michael Lillis convened a leasing marketing staff meeting to update us on GECC discussions. I have not yet seen the video they made for non-attendees, but I hear it was a confidence-draining non-event. On the one hand, it was too soon to report anything finite or even probable, I gather. On the other hand, Mick gave the impression that anything could happen. Everyone seems thoroughly unsettled. We apparently should know our fates in July or August. As always, we wait.

Only the possibility of returning to a nice fat remuneration package keeps us hanging on here, avoiding looking for another job. Prudence would suggest we start searching, but aviation is a small worldwide industry. At our level there would be no secrets and I guess we all want to look as loyal as possible if it helps us to stay in the new order and be personally, financially successful again.

One thing seems clear: GECC is firmly in charge. GPA is a failed company. GECC is the new owner in all but shares. Now we all dance to GECC's tune—it is the only way the hordes of pipers will be paid and GECC absolutely knows it.

GPA is passing. I will continue this diary until the GECC deal is finally signed. If there is a slip 'twixt cup and lip and we are not GRAPEd, GPA will crash and I will be around, *inshallah*, to keep this literary camera turning.

Yesterday there was another board meeting at which it was resolved, or rather the board was allowed, to go ahead and make the June repayment to the unsecured bondholders—some $120 million. The pieces seem to be coming together all right under the GECC banner. John's man this morning declared the banks to be overjoyed at the outcome, i.e. GECC taking over. Talking to PJ Mara this afternoon, it seems there is a press release in the works, due to come out over the next 24–48 hours, announcing the signing of a detailed Memorandum of Understanding between GECC and GPA to cover future arrangements. This will, of course, be conditional upon shareholder consents and the

$150 million infusion.

Jim is in Paris for the Air Show, building and rebuilding bridges, I expect, preparing for a possible new existence. We have noticed that Jim seems to be trying to rehabilitate himself, especially in the direction of marketing. Jim on his own dazzling a customer is a whiz. I have to stand back in admiration at his style. They all love him. But back in a senior capacity in charge of anything—after everything that has happened, it shouldn't be.

On the leasing business front we have another problem. Yesterday at the Monday meeting, Niall called it the 'Canadian Disease'. It is, he reckoned, whipping through the Americas. Canadian Airlines have negotiated a moratorium with us on their lease rentals in respect of their eight Airbus A320s. The monthly lease rentals for these aircraft are in excess of $2 million per month. The airline informed us some time ago they could not resume paying before July.

The Canadian virus is now abroad. Lan Chile, BWIA (Caribbean) and Mexicana have all separately informed us that they are unilaterally declaring a moratorium on aircraft rentals—to avoid bankruptcy. We are trying to cure the outbreak. We all fear where this is leading. Mexicana only took delivery of its final Fokker 100 from us, one of a significant package, last week! This was not an honourable thing to do: to accept delivery on lease of a $25 million asset, knowing, as they must have, that they would be reneging on payment within days.

We should repossess the aircraft. We will not. At such a crucial time in our fight for life, we do not need fleets of newish aircraft decorating Shannon or any other airports. We will soldier on as usual, making the best of a hopeless position, acting on short-term expediency, as we cannot yet have any long-term confidence as to our survival until GECC is locked in. I hope we are all taking names so that when the upturn comes we remember the airline miscreants.

There is a piece in the *Financial Times* today saying that GECC has the option to buy a 65 per cent controlling interest in GPA for even less money than previously thought—$200 million. The article's unwritten subtext is obvious— GPA was dead without GECC.

Monday 21 June 1993

In Shannon. At the morning meeting Bob O'Reilly, senior VP of GECC, sat in as a listener, as he put it. Every time someone spoke, even if it was behind him, Mr O'Reilly turned his head to look at the speaker. We all tried to look suitably steely and efficient—as in hire me I'm good. Phil chaired the meeting.

Bob was to spend the day seeing groups of people. We could not make out what was going on, although Niall said over lunch that Bob was not interviewing, just trying to get a handle on the organisation. Well, maybe. He did not see me. His being there in Phil's office pervaded the atmosphere. Like being visited by minor royalty, you were constantly aware there was someone important in the building, but it was not enough to stop work for.

Strolling around the block after lunch with Mike Barry and Joe Clarkin, we were all full of conjecture as to what would happen next: who would head up the new company and who the existing company—which would be gutted supposedly by the spillover into the new company? The only common denominator was that none of us, and no one that we knew, had the correct answers. We all had our theories and I guess the issue is of such overwhelming importance to us that we talk around the subject endlessly. But it is futile.

Today's *Irish Times* Business section carried an article with a prominent photograph of Colm Barrington. The press release mentioned by PJ came out last Friday. We have now agreed terms with GECC for the setting up of a new management company to be based in Shannon. This company will manage, so said, all the GPA and GECC aircraft and those securitised to third parties. Within GPA Leasing the name of the game is to get on board the new company. There will be redundancies. Where will the axe fall? Already going around the building is—'new Co, old Co, dole queue'.

During the afternoon I speak with a colleague in New York. More information. I feel like the robot in *Short Circuit*—'input, input'. He tells me that last week the talks with GECC did not go well initially, to the extent that it was only during the latter part of the week that the GPA team were able to convince GECC to agree a major presence for the new company in Shannon.

Jim flew to Stamford after Paris and 'wheedled' his way into the GECC discussions. He apparently introduced himself as GPA vice chairman, but stated that his background was predominantly in leasing. When the meeting broke up into subgroups, each concentrating on different topics, Jim joined the leasing subgroup. My colleague's dismay at Jim's attempts to get back in was clear.

Michael Lillis has been deputed by the new guard to negotiate with GECC on behalf of staff interests and has instructed outside advisers to asssist him.

Just before I left to return to London on the 6 pm flight, I saw Phil. I told him I felt like a player on the touchline watching the game, not knowing whether I would be called on to the field to play in the second half or sent back to the changing room for an early bath. He sympathised, reiterating that he did not know what the staff implications were as yet. Nobody was assured. The GPA/GECC report had been submitted to GECC's management. Their report would be put to GE's management by the end of this week. Thereafter we could expect decisions. He estimated that nothing would appear before 16 July, less than a month away.

I get home to Cambridge by 9.30 pm. Just time to eat, pack, write this, sleep. Tomorrow I must be back in London by 7 am for a breakfast meeting with the CEO of South African Airways. Later in the morning I have an Iranian to see, starting up an airline in Belgium. A lunch appointment, followed by an afternoon in the office catching up. In the evening it's off to Heathrow for an overnight flight to Johannesburg, taking in meetings there and in Zimbabwe and Mozambique, before returning on Saturday, ready for Shannon again on Sunday. The doorman at the hotel in Duke Street, where I leave my car, asked me if I ever see myself coming in the opposite direction.

Wednesday 7 July 1993

Things appear to have quietened down considerably. This is probably a fiction.

Michael has continued to discuss the staff position with GECC in

New York, but is sworn to secrecy. No one knows what's going on.

GPA bonds are now trading at 70 cents on the dollar, reflecting the upturn in hopes that the takeover will be finalised.

Backroom work continues to be done on the GECC and shareholder issues. One thing is already apparent: the timescale is slipping. We have not been told anything, but the shareholder board meetings at which consent is being sought for the rescue are now estimated as happening late in August or early September. We were supposed to be getting a report on the 'Newco' management, company location, structure and manning around mid-July. This has now slipped indefinitely.

The June bonus Tony mentioned in his address at the last staff meeting never materialised. There is silence. The staff are humming. Family finances rely on bonuses; payment of share debt relies on bonuses; we all need bonuses.

Incidentally, 17.5 per cent of the outstanding sum is the settlement figure finally agreed by the Allied Irish Banks for its non-recourse share debtors to get out of their onerous share loans. There is even the possibility that the bank will finance the repayment.

On the marketing side, things are also relatively quiet. We have 'cartloads' of MD-83s coming at us, in Phil's words at the Monday morning meeting in Shannon. These should be difficult to move, but the executive responsible has done a great job up to now keeping these new but old technology aircraft out on lease. Overall the market is flat. In Africa it is virtually non-existent—a continent of airline basket cases for the most part. Even my favourite, Flitestar, continues to have a thin time.

Thursday 8 July 1993

Tony has put out a memo to all staff, entitled Restructuring Status. He is a sad man. Reading the memo I get the impression we are still on the cliff's edge. Nothing has been definitively signed with anyone, but GPA keeps shelling out money because it has to, to keep the wagon rolling. It starts off: 'GPA's restructuring is continuing successfully, albeit slowly.'

In June we paid out $263 million to lenders. Our cash balance is now

$191 million. I recall that we are, or rather were, holding nearly $500 million in customer deposits and advance maintenance payments. That money and everything else that GPA can lay its hands on now amounts to $191 million. If we go down, we will take many of our lessee airlines with us. There will be the mother of all rows and an unholy mess— truly a lawyers' and a liquidator's banquet. I am very glad I am not a director.

At the moment we are negotiating final documentation with:

1. our secured lender banks, some 138 in number, regarding the debt rescheduling.
2. the Japanese Club Loan banks to extend a $150 million loan for a further three years.
3. six banks, to provide us with a $92.5 million bridging loan facility.
4. four shareholders—Citibank, Mitsubishi Trust, PSERS and Nomura, who are to underwrite a $150 million loan, which will partly convert into shares. Some $20 million of this loan is coming from the Shannon Development Agency as part of an Irish Government initiative.
5. General Electric Capital Corporation in relation to the $1.35 billion aircraft financing and GECC's option to buy a 68–85 per cent interest in GPA. This is the GRAPE deal.
6. GECC again, in connection with the formation of 'Newco', to manage GPA's aircraft assets.

All of this has to be completed so that shareholder approval can be sought in early August. The approval process will take four weeks, so that everything should be finished, assuming approval by early September.

It is interesting that Newco is stated to manage only GPA's aircraft. There had been expectations that the fleets of GPA, Polaris and GECC would be merged for the purposes of fleet management and that this would be done by Newco—obviously not.

Tony states: 'GE Capital has agreed that [Newco] will have a significant operating presence in Shannon and will provide employment for a substantial number of GPA's staff . . . there will be a need for some redundancies in GPA, because of the reduced level of business. It remains the company's intention to ensure that staff who are made redundant will be treated equitably and sensitively'—then comes the crunch—'within the limits of GPA's capacity.'

There will also be a 'Rebound Bonus' to be paid on completion of the above negotiations, while shareholder approval is being requested. 'All staff who have made outstanding individual contributions to the company's successful turnaround will qualify for consideration for this bonus.'

It will be a complete travesty if any of the board receive any bonus. Further, if anyone connected at top levels with the failed IPO receives anything, it will be a disgrace. I am equally sure these will be just the people to collect the lion's share of any bonuses going. I would have thought it more equitable, if there is any spare capacity, to put it into the redundancy payments pot.

Tony ends the memo by recognising that some people have real financial problems, but declines responsibility. He is right. The company cannot be responsible for people's individual investment decisions, but many of the staff investors were working flat out, heads down, pedalling the money machine. They had neither a good view of the lie of the land beyond the parapets of GPA, nor the experience to compensate. There was pressure to invest; it was the proper thing to do. In the end they saw other people investing and trusted Tony, Maurice, the rest of the board and the sheer level of apparently profitable activity. Tony must at least take that responsibility to his pillow every night.

Tony invites staff with, impliedly, overwhelming problems to talk to Colm Barrington or John Tierney.

Friday 9 July 1993

In Shannon. I have a freight airline's MD and team coming over from the UK to inspect one of our DC-8-71 freighters, now squatting on the ramp outside GPA Expressair. Beforehand I sit in on the 8.30 am meeting, taken by Niall. Afterwards I run into Phil. As I shake his hand in greeting, he winces. His shoulder, he explains. Something wrong. Then, as I follow him downstairs, I see he is limping and ask him is he all right. At the foot of the stairs he turns to reply, half grinning, 'I'm fookin' farlling apart, but I haven't gat HIV . . . yet!'

Monday 12 July 1993

Back in Shannon. At the morning meeting Niall is in the chair. He announces that Phil is ill with a blood infection. He is expected to be off for the rest of the week. Everyone believes he is run down from overwork and worry.

During the meeting, when one of the marketing people says something to the effect that one of his airlines is keen, Niall makes a telling comment: 'This is something we seem to have forgotten about. Sometimes people do want aircraft.' This sums up the situation. Again I think about what could have happened if we had floated the company, raised the equity, raised the finance and taken delivery of all the aircraft Tony had lined up for us in 1992 and 1993. We are having enough problems sorting out the existing aircraft. We could not handle any more. If the IPO had been successful, we would be in a far greater mess. I hope Tony and the rest of the board realise that.

I turn to my neighbour in the next seat and whisper my thought briefly. He whispers back: 'All the directors would be in jail by now.'

Later in the morning the first person I ever met in GPA drops by. He is plainly expecting to be made redundant. He has been in GPA from its early days. His last assignment as henchman to Graham, negotiating aircraft purchase contracts, has come to an end. He has heard that 'Oldco' (i.e the current GPA minus the spillover to GECC) will shrink to about 30 souls. Patrick will be chief executive and the staff will comprise mainly John Tierney's finance people.

With that I go upstairs to see Diarmuid Hyde. He is one of the team looking into staff redundancy packages. He says the package being negotiated is better than the original voluntary one, later watered down by Tony. The extra is to head off possible legal action by disgruntled redundant staff. Plainly Diarmuid feels that the company is on unsafe ground from advice he and the team have received. His manner to me invites legal action if I am to be made redundant and feel unhappy about the settlement. He admits it.

As to redundancy, Patrick and Phil have now drawn up lists of the people they want in their teams in Oldco and Newco respectively. Those not on either list will be made compulsorily redundant. According to Diarmuid, we could all hear our fates next week.

It is very hard at the moment. For example, in the London office the three full-time administrative staff have had a tough time. In the months leading up to the IPO and ever since, the office has been swamped with Shannon financial, corporate, legal and often commercial people, as Shannon is hopelessly off the beaten track, despite what Tony has been able to achieve there. This has meant frantic activity much of the time with the trio bearing the brunt, working all hours. The service to me and the other marketing executive based in London has suffered to the point where I try to manage without a secretary and often work from home because there is no room in the office. Now, though, it seems likely the London office will be chopped. GECC has a London office; so does Polaris, just around the corner in St James's. In these circumstances it is hard for our ladies to be motivated, especially when the sword has been hanging over us all for so long. Bernie tells me the mood among the women in Shannon is the same—knowing nothing and fearing the worst.

So much for the foot soldiers. What of the generals?

Speaking to our helicopter pilot who flies Tony around, he had the impression that Tony still had no real idea what was going to happen to him under the new regime. Colm remains favourite to become CEO of Newco, with Phil as No. 2. The thinking is that Tony could be non-executive chairman. This talk all the time of GPA people in the top positions seems to dismiss GECC's ideas for its own personnel in the management of Newco. We should soon know.

Monday 19 July 1993

I am in Nairobi, Kenya, at an African aviation conference. These are popular with the Africans because they can escape from their offices, usually decrepit, to the atmosphere of a luxury hotel, do nothing and have it all paid for. Thinking about it, maybe that is the motivation for most people attending these things. For me, the attraction is that many airline executives scattered around the dark continent are gathered in one place who would otherwise have taken months to visit individually.

During a break in the conference proceedings I meet someone who has been talking to Colm recently. Colm had obviously been melancholic, saying that the 'deal had looked so attractive' in connection with shares he had so disastrously bought close to the IPO. It has cost him dear. He had also characterised Tony as walking around the GPA offices 'like a ghost'.

In the evening, in the garden, the organisers have put on a gently torchlit alfresco buffet. We drift about in warm soft scented airs under a clear tropical sky, the bright equatorial stars pressing down overhead. Accidentally I eat a mouthful of deep-fried caterpillars. Oh God!

Friday 23 July 1993

Johannesburg. I have flown down on Kenya Airways in a 180 seat Airbus A310-300. The passengers were predominantly black. The inflight movie was *Peter's Friends*, a peculiarly English, class-ridden comedy of manners about one of them contracting the HIV virus. In some macabre way, apt maybe, but I could hardly think of a less suitable film for the average African.

Flitestar is on the brink of closure and is asking us for a 50 per cent cut in its lease rates to keep going. This would cost us nearly $600,000 a month. Such is the lack of market for these aircraft that our Airbus manager is recommending the cut, for a five month period. The aircraft are leased out on five year fixed funding. Getting the aircraft back and breaking the funding would cost us $9 million. The MD of the airline, which is excellently run and managed, tells me that outside the board and three shareholders, only their finance manager knows the true situation. All the other hundreds of their employees are in ignorance of the airline's position, unaware of the real probability of the imminent liquidation of the company. It makes me wonder, likewise, how many of us in GPA really know what is going on.

Monday 26 July 1993

In Shannon. Flitestar's chairman and MD are coming here to plead their case. Today they are with the South African Minister for Trade & Industry, telling him the politically promised level playing field between them and SAA has not materialised. I saw the Minister's top policy adviser in Pretoria last Friday and he was not helpful.

So far as GPA is concerned, we still wait on events. John Redmond tells me GECC are twisting our balls to get a better deal for themselves all the time. Current issues are staff levels: who does what, who goes where, and who goes? There is the inevitable slippage, so we will not hear anything by month end. Remember Phil told me mid-July was the likeliest date. Well, at least one thing has not changed in three years.

John says we cannot count our chickens yet, but he expects the deal to go through after some more armlocks on us. He reckons the atmosphere in the company is post revolutionary. Lines of command are blurred. There have been shifts in the corporate power landscape. There is some paralysis as a result.

Patrick and Colm are the company's principal negotiators with GECC on staffing. Whither Michael Lillis?

Phil is back but looks very pale. I ask him how he is. 'Recovering,' he growls.

The $20 million that the Irish Government is prepared to put into GPA, to fill the gap left by a penniless shareholder, Aer Lingus, is consequent upon a certain number of Irish jobs being retained, together with a Shannon presence. I reckon my chances as a Brit, living in England, of being given the boot have jumped.

Walking around the block on the development estate after the usual quick lunch in the GPA dining room, Graham answers my query about Tony's retention of day to day power by saying there is still a weekly chairman's meeting, which Tony takes. Maurice, Colm, Jim, John and the old guard attend. They go through an agenda. The pecking order is retained. All seems normal, according to Graham. I wonder how that can be, given the coup and the GECC presence. Is it all essentially a charade? Another case of people hanging on to their usual routine in the absence of anything else to do? Of remaining normal in the face of—what?

John Redmond ventures that we should close the company for 15 days, save for a skeleton staff, to give everyone a holiday. It certainly is true, by our standards, that nothing much is going on. Everyone is demoralised, anxious. How much longer before we know our fates? Someone has even coined a name for it—Shannonitis.

Tuesday 27 July 1993

I spoke with Phil in the afternoon and we discussed the GECC situation. There will, he confirms, be a significant Shannon presence, with the Operational, Technical and Marketing departments centred here. The GPA regional offices are at risk. There will not be two offices in London, with the GECC/Polaris offices a couple of hundred metres away from our own. The GPA New York office will, at best, move to Stamford— coincidental, as that was where Graham started up GPA Inc. a decade and more ago. There may be a new Hong Kong office to act as a more convenient portal for SE Asia.

Phil continues: by the end of this week there could be a memo setting out the top management structure of Newco. After that, those top managers named would settle the staffing. I ask if the staff lists have yet been drawn up. He replies, definitely not. I asked if when the lists were being compiled, whether people would be chosen on their merits. He said, not always. Some will go for purely location reasons.

Phil emphasises that no one really knows what is going to happen, from Tony down. Even Phil is not sure about himself. He says the GECC people are savages, going for the best terms they can get, bar nothing. 'If what GE is doing to GPA was being done by one person to another, it would be a criminal offence. It's sodomy. We're being buggered.'

I asked about Tony's position. Phil says that GECC told our negotiators they didn't care what Tony did, but they were not going to pay for him. If Tony is to stay, GPA would have to foot the bill.

Phil is obviously under a great deal of stress. The skin on his hands is peeling away. 'Stress, the doctor says.' I believe he feels responsible for the people under him. Us lot. He knows we cannot all survive, but he is doing his best and the strain is telling. Also I expect financially he has a large amount riding on the dice.

Wednesday 28 July 1993

In Shannon. I have the embattled Flitestar chairman and MD in town, cap in hand, through no fault of their own. Phil joins us for lunch and hosts dinner later. He explains the GECC situation to our visitors. He paints a picture of the GE corporate culture colliding with GPA's freewheeling style. This, he says, will be our greatest challenge. Phil already seems knowledgeable about GE and its house style. We inside GPA know nothing. We can only guess that it could be typically American—hard assed, hard faced, devil take the hindmost, corporate jungle. Suddenly the old GPA, with all its faults, looks very appealing.

I hear separately that the redundancy terms are sorted. For me with eight years before the GPA mast it would amount to some 22.5 months' basic pay—it might just cover one year's mortgage and school fees after tax.

Friday 30 July 1993

Phil had predicted we might hear today the structure and top management of Newco. Nothing has emerged. There is a GPA board meeting in London today. Maybe Tuesday we will hear. Monday is an Irish bank holiday. The latest variation is now Newco, Oldco, Noco— how to conjugate your future!

Tuesday 3 August 1993

PJ Mara is not on standby for a press release, but he has just come into the office, breaking his holiday, just in case the Newco structure and management is announced today. He is jaunty as ever, with tie to match—a very appealing character.

I met Michael Hayes coming out of Phil's morning meeting. Apparently GECC thought up some more genital-garrotting issues last Friday and so the management services contract for Newco is still not signed. We will hear nothing today. He foresees a two stage memo: first, on structure and top management for Newco and Oldco; and second, the big R memo. He believes plans are already laid as to who will go and who will stay. Even he, who has made a real impact as chief debt collector, is clearly unsettled and worried like the rest of us. I told him

I had looked around the table at the morning meeting and saw the same old faces. Throughout all the traumas we have all hung in there. He agrees and adds that there are no wasters among them either. Yet we both know the axe is going to fall.

Wednesday 4 August 1993

In the London office. Nigel Wilson pops in to say hello. He is now Group finance director of the large US-owned Waste Management International Plc. Fallen right on his feet. He looks happier and more relaxed than I have ever seen him. We agree you never know what is around the next corner.

Our conversation naturally turns to the state of GPA. I say, 'Tony overbought and was surrounded by yes men.' Nigel says he wrote a memo to Maurice advising on the way the IPO should be handled, stating the need for flexible pricing of the shares, which he saw then as overpriced, and an April flotation. This was just before he even joined GPA. Apparently Maurice and John Tierney agreed with him, but not Tony. Tony, he said, saw any disagreement with himself as disloyalty. There was not even the chance for debate. It was Tony's way or nothing. He recalled Tony getting 'ratty' with him for not agreeing to certain things. Nigel went on to contrast the way GPA's IPO went with the smooth IPO of his present company, which had floated in April of the same year. How does it go? Sell by May and go away.

Colm is in the office. I ran into Patrick leaving as I arrived. The girls say he has been in a foul humour all week, barking around the office. Latest is that GECC's lawyers are concerned about how GECC is going to effectively run the company without getting embroiled in any of GPA's liabilities.

Everything seems a complete mess. Lessees are failing; lessees are not paying, there is huge overcapacity in the market; financing edifices are creaking; GPA has no money; and there are new aircraft we can neither finance nor place, which are costing us dear—B767s, B757s, A320s. There seems no end in sight. I wonder if we can make it, even with GECC's $1.25 billion. At this rate I can see it all getting much worse and the money running out. If GECC believes it will not come good, they will pull out, taking just the best of us to manage their own portfolio of aircraft, and what is left will sink. If this is what is staring Patrick in the face as he prepares to take over Oldco, no wonder he isn't great company right now.

Thursday 5 August 1993

Still in London. Patrick is here and has been continuously for four weeks, without returning to Ireland. He describes completion of the GECC deal as a 'high risk closing'. He agrees there are problems everywhere on the leasing front and says the GECC deal is no guarantee that we will make it.

Later in the evening I pitch up at the Aer Lingus Gold Circle lounge at Heathrow, on my way to Shannon. Already there is Patrick, John Tierney and two of his team. John tells us he is reading a book on the fall of the Third Reich. He has now reached the part where Hitler and his cronies are finally in the bunker near the end of the war. Wryly and dryly he says there are certain parallels. We laugh too heartily. They all look worn out. One of them says the Operation Rebound bonus may be the last dip in the honey pot—for all time.

Friday 6 August 1993

In Shannon. The place is jittery. People are living on their nerves. What am I doing here? everyone asks. Friday is not my day for Shannon. Have I been called in for a chat? The fact is I am trying to get away on leave this weekend and Shannon is an efficient place to tidy things up preparatory to that.

Everybody is waiting for the memo. Everybody is anxious. We all know GECC is being even more difficult over the terms. We are all pessimistic about life under GECC. No one seems to see a Shannon headquarters as a permanent feature of a successful GECC subsidiary, with such vast amounts of money involved. They will want it back in Stamford.

Michael Hayes and I agree that the high credit risk lessee chickens we have specialised in are tending to come home to roost. We further agree that the reason we have such lessees on generally low return leases is because we cannot get down to a commercially interesting price with decent credit airlines and make a return. Our costs, of aircraft, of financing, our numbers of aircraft, force us into the rubbish end of the market, and now it's falling apart.

Mexico, with many of our aircraft, is a disaster area. Too many aircraft, mostly ours, forced into new, shaky carriers. Canadian Airlines has rescheduled its lease payments. Whether they will pay is another matter. America West is prey to any competitive push by a major US airline. Elsewhere the airlines are hanging in, owing us large, growing amounts. We should have already repossessed a raft of aircraft, but we have desisted.

GECC has done a thorough due diligence on us, so they must know all about our potholes. No wonder they don't want to acquire any of our liabilities until we manage to escape from the woods—if we ever do.

Michael, once MD of Bahamasair, believes our strategic management has been a dismal failure. 'Don't talk about it', he says. Dealing always with the depressing offenders and delinquent payers, Michael's usually cheerful indefatigability breeds respect.

I put in a late leave request to Niall, finally believing I could possibly disappear for a fortnight. Niall responded by coming round to see me in Graham Boyd's office, where I was today, wagging a finger at me, adjuring me to the strictest secrecy. He told me that as I was about to be away for a fortnight, for my peace of mind and subject to any changes, which could well happen, the following. The London office will probably be closed, but that will not affect my employment with GPA, i.e. I will be in Newco. I have made the cut. Looking me firmly in the eye, as if to seal my lips, he said he would absolutely not say anything further at this stage. What a nice person he is.

Thursday 12 August 1993

I am at the fiendishly expensive Don Carlos Hotel near Marbella on a family holiday booked just last week.

My secretary calls me. The redundancies have happened. There is no memo as such; people have been informed individually. She sends me an unofficial list of those affected. It is not complete but gives me a good idea of who has gone. There are 33 names on the list. I am surprised it is not more and feel that this is maybe only one round in the process. The most senior person and a real surprise is Peter Denison-Edson. Bernie says some of the people are really upset. I can believe it.

There is still no word on the management structure of Newco. Phil gave the marketing staff a talk on the redundancies this morning.

Monday 23 August 1993

Back to reality. Up at 4 am to catch the 7 am to Shannon. In the lounge I run into a youngish GPA man. He has just been made redundant and is going back to clear up a few things. He is very unhappy but says his bitterness has decreased over the period since he first learned the news. I sit quietly murmuring sympathy. He cannot understand why he was let go, in view of the specialist work he does. He is a sad Tigger, a sorry Tigger.

I make it to the morning meeting only a couple of minutes late. Normally, being late I would have had to seek a standing position somewhere at the back and make my contributions from there, but today I am able to walk right to the front row to a seat at the table facing the screens. We are very thin on the ground. Niall is taking the meeting. The mood is dispirited. There is not much happening on the screens. Hardly anything seems to have changed since my absence. At one point a colleague in the next seat starts browsing the *Financial Times*. The meeting breaks up early. Niall comes over to greet my return. We go back to his office.

The Wednesday of the redundancies had been a horrible experience. Niall is quick to point out that it was horrible for those going rather than for him and Phil, in terms of where any sympathies should lie. I ask about the London office. No decision has yet been taken. Patrick may take it on in Oldco (GPA), maybe sharing it with Newco. I ask about the GECC aviation people in London. Niall implies they may all get the push. He says the redundancies are the final round: that GECC had looked for a total of 160 jobs to go. With the voluntary leavers, those coming to the end of contracts, consultants not being rehired and the redundancies, that figure has been achieved.

GECC has still not given its word on the structure of the company or its management, so he and Phil were still in the dark. I asked if the expected changes in the marketing territories would still be implemented. Niall replied that hopefully they would be, but that GECC would have to approve them. He thought the GECC deal could be signed that afternoon or maybe tomorrow.

Elsewhere I found that 'Black Wednesday' was just that. People were called in individually during the afternoon to be given their bad news. There were scenes. One person stormed out of the office. Another refused the situation. One was getting married the next week. One was supported by colleagues who have professed solidarity. One of our marketeers was actually telephoned at his hotel on holiday to be given the news. And so on.

I am told I chose the best two weeks of the year to have a holiday.

During the morning I looked up Peter Denison-Edson. Affably, he rationalises his redundancy as an opportunity to take a sabbatical, during which time he will see what the prospects of life are in academe. Still waters.

Peter shows me a draft press release due to go out following the signing of the GECC deal. The draft has Maurice's reference on it. It says all the non-executive directors will resign—John Harvey Jones, Nigel Lawson, Garret FitzGerald. Peter Sutherland resigned earlier when he became GATTman. Tony, Jim and Colm are all also coming off the GPA board but will have senior positions within Newco. I am filled with disappointment. We have the triumvirate, fresh from wrecking one company, about to be let loose on another. Once more the old guard has looked after itself.

Patrick is to be head of Oldco—i.e. what is left of GPA—with John Tierney and Brian McLoghlin. Maurice will retire from Oldco next March on his contract's expiry.

Tony is jumping ship from GPA (Oldco) to join Newco.

None of this seems to take GECC into account. Maybe, hopefully, they may have alternative ideas for Newco, which may not match Tony's expectations. The prospect of having Jim running the Leasing department of Newco under Tony is too much to contemplate, given his previous performance in charge of GPA Leasing.

Ominously, Phil is nowhere mentioned in the release. If Phil does not get his just reward in the reshuffle, there will be a marketing mutiny, no less.

In the afternoon I return to the London office. The first person I see is Nigel Lawson. A surprise board meeting has been convened. Maybe this is it.

Tuesday 24 August 1993

It isn't. I leave for Johannesburg. Flitestar is threatening closure by the end of August. I hope to see the South African Minister of Transport on Thursday. We do not want four A320s back on our hands.

Thursday 26 August 1993

Somehow the press release contents have leaked and the story appears in the *Financial Times*. Here it states Phil Bolger will be given a senior role in Newco, here also for the first time in public called GE Capital Aviation Management Limited—GE CAML. Perfect, a leasing company invented by a committee.

Sunday 29 August 1993

GPA is the lead story in the *Sunday Times* Business section; the *Sunday Telegraph* also reports Tony leaving the GPA (Oldco) board, as in end of an era—which it is.

The appointment of Dennis Stevenson as the new chairman of GPA is reported. I have never heard of him. A typical annual report-type photograph of him is printed. Stevenson's austere visage looks the part—like a cross between Sir Colin Marshall and Charles Hawtrey— competent flintiness personified. The fact that he is trying out a sickly grin fools nobody. This face radiates asceticism—the new face of GPA after the years of excess.

Monday 30 August 1993

On the 7 am flight out to Shannon, I am sitting next to Colm. Beaming, expansive, bulky, solid, curly haired, he resembles a clean-shaven Neptune. Goes well with his sailing image. Colm is secure in himself and needs no airs or affectations to underline his position in life— apart maybe from the big cigars. His suits look as if he gives them a hard time, probably because he fills them out. He gives you the excellent impression that if you were ever to find yourself in dire peril on the sea, he would be the man to have in your boat. Quite how that translates into dire peril, or even everyday life at GPA, is not so clear. His radiant confidence is unsinkable. Colm is outwardly a very nice person.

He tells me the GECC deal has been signed. Mostly. It happened at the end of last week. There are still some affiliated agreements to be executed, e.g. the Underwriting Agreement and GPA shareholder consents have yet to be obtained, but it all seems to be coming together. He says he wants a two month holiday. John Sharman of Spectrum Capital (remember Eaglet?) will be joining GPA's (Oldco) board—an ironic return considering his earlier sacking by Tony—representing $150 million worth of new shareholder. Colm is also somewhat unhappy about our lack of negotiating skills, believing we have given in too easily to GECC's demands. The way I have been hearing it, however, there has been little scope for negotiation. GECC has simply said, that's the way it is or goodbye.

We talk about the press coverage. Tony has been named there as executive chairman of GE CAML. I wonder aloud to Colm whether Tony will run CAML in the same way as GPA or whether his style will change. Colm answers quite definitely that Tony will not be in charge of CAML, whatever his title. He believes a GECC person will come between the chief executive and Tony. I enquire then about Jim's possible role, given his ultra close association with Tony. Colm says he is not at liberty to discuss top executive positions and clams up. Oops. He believes nothing will be announced regarding the top management structure for another 15 days and that CAML will not begin until mid-October.

From recent statements, the implication is once again, from references to the failure to float GPA, that the subsequent collapse in fortunes was due to that non-event. I say to Colm that Tony seems to want to rationalise the whole situation to that failure, with the implicit message that the public flotation was something he had entrusted to others in the company to carry out successfully and they had not. I continue, asking Colm's view, whether he thinks that if the IPO had been successful, so that we had been able to finance lots more aircraft in 1992 and 1993, we would have been in a far worse situation now, with large numbers of unwanted aircraft around our necks. Colm agreed that might be so. The trouble was, he said, that we had got so large we ended up floating on the industry's tides, going up and down with them. I pointed out that size was central to Tony's strategy. He told us at an annual conference some years back that by the end of the century he wanted GPA to be the American Express of the aviation financial services world. Colm recalled the occasion. I also privately remembered Phil peddling the party line early in 1990, going on about reaching 'critical mass', so that we would be out of reach of the vicissitudes of the market. What a lot of expensive hot air has been talked by us over the years to prop up untenable policies.

These people are still going to be in charge.

I ask Colm if a snappier name is being thought of for the new company. He says it will be called GE Capital Aviation Management. GECAM. I say it sounds like a video system.

Colm asks me if I have a share loan. I have not. I wonder if this excludes me from some special club of the suffering. Are we now to have this—only those who have gone through the holy expiatory ritual of the unpaid share loan, with its attendant confiscation of shares, will be considered worthy enough to be given high office in the GECAM which is to come. It wouldn't surprise me. Having no share loan marks me out as an unbeliever in the GPA that was.

Colm also believes that because of GECC's option to buy GPA at a knockdown price over the next few years, value will never come back into GPA's shares—maybe $1 at most. Ah well, so much for my 20,000 share options, at one time worth the best part of $1 million to me. *Sic transit præmium mundi.*

According to Colm, all of Tony's shares have gone to his bankers as part of the price for extrication from financial entanglement. It is difficult to imagine Tony without a GPA share, when he had so many representing so much paper wealth.

I ask after Peter Ledbetter's well-being. He is apparently in discussion with his banks.

Later at the morning meeting Niall runs through the GECC signing and outlines what still has to be done. At least there are more of us here than there were last week, but I still get a front row seat. Like the sun at the last stages of sunset, the remaining form of the old GPA is quickly slipping below the horizon.

Sunday 5 September 1993

The *Sunday Times* and *Telegraph* both ran stories in their Business sections about senior politicians who take City posts. Nigel Lawson figured in both as an example of what can go wrong with this strategy. Elsewhere there is coverage of the board departures, stating that GPA is losing its star-studded board.

Goodbye. You were useless to us.

Wednesday 8 September 1993

Since returning from my holiday on 22 August I have slept in my own bed three times. I am back in Johannesburg on my third visit since Marbella. I am exhausted. This week we have been working each day both in Johannesburg and Pretoria, 40 miles away, up till 3 and 4 am followed by early starts. Each week of this for me has begun and ended with 11 hour overnight flights between London and Johannesburg.

I hear that GPA board meetings continue back home as the GECC deal reached finality. Still no one knows just what is happening or the new command structure. Phil gave a brief update to marketing, but the prevailing message appeared to be one of lack of knowledge.

Monday 13 September 1993

I travel down to the London office during the morning. My idea, to catch up on some business before flying back down to Johannesburg on the evening BA flight. Upon arrival at the office I find it packed out. For the few minutes I am there I sit on my secretary's seat when she isn't using it. The Shannon heavy hitters are in town taking up the space. Colm, Patrick, John, Brian McLoghlin—even Maurice is banished to the little goldfish bowl office at the far end of the open plan area, where he sits uncomfortably on display. How things have changed.

Some of them have brought their secretaries. I speak to one, asking how things are going. 'It's out of control,' she says, meaning the endless rounds of meetings and negotiations. The sheer complexity of all the things that have to be done to satisfy all the parties to the restructuring is mind-boggling. The expense likewise, as GPA will be footing the bill for one of the biggest feeding frenzies by professional advisers ever seen.

Everything impacts on everything else, so the consequential agreements and changes that have to be taken into account, the requirements of GECC, banks, shareholders etc. seem to be legion. This has been going on, unbroken, for months. The costs, even this financial year, to GPA will be enormous.

I also hear some bad news. Two of our brightest Latin American region marketeers have left over the weekend, to set up their own aviation leasing consultancy based in Miami. They are a loss, another indication that the glue holding the marketing team together is disappearing.

Thursday 16 September 1993

Today I have been making a speech at an aviation conference in Gabarone, Botswana. At the end of the day, talking to a colleague on the Trading Floor about a prospective customer for a DC-8-71 freighter, he says he has heard that the forthcoming prospectus, to be issued in respect of obtaining shareholder consents to the GECC/GPA takeover and restructuring, has some interesting passages. Apparently pages 85 and 86 detail payments to be made to Tony and others in relation to the restructuring—along the lines of $2 million to Tony for agreeing to transfer from GPA to Newco! I ask who the 'others' are. He doesn't know, but he thinks the other directors.

Surely this cannot be. The persons who effectively brought us to this desolate pass receiving a golden handshake?

Saturday 18 September 1993

I arrive back from South Africa to find that Bernie has thoughtfully sent me some press cuttings on my fax machine. One is dated 16 September and is headlined 'GPA's *Annus Horribilis*'. It consists mainly of a leaked estimate of the year's losses for the financial year ended March 1993, the year of the IPO and its aftermath. The estimate is $600 million. 'And the rest' is my immediate thought. There is mention of the imminent 400 page prospectus, but nothing about payments to Tony and others. As a shareholder I am looking forward to getting a copy to see for myself.

Sunday 19 September 1993

In the Gold Circle lounge at Heathrow, *en route* to Shannon, I am pleased to see Graham Boyd walk in, florid from a day spent sailing his 38' Baltic yacht Stratocruiser in the Solent. We have not seen each other for a while. The prospectus straightaway becomes the topic of conversation. In a later draft it is now on pages 88 and 89. Graham tells me the figure for Tony is $1.8 million, but there are other increments. There are also bonus arrangements for Patrick, John, Brian McLoghlin and Maurice, running into millions of dollars for each of them if they can successfully steer GPA's course going forward. The prospectus is due to be issued tomorrow.

Last week at the conference I heard someone describe rumour as advance fact. There are plenty of rumours about as Graham updates me.

The GECC advance idea of structure for Newco was a company of seven divisions, all but one to be headed by GECC people. The one exception was the Operations division, to be led by Colm, with Phil under him. Marketing was to be a separate division, with a GECC man in charge. This was hardly what Colm was expecting. He had been tipped as chief executive of the whole of Newco and his remarks to me in the plane several weeks ago confirmed his expectations. Under the GECC plan, Tony would be chairman, with Jim as his deputy, for the first 12 months. Whether these posts carried any executive responsibility or were just face saving was unclear. Apparently Colm had written to

Dennis Nayden of GECC stating that Marketing should come under Operations, but Nayden (No. 2 at Stamford under Gary Wendt) had refused this suggestion.

The next piece of news is that GECC is rethinking its involvement: to the extent that Polaris would not have its fleet merged with GPA's and GECC's within Newco. Neither would Newco look after GECC's fleet. This would leave Newco (GECAM) looking after GPA's fleet and the aircraft GECC had cherry-picked from GPA, the sale proceeds from which formed an essential part of the rescue of GPA—rather different from what had been envisaged. This ring fencing would amount to a strict quarantine of GPA and its operations, whilst those operations would be under the control of GECC, through GECAM (Newco).

I do not find it difficult to believe this might be true. In crawling all over us for the purposes of GRAPE, GECC must by now know almost all of the horrors our shop contains. Many of these are ongoing. In GECC's shoes, I would be very circumspect about jumping into anything linked to GPA. Neither would I be necessarily trusting about representations given to me by the GPA board.

If GPA (Oldco) and GECAM (Newco) are to remain in bed together, without any new business there is even less reason for payments to Tony. Not that there is a single reason for them anyway and plenty against.

Monday 20 September 1993

Arriving at the Shannon offices at 8.10 am for the marketing meeting, I am struck by the empty car park and no lights on in many of the office areas. People are not hard at it as formerly.

Feeling about the payments is centre stage and hotting up. I see the part of the draft prospectus which relates to the payments, but in the brief time available do not take it in, preferring to see the final version so I can study it properly. The detail is such that plainly it will have taken a lot of time to put together and negotiate. I am afraid I deeply resent the time spent on this issue, in view of what has been going on elsewhere.

At the morning meeting, which I have not attended for a month, it becomes clear to me that our Latin American business, of which we have a large amount, is coming apart. Latin America, from Mexico southwards, has been an area of huge growth for us over recent years. So inspired was Tony by Mexico, he even bought a beautiful house there. We have stuffed mainly new aircraft into established and new carriers all looking for growth. Many of these airlines are now taking a pounding: some due to competition from us mega carriers, some from bad management, recession and a combination of these factors. It is a dismal picture.

Our debts receivable lists are lengthening. Quite apart from the VASP and Transbrasil debts, which have long since been removed from the screens, we are owed currently another $25 million in Latin America, just looking at the major debtors. Part of my area, Africa, owes some $7 million in total (nothing is owed by the Middle East). Aerocalifornia is still in there at $3.3 million, whilst Hawaiian Airlines is going to declare Chapter 11 tomorrow, we hear, owing us $10 million. Air Ukraine's debt is now over $3 million. So it goes. On and on.

At the end of the morning meeting, chaired by a slimline Phil—under doctor's orders to exercise since his bout of ill health—he is asked about the announcement of last year's results. This will become public knowledge with the release of the prospectus. The questioner is concerned at the adverse effect it may have on customers. Phil replies saying that we must accentuate the positive by concentrating on the GECC side of things, i.e. their financial strength.

After the meeting an old guard inner fringe figure in the office next to the one I am using sidles in. The loss figure for the year, he informs me, will be $1.05 billion. The turnaround from the previous year's profit of $350 million is therefore a $1.4 billion loss. The management responsible for those results is even now busy negotiating bonus payments for itself worth millions of dollars. It is scandalous and I say that to him.

In yesterday's business sections, the Sunday papers were full of a £60 million loss made by Spring Ram, a company dealing in fitted bathrooms. Headlines such as 'Exodus At Spring Ram' gave the news that the board of directors and some senior managers had been fired for the bad performance. Those figures pale into absolute insignificance set against the GPA losses. But do we fire those responsible? Do they feel guilty? No way. They're not only all still here, but they're expecting top positions in the next round and trying to collect millions in bonuses and other arrangements.

I apologise for the increasingly embittered tone of this diary, but the antics going on way above me are vexing.

A GPA board meeting was held last Saturday at which the various important resolutions were agreed, passing the contents of the prospectus, including the payments to directors. Tony's shares, it has been reported in the press, have been transferred to Merrill Lynch as part of the rescheduling of his personal loan with them, but apparently Tony reserved the right to vote one last time as if the shares were still his.

More news. Jim and Graham have settled the $40 million advance credits tussle with Pratt & Whitney, one of the conditions being that GPA has to have PW engines in at least 40 per cent of its widebody aircraft to be delivered between now and 2005. As GPA is not expected to buy any more aircraft, this hardly seems to be a problem. The good news came through over the weekend and the Saturday board meeting was interrupted to hear the tidings. Apparently the board heard the news impassively. Either they are shell-shocked or their minds were too busy carving out directors' bonuses. Graham is feeling miffed that hats were not thrown in the air or yippees heard behind the closed doors. Actually, maybe there were some yippees, but not for him.

Another mailshot to lessees is to be prepared. Already I can see this will be a masterly work of art, probably conveying an alternative reality close to our own universe, but not in it.

At lunch with Phil, Graham and two other senior guys, one a lawyer, the prospectus is discussed. It turns out that successive drafts are changing the parts relating to the payments to Tony and the rest of them, inasmuch as detail is being cut out and the meaning 'obfuscated'. It is obviously a very sensitive issue and the maximum is being done to play it down in the prospectus. No wonder. Writing this, I also recall the question of Operation Rebound bonuses. I have not heard any more about them, but I remember thinking that Tony & Co. would probably award themselves the lion's share. Will these still be paid, on top of the prospectus payments? Is there to be no end to the greed?

The legal man says morale is at rock bottom. Numbness has set in, according to him. Phil, who had been fairly quiet during the discussion, said something was needed to get people going again, though he used an earthier expression. Ironically, a good number of those made redundant in August are back among us—as consultants. This has not improved spirits, I hear, as they are now being paid more than before. Plus they have their packages.

It turns out that in the prospectus the incoming chairman and non-executive directors of GPA Oldco, Stevenson, Houstoun and Davies, are also being welcomed aboard with their packages linked to GPA's profits. Well, this seems fair enough. Joining the board of GPA nowadays would need some enticement. Also I exclude Patrick from any opprobrium in terms of bonuses. If he can earn any from turning GPA around, good luck to him.

I can only hope the press, once it sees the prospectus, will give Tony and his crew and those agreeable to the deal, a lashing that will outdo the criticisms made against Gerald Ronson over the deal he wanted to cut to continue running Heron Corporation.

GPA is due to make another payment to the unsecured bondholders on 28 September to the tune of $110 million. We have enough funds in the bank, some $200 million plus, but as always those funds represent what is left of the lessees' maintenance reserves fund holdings etc. The mindswitch at top management level for the last few months, i.e. since it became necessary, is that it is all right to use these funds as long as GPA can pay maintenance bills as they fall due. No longer is there a requirement, even a moral one, to regard the reserve funds (or the refundable lessee cash deposits) as in any way separate. They are there to be used for any purpose thought fit at the discretion of the management. Okay, but try telling that to the lessees if this all goes wrong. In essence, despite the 'commingling' words, I would say we are trustees for that money, not the beneficiaries, in these super-abnormal times when insolvency looms.

The latest spin is that GECAM will not take over looking after the fleets of GECC and Polaris until spring 1994, because GECC will not be able to reorganise itself to accommodate the new structure before then. The picture coming across is of an uncaring GECC—uncaring that is, as regards people. Their head of human resources is coming across to Shannon this week to hand out envelopes with job offers, so it is said.

Graham, in the office on the other side of me, came in with a calculation which showed that had the IPO succeeded and we had financed the next tranche of aircraft, we were contractually due to take delivery of 138 new aircraft in 1993 and another 151 aircraft in 1994 (never mind later years)—these in addition to remarketing existing aircraft coming back off lease either on expiry of leases or via unscheduled terminations. It would have been a completely impossible task in the circumstances, given the sharp recession. I launch into my well-worn spiel that a successful IPO would have been an even worse result than a failed one. The failure was a blessing in the heaviest of disguises. If the IPO had been achieved, we would already be out of business, swamped with aircraft, in even greater debt than presently, with directors probably facing huge responsibilities, given the contents of the IPO prospectus, and having left an almighty mess for a liquidator and creditors to sort out. Yes, we would have tried to reschedule aircraft deliveries, but the fallout would have been even more unbelievable than the present circumstances. Tony however still, publicly, believes that the IPO cock-up (for which he had great culpability—mistiming and insisting on too high a share price) is the cause of our present predicament. Inside his own mind though, he must realise the truth. He overreached and he and the board of GPA woke up to it far too late.

Tuesday 21 September 1993

It is a warm evening at home in Little Wilbraham, just outside Cambridge. I take both little pleasure and real pleasure in the old sixteenth-century house, the garden, the pool, the tennis court, the paddocks—the usual accoutrements of a GPA executive—because I constantly think, how much longer can we afford to live here?

Paradoxically, although over the past three years I have been chronicling the death of GPA, this diary itself is starting to feel like a pregnancy, a growing, living weight I carry round with me.

Wednesday 22 September 1993

11 am. According to Bernie 'they' have all gone round to the offices of lawyers Clifford Chance for yet more finalising of the GECC deal, which will then be complete, subject only to the shareholders' consent. I understand the prospectus for the shareholders has been printed and will be distributed today. There will also be a press release issued today. Maurice is all booked up for press interviews in London tomorrow. Jim is in Dublin for the Irish press. Don't know where Tony is, hiding probably, hoping he can get away with it, into the next well-paid phase of his life.

I expect the City journalists are salivating at the thought of what is going to hit the streets tomorrow. I am sure they have a pretty good idea of what is about to come down. I hope so. Somewhere in all this, someone has to be responsible for the astronomic losses about to be announced. Maybe this occasion will see people being forced to acknowledge that responsibility—and go—without the gilded parachutes.

Last thing in the afternoon a memo has gone out to all staff from Tony. It is a classic. Here it is in full.

'To: All Permanent Staff
From: T.A. Ryan
Date: 22 September 1993
Subject: Restructuring

PROJECT REBOUND
I am pleased to confirm that last Friday the Board approved the various elements of Rebound and on Saturday agreements were signed with GE Capital and with the four shareholders and Shannon Development who have agreed to subscribe for $129 million of new loan and convertible stock. We signed the bank agreements on 13 September. The agreements with the manufacturers have also been completed.

A shareholders circular and prospectus has been issued today and it is proposed to hold an Extraordinary General Meeting of shareholders on 18 October at which time shareholder approval for the transactions will be sought. Subject to the receipt of shareholder approval, consents from third parties and completion of other conditions precedent, the entire series of transactions is expected to close by the end of October. Each of the transactions is conditional upon the closing of the others.

This has been a long and painful process for all of us. I would like to thank all those of you who have devoted so much of your skills, energy and time to achieving the current position and also to recognise those families who have had to endure unusual disruption, particularly during the summer holiday period. There is still a considerable amount of work to be done to close the transaction and I encourage all of you to continue your efforts so that we can put this episode behind us.

In recognition of the successful efforts of staff, the Board has confirmed the availability of a total of $5 million as additional compensation for those staff who, through unusual effort and achievement, have made a significant contribution to the completion of Rebound, to maintaining our liquidity and our aircraft leasing business and to the Company's performance in general in what has been a very difficult period. The process of performance evaluation has already been initiated by managers and we plan to be in a position to inform staff in more detail of the allocation of this sum during the next ten days.

GE CAPITAL AVIATION SERVICES

The new GE Capital management company, GE Capital Aviation Services Limited ("GECAS"), will commence operations as soon as the overall transaction closes, which is expected to be before 30 October.

GE Capital has stated that it does not now intend to merge the management of GPA's, Polaris's and GE Capital's aircraft for the time being, but rather to maintain three independent management entities: GECAS–Shannon, GECAS–Stamford and GECAS–San Francisco. This arrangement will be reviewed again early in 1994. The result of this is that, at least for the time being, GECAS–Shannon will be responsible for the management of GPA's assets only and there will be no immediate merger of the GPA, GE Capital and Polaris management teams.

GE Capital has stated that its representatives will visit Shannon during the week of 27 September for the purpose of meeting with staff and making employment offers to the 160 GPA staff who will be invited to join GECAS. The remaining employees will remain with GPA. GE Capital has indicated that the GECAS offers will constitute the September salary review for those staff who will transfer and, as agreed, the revised salary levels will be back-dated to 1 April 1993.

FINANCIAL RESULTS—FY 1993

The Prospectus and financial statements will show a loss of $980 million for the financial year ending March 1993. This is the first year in GPA's 18 year history that we will have incurred a loss. The loss is primarily as a result of the reduction in confidence in GPA following the failure of the IPO but also reflects difficult trading conditions particularly in relation to lease rates, non-performing aircraft, receivables, aircraft values and aircraft sales. The company did make an operating profit of $48 million in the period, before deduction of the substantial restructuring provisions and charges referred to above. Much of the loss is in respect of non-cash items and GPA also retains net worth of $247 million.

While market conditions are unlikely to improve before 1995, I am hopeful that the arrangements with GE Capital will engender an increase in confidence in GPA, which together with GE's assistance in launching ALPS funds should generate increased liquidity from the sale of aircraft.

Finally I want to congratulate all of you on the courage and resilience that has been shown over the past year. Third parties have expressed considerable surprise at the level of morale that has been maintained throughout this difficult period. We should all take pride in the fact that despite the predictions of most third parties we have continued to meet all our obligations and maintain our business. I am now hopeful that we can build on our past strengths and develop our business again in the future.

T.A. Ryan
Chairman and Chief Executive'

Is that memo not amazing? Tony Ryan and to a lesser extent his board and top management have been responsible for:

- a one billion dollar loss in one year.
- a massive public flotation which aborted.
- company net worth reduction of 80 per cent.
- half the company's employees gone.
- the company rescued from imminent bankruptcy on terms it describes as 'corporate rape', broken up and its operations under outside control.
- employees' and retirees' shareholdings rendered worthless. Numbers of past and present employees ruined and being pursued by lenders for repayment of huge amounts.

Yet nowhere in that memo is there a scintilla of culpability anywhere, on anyone's part in the company. Not a whiff of acknowledgment of responsibility. Not a whisper of apology. Nothing. And there never has been. Yet again Tony and his directors present the situation as an achievement.

We who remain will all have, with any luck, 'attractive' job offers from GE Capital. But Tony, why didn't you tell us about the $1.8 million your board of yes men voted you personally to transfer from GPA to GECAS? Not to mention the other benefits of that little package. Not many guesses needed to figure out where a good share of the $5 million Rebound bonus is going—to the team that brought us the necessity for Operation Rebound in the first place.

Thursday 23 September 1993

The press release is published. It is not just a press release, it is GPA's death notice. This is the text:

'Information from GPA
GPA calls EGM to Approve Restructuring
Shannon, Ireland, 23 September 1993:

GPA Group plc ("GPA") announced today that it had convened an Extraordinary General Meeting of its shareholders for 18 October to approve the arrangements for its financial restructuring.

GPA said that conditional agreements on the restructuring had been executed, *inter alia*, with certain secured creditors and certain manufacturers, with subscribers to an issue of new capital and with General Electric Capital Corporation ("GE Capital").

GPA said that the proposed restructuring was the first step in a programme to regain the confidence of the financial markets and to enable the company to resume aircraft sales in significant volume—both of which are essential if GPA is to continue to meet its obligations to creditors and regain some value for shareholders. GPA added that implementation of the restructuring was the subject of various approvals, including regulatory consents, and to a substantial number of closing conditions, many of which are not under the company's control.

Restructuring Proposals

The restructuring proposals comprise a number of interconditional elements, including:

- reductions in GPA's future aircraft purchase obligations
- increased short and medium term liquidity, *inter alia*, through the deferral of certain repayments of secured debt and the sale to GE Capital of up to 44 aircraft
- the management of GPA's assets by a newly formed Irish subsidiary of GE Capital
- the granting to GE Capital of an option to acquire control of GPA
- the raising of new capital

Aircraft

GPA's agreements with aircraft and engine manufacturers reduce the total committed aircraft orders of GPA and its affiliates for delivery after 1 January 1993 from 242 aircraft with a total cost of $11.3 billion to 57 aircraft with a total cost of $3.6 billion. This represents a significant reduction in GPA's future liquidity requirement.

GPA and certain subsidiaries are in litigation with McDonnell Douglas Corporation arising out of certain aircraft purchase and other agreements. Trial of the issues is not expected before late 1994.

Lenders

The arrangements agreed with GPA's principal secured lenders include:

- the deferral for up to three years of approximately $750 million of loan repayments together with the provision of further liquidity of $150 million
- new lending covenants which focus principally on cash flow
- improved terms for the lenders

GPA is permitted to purchase aircraft under its amended order book. GPA said that it had to date met all its financial obligations to secured and unsecured lenders and that the primary objective of the restructuring was to enable it to continue to do so. There are no proposals to modify the terms of any of GPA's unsecured capital markets obligations or of any other obligations except those now being restructured.

GE Capital

The arrangements with GE Capital include the following principal elements:

- The sale to GE Capital of up to 44 aircraft
- The setting up of a management company to manage GPA's assets
- Assistance with further aircraft securitisation ("ALPS") transactions

Dr T. A. (Tony) Ryan. (© *Kevin Dunne*)

Maurice Foley. (© *Kevin Dunne*)

Juan O'Callaghan and James (Jim) King. (© *Kevin Dunne*)

Colm Barrington and Peter Ledbetter. (© *Kevin Dunne*)

John Tierney. (© *Kevin Dunne*)

Graham Boyd.
(© *Kevin Dunne*)

Patrick Blaney. (© *Irish Times*)

Philip (Phil) Bolger.
(© *Kevin Dunne*)

Brian McLoghlin and Niall Greene. (© *Kevin Dunne*)

Liam Barrett. (© *Kevin Dunne*)

Trevor Henderson. (© *Kevin Dunne*)

The author, Chris Brown. (© *Kevin Dunne*)

- An option for GE Capital to acquire a controlling shareholding in GPA

No responsibility is being undertaken by General Electric Company, GE Capital or any of their affiliates for any of the liabilities of GPA or any of its affiliates.

The aircraft transaction comprises up to 44 aircraft, including 17 aircraft on order by GPA. On acquisition of the aircraft, GE Capital will pay GPA approximately 85 per cent of net book value of the aircraft, with GPA reflecting as an investment an amount approximately equal to the remaining 15 per cent payable. The value of this investment will be realised as a deferred payment, the amount of which will depend, *inter alia*, on the price at which the aircraft are sold at a future date. This transaction is expected to provide approximately $465 million of gross liquidity to GPA, which will reduce to a net $331 million in the medium term. In addition, a GE Capital affiliate purchased an aircraft from GPA in July.

GE Capital Aviation Services Limited, an Irish subsidiary of GE Capital to be established in Shannon, Ireland, will provide certain management services for GPA's aircraft under a 15 year contract and will also acquire certain related GPA assets. The management contract will become effective when the restructuring proposals are implemented and GPA expects that about 160 of its current employees will be offered employment by GE Capital Aviation Services. The remaining employees, about 25, will remain with GPA.

GE Capital will be granted an option to subscribe for new GPA shares, exercisable up to 31 March 1998. If exercised in full, and if only the minimum $129 million were raised in new capital offers (*see below*), GE Capital would acquire approximately 67 per cent of GPA. The exercise price is based on a formula related, *inter alia*, to the date of exercise and the value of GPA's Ordinary Shareholders' funds at the time, but subject in the event of exercise in full to a minimum price of approximately $110 million and a maximum of approximately $165 million. If GE Capital exercises this option in full, it may during the following three years exercise a call option over all GPA shares then held by subscribers to the new capital issue or their transferees. The call option may be exercised at fair market value, subject to a floor price. If it exercises the call option, GE Capital will also offer to buy all existing Ordinary shares on the same terms except for the floor price.

New Capital Issue

The Company plans to raise up to $150 million before expenses through the issue of Convertible Notes and Non-convertible Notes, to be offered exclusively to existing shareholders. There will be two separate offers, one for $129 million and the other for $21 million. Citibank N.A., Mitsubishi Trust International Limited, Nomura International plc, Public School Employees Retirement Board (a pension fund of the Commonwealth of Pennsylvania) and Shannon Free Airport Development Company Limited have conditionally agreed to subscribe for all the Notes offered under the first offer to the extent that the offerees do not do so.

The Convertible Notes, if fully subscribed, will be automatically converted into approximately 25 per cent of GPA's equity on full exercise of the GE Capital option. If only the minimum $129 million is raised, the Notes would convert into approximately 23 per cent. If the GE Capital option expires, the Convertible Notes may be converted into 90 per cent of GPA's equity, at the option of the holders, up to their maturity in 2001.

The practical effect of these arrangements is that, if it exercises the option in full, GE Capital will own approximately 65–67 per cent of GPA and the Noteholders approximately 23–25 per cent. The balance of 10 per cent will be held by existing shareholders. If GE Capital exercises its call option, it will own between approximately 90 per cent and 100 per cent of the Company.

Future Management

GPA's non-executive directors will retire from the board on completion of the restructuring, as will Dr Tony Ryan (Chairman and Chief Executive), Mr Colm Barrington (Assistant Chief

Executive and Operations Director) and Mr James King (Vice Chairman). GPA expects that Dr Ryan, Mr Barrington and Mr King will be offered appropriate positions in GE Capital Aviation Services.

Following completion of the restructuring, it is intended that Mr Patrick Blaney (who is at present Chief Operations Officer) will become Chief Executive of GPA and that Mr John Tierney will continue as Finance Director. Mr Blaney and Mr Tierney will continue to serve on the board. Mr Maurice Foley will relinquish the position of Deputy Chairman but has been invited to remain on the board, in a non-executive capacity, after his planned retirement from executive duties in March 1994. Mr Brian McLoghlin will continue as Chief Legal Officer and Company Secretary.

The following have been invited to join the board as non-executive directors from the completion of the restructuring: Mr Dennis Stevenson as Chairman, Mr Michael Davies as Deputy Chairman and Mr William Houstoun. While discussions are at an advanced stage, they have not yet agreed to join the board pending completion of their due diligence and agreement on remuneration and the other terms of their employment.

Financial Results for Year to 31 March 1993

GPA made an operating profit of $48 million in the year to 31 March 1993 (compared to $262 million in the prior year), on revenues of $1,742 million ($2,010 million), after interest but before exceptional charges and restructuring provisions. After all such charges and provisions, the loss attributable to Ordinary shareholders is $993 million (compared to a profit of $249 million) which reduces net book worth to $234 million ($1,230 million). GPA's cash flow from operations was $932 million ($1,572 million).

Provisions and charges of $737 million have been incurred in connection with the restructuring. These include $462 million related to the restructuring of the aircraft order book, of which $71 million is GPA's share of affiliates' costs. Exceptional charges and provisions of $234 million have also been incurred as a result of the very difficult conditions in the civil aviation industry. The exceptional charges include $128 million of additional aircraft depreciation. This represents about 2 per cent of the book value of the owned aircraft portfolio on 31 March 1993 and arises because of GPA's policy to reduce the carrying value of specific aircraft to market value in certain circumstances even if the portfolio as a whole is valued in excess of book. GPA said that independent valuations indicated a 'going concern' surplus of over $1 billion (about 15 per cent) for the portfolio as a whole on the same date, which is not reflected in the balance sheet.

COMMENT FROM THE CHAIRMAN
Commenting on the restructuring, Dr Tony Ryan, Chairman and Chief Executive, said: "I am pleased that we have at last completed the documentation of the proposals which we announced in outline in mid-May. This has taken much longer than we and the other parties had hoped, because we have had to resolve some extremely complex issues and reconcile the differing interests of the many participants in the process."

Dr Ryan said that the restructuring proposals were an essential first step in enabling GPA to continue to meet its obligations and regain some value for shareholders and that, if they were not approved and subsequently implemented, the company would probably have to seek court protection or take other insolvency action.

Shareholder Circular and Prospectus
GPA will post a circular and prospectus to its shareholders today and these documents have been filed as required by applicable law.'

GPA is bust to the wide. A financial reversal in simple terms of a billion and a quarter dollars in just one year—through sheer strategic mismanagement of a foreseeable situation. Again, not one word or indication of blame, contrition or even explanation in the chairman's comments.

If this release gets through the press without scathe, it will be the biggest confidence trick I have ever witnessed.

The entire executive board of GPA are expecting to either retain their positions or be awarded other appropriate positions. I can imagine my idea of 'appropriate positions' might not equate with their own.

The figures are only to 31 March. Another six awfully expensive months have passed even since then.

If the GECC deal does not go through, GPA folds. If the GE deal does go through, GE has the option to acquire 100 per cent of the company in the future if it is worth anything after the dust settles. If we include all the costs and provisions, probably the best part of $2 billion has gone up in smoke for GPA, its business partners and shareholders, but there are apparently no culprits.

Friday 24 September 1993

The fabulous GPA New York offices are closing today. Staff remaining on the payroll will work from home until further notice.

Sunday 26 September 1993

Tony appears to have got away with it. Nothing in the *Sunday Times*; a very small piece in the *Sunday Telegraph*; nothing in the *Observer*. The Irish papers, notably the *Sunday Business Post*, carry stories, but they lack real bite. So much of it has been dragged out before, and the real issues this time around have been cleverly deflected into the restructuring effort, so they have escaped the attention they deserve. Tony's compensation or rather transfer fee to GECAS is not now $1.8 million plus amounts for pension, car etc. but is nebulous, something to be decided on arbitration—and not even how much, but whether and if so, how much.

The question of $5 million being available to staff as a bonus, even in the face of such losses, is explained away as necessary to keep a talented workforce together and to reward the staff for having remained loyal throughout a difficult year. The bonus will be widely shared among us, not concentrated on a few, the press has been assured by our spokesmen, Maurice and Jim. On that basis the press seems content. We know the whole purpose of the Rebound bonus is to direct it mainly to a particular bunch and my fears on that score are well documented here, but Maurice and Jim state otherwise. We shall see. The press made it out to be about $25,000 per person, if evenly shared. I will keep you posted.

Once again the reason for the loss is given as the collapse of confidence in the company following the IPO failure. Nothing is ascribed to pre-IPO strategy, where Tony simply bought too many aircraft for the company to stomach and where by early 1990 I believed the company was doomed because of it.

Tony seems nowhere quoted in the press coverage. He is keeping his head well down, as I suspected he would. There were though large photographs of his fall guys in this exercise, Jim and Colm. I understand Colm is none too pleased at the exposure, bracketing his name with the losses. Objectively he was daft to agree to it. Tony should have been called out to face the press, but even in this, at the very last, Tony gets his way. His spell continues, because Jim and Colm need his shreds of patronage to secure their places at GECAS. So it ever went.

Monday 27 September 1993

Tony appears at the morning meeting and sits through most of it. He makes an introductory speech, about him being chairman of the new company and Colm being president. That we should all be positive and go forward to new glory. He also tells us that his mind and those of his very senior management (Jim and Colm) have been focused on other aspects of the company's business for the past 12 months on Operation Rebound, but that now they're back and able to give Leasing the attention it has been without.

Sweet Jesus—the arrogance of them.

Larry Toole, Human Resources director of GE Capital, is also there, next to Tony. After the opening speech, Tony our old/new chairman keeps fairly quiet. As far as I can see, no one is intimidated by him. What a change. At the end of the meeting, though, Tony speaks again, complaining that the meeting format has been too recitative and stating that we ought to make an example of one of our biggest customers, Mexicana, who owe us several millions, by repossessing our aircraft. Typical Tony—back to the old routine—criticism and kicks in the bollocks all delivered from the hip with his usual quiet but intense asperity.

Talking afterwards to several colleagues, there is a bad reaction to Tony's presence. People did not want to see him there, especially seeming to belittle the results achieved by Leasing—universally recognised as having held the company together and given credibility to the restructuring by its continuing achievements in the face of collapse—while his attention was elsewhere. We think we did better than other parts of the company, considering. No one thinks we will do better with him in charge.

Our PR guru, PJ Mara, is in. I say to him, 'Tony got away with it', referring to the relatively benevolent press coverage following the press release, in view of what could have been expected. PJ looks straight at me and says flatly, 'Tony got away with murder.'

Apparently the reason why the draft of the GE rescue prospectus particularised Tony's payout whereas the final version mentioned arbitration seems to be the stance taken by PSERS, an investor. It is the pension fund representing retired schoolteachers of Pennsylvania. PSERS is not a fan of Tony. It wants him out without compensation. The compromise for the purposes of the prospectus is the arbitration clause. This story runs.

During the morning I find out there is a special meeting going on with Larry Toole. It transpires that 15 people, some of them in marketing, are going to be held back in GPA for a while. GECC's lawyers, as part of their exercise to ring fence GECC away from GPA's liabilities, have insisted that Newco-GECAS does not market or otherwise deal with any aircraft not belonging to GPA, but which GPA manages on behalf of the aircrafts' respective owners. This affects aircraft which are owned by the GPA joint venture companies, those we have securitised, aircraft we may have leased in, and other situations where we look after aircraft for fees or whatever. These people therefore have been picked out by Patrick to stay behind to look after these aircraft until the owners have consented to GECAS taking over, on terms which will indemnify GECC from anything which may have happened pre GECAS taking over.

It turns out Patrick did not consult at all with either Phil or Niall before naming the so-called DTES—Deferred Transfer Employees. The DTES are unhappy. They feel isolated and somehow second class by comparison with shiny new GECAS. Neither will they want to risk losing their place in the new hierarchy. The trouble is no one can predict with real certainty how long it will take to clear all the consents. For example the MDC aircraft in Irish Aerospace, our erstwhile successful JV with MDC, may be caught up by the litigation now going furiously on with MDC over the MD-11s and drag on for months.

Staying with the MDC case, we have made a provision in the billion plus dollar loss of $144 million to cover the possible cost of the lawsuit. I hear it may cost us this. MDC is suing us for not taking their aircraft; we are counter-claiming that the aircraft do not perform as represented. Unfortunately, as previously set out here, we did not obtain performance guarantees. Heads rolling over that? Not that I see. We ordered 18 new untried aircraft at approximately $110 million each, some anyway with no performance guarantees.

Graham thinks I am being harsh on our chief strategist, with whom he is friendly. He says 'your man' did warn Tony of oversupply of aircraft before the IPO, but went along with Tony's view on the basis of collective responsibility, i.e. you agree with the majority or resign. I reply that as he was acting as a professional expert to the company, he has a different standard of care. He should give his view and stick to it, not cave in and go along with the board, even though it takes a contrary view. Third parties were relying on his objectivity. He did not tell them the opinions he was expressing were not necessarily his own. Large amounts of money are involved. On the other hand, this same person wrote a 'humungously' (his word) large cheque for GPA shares on the eve of the IPO and was hugely relieved when he somehow got his cheque back—uncashed—after the IPO was pulled. So he must have believed that the company's prospects were good, whatever the scale of aircraft orders and the industry's woes at the time—or maybe it was just participation at the last moment, carried away in the general greed and optimism everyone seemed to be indulging in at the time.

Which brings me on to the next subject. We are being sued (this seems to be open season) by purchasers of $40 million of our public debt in the us. Aggrieved bondholders, they are alleging that our prospectus, issued in connection with the offer for sale of these bonds, was misleading. I have not seen the document, but I can believe they may have a case. Let's face it, the IPO prospectus itself must have been a masterpiece, to paper over the serious structural cracks which were already apparent in the organisation and its prospects. If the IPO had been successful, as someone said somewhat tongue-in-cheek, all the directors would be in jail by now.

I have a fairly heavy week ahead. To London this afternoon, then off tonight to Harare, followed by Maputo (Mozambique) and on to Johannesburg, returning to the UK on Saturday and back to Shannon next Sunday. I will be in the air on every one of the next seven days. Two whole nights will be spent trying to sleep in an aircraft seat. None of it is marketing. I will solely be chasing receivables, debts, threatening repossessions, nursing sick airlines. I am a glorified bailiff.

Thursday 30 September 1993

I flew to Maputo this morning from Johannesburg, only to be refused entry to the country and escorted straight back across the tarmac to the aircraft I arrived in, to return to South Africa. Mozambique has suddenly and for no published reason changed its visa requirements. No longer can I get a visa on arrival for $30 as usual. The Lineas Aereas Mocambique duty officer goes nuts with the immigration officer when he realises I am there to see his boss, the director general of the State airline. To no avail. The Third World strikes again.

Sunday 3 October 1993

In Shannon. I have with me the brown envelope—the GECAS job offer. I have not read it yet. Why can't I summon up the enthusiasm? Because I have a sense of foreboding.

Last night I went with the family to the cinema to see *Sleepless in Seattle*. Now there is a title I can empathise with.

Monday 4 October 1993

I learn afterwards that Tony stood at the back listening to the morning meeting. There was no seat left for him next to Phil, who chaired and gave no acknowledgment of Tony's arrival.

The GECAS job offer spawns various questions, but I shall not bore us with these. I guess I am lucky to get it. People are wondering if Colm will accept the GECC offer. Jim apparently will not be in the Leasing chain of command. GECAS's structure is still unknown despite the brown envelopes.

Thursday 7 October 1993

I call John Jones, now a consultant, having heard he is talking to Sir Freddie Laker about a new transatlantic operation. He is very *au fait* with the market. Disturbingly so. He rebuffs my offers of aircraft and lease rates with truths. These are that the market is inundated with people trying to offload aircraft, even very good ones, for next to nothing. Or even for nothing, but just the hope of something (i.e. pay by the hour and no minimum hours). There is nothing out there. Maybe the odd pocket of demand, but basically the world is awash with aircraft. In the air and stuck on the ground.

Manufacturers and lessors need healthy developing airlines; airlines need more proper fare-paying passengers; passengers need more money or economic imperatives to fly. Near the top of our food chain we suppliers sit like predators, starving and stranded by a lack of prey.

This deep global recession has been around now for two years, getting worse during that time; the same time Tony had us down for taking delivery of hundreds of new aircraft we had already bought in 1989, if the IPO failure had not intervened to prevent it by collapsing confidence in GPA. If the IPO had succeeded, afterwards we could never have drawn down on financing or taken delivery of more than a relatively few aircraft comprising our mega order, before there would have been more breaches of the financing covenants than fleas on a mutt. What hell would then have broken out? Remember we were living on waivers of our AOG covenant way back in May 1990.

Monday 11 October 1993

In Shannon. Most of the morning meeting is taken up with dealing with problem cases, not new deals. By the end of this week, even with our depleted fleet, we shall have 25 aircraft AOG. Phil gives the clear impression that GE Capital wants them all flying by the end of the year. Can you imagine if the IPO had come off, the number of unplaced aircraft which would be around somebody's neck? The mind boggles.

The meeting is told that Airbus Industrie seems to have written GPA off as a future customer for its aircraft. Airbus is terminally fed up with us. It has taken back two of the three new A320 aircraft we were having stored and deferred at Toulouse. They were past their contractual delivery dates but we could neither finance nor find lessees for them.

I also heard, outside the meeting, that Patrick had written to Airbus asking for cancellation of 1995 deliveries, deferral of 1994 deliveries into 1995 and deferral of 1993 deliveries into 1994. The uncompromising answer had come back—yes, no, no. All this underlines the emptiness of assertions during Operation Rebound of the valuable future delivery positions GPA was holding, ready for an upturn. The truth is that each time we cancel an aircraft we lose more millions of dollars of already paid pre-delivery payments, our level of bulk discounts reduces and therefore credits are reclaimed if already paid.

There is a GPA board meeting in London today. Tony, Maurice, John and Jim are there. Colm is on a week's vacation. He is reported to be using the time to look around for another job.

I believe there is also a meeting of the Compensation committee, which is chaired as always by John Harvey Jones. One might reasonably wonder what the agenda for the meeting could consist of—distribution of the $5 million?

I speak to Phil during the morning. He seems to be in charge of putting GECAS together. I do not detect the hand of either Tony or Colm at work. Phil talks about the structure of the company he wants. The so-said very top seems to be shaky. I hear the US shareholder Prudential is not in favour of Tony.

I ask Phil about continuing in the London office, which looks like it will be kept open by Patrick and John in GPA (Oldco), if they can afford it. Phil says that GECAS staff are not to set foot in it. Period. Again because of the fears that the two operations could be deemed to be operating as one and therefore GECC could become liable for GPA debts. GPA House in Shannon though will house both GPA (Oldco) and GECAS (Newco) under the same roof. It will be interesting to see how the building is segregated. Instead of interior designers, we'll have interior lawyers looking at it.

Tonight we had a farewell dinner for the London office. Jenny Brown, our office manager, will be staying with GPA and be its longest serving member after the GECC deal finally consummates. We all had a good evening at the Mayfair Hotel, where visiting GPA staff stay whilst in London. There was much merriment, not to say envy, over the recent news of a previous GPA London marketeer getting engaged to Koo Stark, Prince Andrew's former and delicious squeeze.

I am being chased for my proxies for the shareholders meeting on 18 October. The Great Vote.

GE Capital is also chasing me, to return the signed contract accepting their job offer.

My bank is also after me. To refill my exhausted account. Like the account, I am drained.

Wednesday 13 October 1993

I call Brian McLoghlin to ask him about my GPA Options. I still have some 20,000 odd at $5 a share—way below the IPO price. They're supposed to lapse if I leave the company. I'm about to go to GECAS, so what is the position? He'll enquire and get back to me.

Thursday 14 October 1993

In the morning I am visited by the GE pensions lady, in the London office. She is the first GE person I have spoken to in this whole episode so far. I am bursting with questions. She has few answers. She is the pensions lady.

Friday 15 October 1993

All this week there has been increasingly frantic activity focused on getting next Monday's resolution on the restructuring and takeover through the shareholders EGM. Because I hold ordinary, convertible redeemable and some other type of shares, I have to fill in red, blue and yellow proxy forms. Because some of my shares are still with a nominee company, I have to instruct them how to vote those shares. As the par value of all the remaining shares I hold in GPA is less than $10,000, you can see the scale of the performance to rake in every last vote. We are told the fate of the company depends on it. Funny, I thought the fate of GPA had already been sealed. Surely it has gone. At best only a heavily lobotomised patient will remain, with Patrick in attendance as chief white coat.

Sunday 17 October 1993

I am literally in the act of leaving home to catch the 6 pm SAA flight to Johannesburg and then on to Harare, when the telephone rings. It is someone in John Redmond's department. Have I seen an email sent to me in the London office at 22.32 last Friday night. No, I have not. How could I? 'Ah,' she says, 'sorry.' By it I am summoned to attend Shannon on Monday. It turns out I am a rarity, a rhesus negative of the GPA share-owning fraternity. I have some of every type of share. Therefore I and a few select others have been chosen to form the quorum for the EGM, to keep the numbers down. This needs explanation. The EGM will apparently be heavily attended: so heavily it will need to be held in the Southern Hotel at the airport. Before that bit of it gets under way, however, the EGM will start off in the GPA Shannon boardroom with a necessary few and adjourn to the hotel to admit the masses.

Crikey, I am needed. That I should live to see this day. From a cog to the crown. It is almost a poignant moment. I am robbed, of course, by my necessity to go to Harare to have an important million dollar meeting with the Minister of Transport. It takes the next 45 minutes via telephone calls to both Brian and John Redmond to ensure that I can be dispensed with after all and so go to Harare.

Checking my fax at home to make sure I had no notification of the Shannon tryst, just to cover my backside, I find a short message on the machine to say that one of my airline contacts, a 39-year-old executive

VP of Planning at Gulf Air, has suddenly died. I am seriously shocked by this news, but can hardly take it in during the kerfuffle over going to Shannon or not. Later in the car on the way to Heathrow I reflect on the awfulness of the tidings. I remembered that half the time when I rang, he would be out at prayers. I must find out what happened. I suspect a heart attack because of the suddenness. By now I am really late for my flight and arrive at Heathrow in a lather—a great way to start a 16 hour journey.

To cap the afternoon, where I park my car, the reception is not holding a set of documents supposed to have been sent to them by courier from Shannon to await my arrival.

I am actually disappointed to miss the proceedings in Shannon, especially now that I know the EGM will be a big affair. Maybe, just maybe, someone will get up and actually criticise in public what has gone on and the mismanagement of the company. I hope so. I get John to promise me a blow by blow account of the proceedings.

Monday 18 October 1993

In Harare. The big day. Isn't it strange that coincidentally I seem to be in Harare whenever something important is going on over in Shannon: IPO day, the GECC rescue announcement, and now the make or break EGM.

In the morning I call Jamila in Bahrain. She tells me the sad details. A heart attack. I organise a letter of condolence to go from Shannon.

Dennis Norman, the Minister of Transport for Zimbabwe and a farmer, is the nicest minister I have ever met anywhere, and I have met a fair few. He is also the most effective minister in the Cabinet. We have a good meeting. I need him to save Affretair, of which his government is the sole shareholder. $1 million plus of funds urgently need to flow. He will see what he can do.

Wednesday 20 October 1993

In Maputo, this time no visa problem, and straight through Immigration, even though the visa is issued on my arrival at the airport as per usual. Don't ask—TIA—This Is Africa.

Friday 22 October 1993

I hear next Thursday is scheduled to be the closing date for the GE Capital transaction. Another showstopper for Patrick.

Friday 29 October 1993

The GECC deal closes. This has been an absolutely mammoth task. Patrick's team will probably get their first rest in months. So many people have been involved. I hear the outside professional advisers' fees alone will be some $130 million.

Sunday 31 October 1993

Graham Boyd is on the flight over to Shannon. Later in the bar at Bunratty I learn that Tony has made it. He is to be executive chairman of GECAS—Shannon. Jim King will be vice chairman; Colm Barrington, president. Apparently Colm, on hearing the news last Wednesday, promptly shot off to Stamford and returned as president and managing director. What will Jim do, I wonder. Graham warns me that everyone has their own agenda, including Phil, and I should remember that. Graham has handed in his notice. Honourable as always.

| GECAS 1993–1995

Monday 1 November 1993

GECAS starts. I am in Shannon, having just returned from a week off in South Africa. I was not expecting to find all the ballyhoo of the first day. The Trading Floor is packed for this first meeting of the new order. I have a ringside seat. Colm is in the chair, flanked by Bob O'Reilly of GECC and Phil Bolger. Other GECC people I have never seen are in the large open plan room.

Colm gives the big welcome speech. The message: *le Roi est mort; vive le Roi.* We are all back in the big time courtesy of GECC. Using the screens, he gives a presentation of the new company. Tony is to be the executive chairman; Colm is to be president and managing director. No mention at any time of Jim King. Neither does his name appear on the list of management in Colm's presentation material on the video computer screens, although we know for sure he is vice chairman. Neither he nor Tony are at the meeting.

Under Colm there are various heads of divisions: Leasing, Legal, Finance, Capital etc. Several of them are TBA—to be advised. Phil Bolger is to head Leasing. I recall Phil telling me he was going to be managing director of GECAS. He is not, but he should be. Already there must be friction. Already an old pattern is beginning to reassert itself. We know who the chiefs are—the old guard. The rest is not yet determined.

Colm tells us the old GPA was 'too arrogant'. Now we must be different. We must also be critical, of him, of the company if we feel the need, and so on. Terrific, isn't it?

After the meeting I turn to Trevor Henderson and remark how truly amazing it is after everything that has happened—the hopelessly misguided overbuying of aircraft, the botched public flotation, the bankrupting of the company, the billion dollar loss, the staff losses, the rescue by GE Capital and the complete eclipsing of GPA—how the old guard have managed to retain their positions. Tony is still at the top; Jim is next; Colm next. In GPA (Oldco) John Tierney remains Finance director, his usual post. Maurice Foley is still there as a director too until his retirement next year. All of them were executive directors on the main board of GPA during the crucial years. Not one of them has had to walk the plank.

Trevor turns to me and says it isn't just amazing, it's a miracle on a par with the raising of Lazarus.

During the day senior GECAS marketing staff have 'getting to know you' meetings with our counterparts in other sectors of GECC's aviation empire. In the evening we all go out to dinner at Durty Nellys, a well-known local hostelry. At my table sits John Flynn, ex-head of Flying Tigers (a major US freight airline) and No. 2 at Polaris Leasing. He has been making short telling comments all day. He has another one for us specifically aimed at Tony. He says: 'One should never confuse intelligence with a bull market.'

Tuesday 2 November 1993

Patrick, now chief executive of GPA (Oldco), has put out a Rebound Closing Memorandum. In it he says:

'Many of you do not realise that Project Rebound was one of the largest, most difficult and complex restructurings ever completed, worldwide, and that, at most times during the process, up to 100 people were involved full-time in its various tasks. It is a remarkable achievement for each of us in GPA that we were able to successfully restructure under the most difficult circumstances in the way that we did. . . . I am amazed at the abilities, commitment and perseverance of GPA's people and particularly the new skills and talents which have surfaced through this epic struggle. It is also a somewhat sad occasion where the benefits, extraordinary success and accomplishments of this unique Irish organisation founded by Tony Ryan pass to GE. It will never be quite the same again.'

There is this recurring theme—our attempts to pick up the pieces after disaster are presented as triumphs. The rescheduling, restructuring project was indeed ultra difficult to achieve and it was achieved with the greatest effort and expense. On its own, as an exercise, a project, it was well worthy of a triumph, a stupendous undertaking by Patrick, leading his team. But, but, but, it was also the most colossal waste of money, effort, time and opportunity, all caused by the mismanagement of GPA Group plc by its board of directors, all of whom either endorsed the ideas of Tony Ryan or were unable to say no to him.

Thursday 4 November 1993

On my computer screen is a farewell note from Peter Denison-Edson. He had hoped to retire, he says, at 50, a millionaire. In his typical dry manner he admits he is short of both targets. We understand. He is off to write the definitive Japanese novel. I reply saying I hope to read the novel and recognise some of the characters in it.

Tonight there is a party. We have had about two days' prior notice. It is to mark the successful completion of Operation Rebound. Patrick's do. It is to be held at the Dunraven Arms in Adare, where I first attended a GPA annual meeting in May 1985 to learn about the company and its just achieved $12 million profit. GPA was 40 people then. It had already taken ten years of hard slog to get that far.

Of course, Sod's Law means that I have two customers in Shannon for meetings on Thursday and Friday. Properly I take my visitors out for dinner in the evening. We have a full night. They end up the wrong side of several pints of Guinness and two bottles of claret, with two Durty Nellys T-shirts and headaches to add to their jet lag. We break for our adjacent hotel rooms at around 11 pm. Ten minutes later I am in the back of a taxi heading out to Adare.

I have missed the dinner but arrive for the speeches. Patrick first, Colm second. Patrick's goal is to survive until 1996, to pay out the bondholders, satisfy the lenders' rescheduling conditions and get GE to exercise its option to buy out GPA. Colm's goal is to help him do it. There's ne'er like us. All ra-ra stirring stuff. We clap, cheer, stamp. The spirit of GPA lives on. We may be down but not out. It is the liquor-enhanced mood of the moment. Several of the redundancees are present, including Peter. I wonder what he thinks of it. Neither Tony nor Jim is there.

Friday 5 November 1993

The morning meeting is cancelled by Phil. People arrive in dribs and drabs at the office. There is a heavy demand for bacon sandwiches from the dining room. I have my visitors, a managing director and a deputy executive chairman of an ailing airline. They need our help. Back to business as usual.

During the day the Operation Rebound bonuses are released—the famous $5 million distribution. After taking into account the advance 'redundancy' payment I and others received during the summer, my bonus is actually a *minus* amount. So much for that. I will never know what Tony and his fellow directors collected.

The Zimbabwean Minister of Transport comes through though. $1.5 million is being transferred today. Situation saved.

Sunday 14 November 1993

A headline in today's Business section of the *Sunday Tribune*, a major Irish newspaper, reads: 'Troubleshooter Under Fire'.

It is an interview between Rory Godson, the Business editor, and Sir John Harvey Jones, GPA's recently departed deputy chairman. I was delighted to see, at last, a public utterance from JHJ about his GPA experience. I will quote from it, being careful not to distort the context. The article begins:

> 'Sir John resigned from the GPA Board [a year after] the aborted flotation. Television's Troubleshooter says what went wrong and why.'

Regarding over ordering of aircraft:

'I think the non-execs were the whole time wanting the executives to cut back on the order book. On the other hand, I don't think the order book led to our failure—everyone over ordered.'

The last observation is both wrong and misleading. Our principal competitors ILFC and Polaris did not over order and no one placed orders on GPA's titanic scale. Our multiple 1989 order for $15 billion worth of new aircraft, bought at the top of the market, remains to this day the biggest of all time.

JHJ gives as the reason for GPA's downfall, the private placement of shares at $32 per share in late 1991. He says the share price was too high, thus preventing freedom to price shares realistically for the later IPO. Also he says by the time of the IPO GPA's position had become complex, its need for cash more urgent. JHJ and Peter Sutherland had argued for a late 1991 IPO. As to the share price issue, later in the interview JHJ says:

'In the event, my understanding is that there was not a price at which the amount of money we were looking for could be raised.'

This is the truth—the IPO was years, not months, too late.
On the IPO:

'In fairness to the board we had no advice of any sort from any adviser that the offering was likely to fail until days before the thing was pulled and at that stage we had no contingency plan which was a mistake.

'We'd still have had hellish problems if we hadn't tried [the IPO] but the problems were enormously worsened by the withdrawal of public confidence in the company.'

Regarding the IPO aftermath JHJ describes the deteriorating financial situation over the last months as a 'holocaust'. In answer to a question why it took so long for the board and executives to realise what was happening:

'We did not realise the immensity of the catastrophe that was hitting us for quite a while and business went on as normal. When things started to go, they moved very fast indeed.'

JHJ also says that they expected the downturn (the recession) would hit old aircraft rather than the new (i.e. GPA) aircraft.

On the non-executive directors' ability to advise on GPA's management:

'The board was given every chance to discuss things. All of us who were on the board at the time must accept our share of the responsibility. The non-execs had significant impact on the decisions of the executives but obviously not significant enough.'

Speaking generally in the context of the GPA experience he says:

'Companies go bust because of bad management—it's not rocket science. It is not a great philosophical point but the job of management is not to go bust. It is generally accepted as being a bad thing if you do. The irony is that companies go bust not because of one specific bad thing they do. By and large these things happen because of a particular accumulation of particular behaviour patterns which grows and grows.'

On Tony's personal influence over the company and the issue of 'yes men':

'The problem is you can't split them [GPA and Tony Ryan]. If it wasn't for Tony's vision the company wouldn't exist. It wouldn't have remained in Shannon, it would not have had the potential it looked as if it had. You can't have the good without the bad. Inevitably companies built by individuals are very influenced by the individual. Until I joined the board the selection of directors was decided entirely by Tony on his own.

'Several large entrepreneurial companies rose to prominence in the late 1980s only to subsequently crash.

'Inevitably the entrepreneur who sets up and runs his own company has a disproportionate influence within that company. He looks on it as his property and people defer to someone in that position more than they would to a hired hack like me. The professional manager is just that, a professional who, at most, will own a very tiny part of the operation. He is not viewed as the father of all.'

On management performance at GPA:

'Well, at least the company is still alive. At least it has an ongoing presence in Ireland. So something is saved from the wreck. But it is not a situation which any of us can be proud of.'

JHJ is elsewhere reported as having lost a quarter of a million pounds on his GPA shares.

Regarding resignation of directors:

'I was never asked directly by anybody to resign but I felt it totally inappropriate that we should stay on. If you are a director of a company which fails then I think the shareholders are entitled that you should go quickly and quietly. The question is when? All of us believed it was our responsibility to stay with it till whatever had to happen did happen. And a bloody tough year it was too. Mind-boggling.'

Sir John, I have news for you. All the GPA employed executive directors on the GPA board throughout the period covered by this diary and when you resigned are still inside GPA House. All of them are still executive directors, either of GPA in the case of Maurice Foley and John Tierney, or of its successor GECAS in the case of Tony Ryan, Jim King and Colm Barrington.

With the old guard at GPA, normal rules do not apply.

Monday 21 February 1994

At the morning meeting, Phil, in the chair as usual, announces the long-awaited and overdue news that GE Capital has now chosen someone to be the overall head of GECAS, to be in charge of GECAS Shannon, Stamford and San Francisco. It is Herb Depp, head of what was Polaris Leasing—now renamed GECAS San Francisco. He is to be based in Stamford. It is almost humorous. All through the GRAPE sequence the word from on high in GPA was increasingly that GECC was unhappy with the performance of Polaris and was looking to the Shannon people to run the GECC aviation business, as we were seen to be of better calibre—another wrong judgment. After taking a good look, GE has discarded Tony, Jim and of course Colm. Their positions today seem untenable.

Once again we, the foot soldiers, survivors of the thinned ranks of GPA, await our fate, not knowing the future shape, location or slant the new organisation will take under our new leader. The word at Shannon today is that we shall all be safe because people are needed to operate the business. Once again I am not so sure. Polaris as an organisation resents us. I think it will show. Our humiliation is about to enter another phase.

It really is time to go . . . but where?

Thursday 3 March 1994

Colm Barrington has resigned. I cannot feel sorry for him. He played the corporate game for all it was worth and has lost.

Tuesday 22 March 1994

Herb Depp has put out a list of his senior management for GECAS, the people who will report to him. This is the list.

Title	Name	Base
President	Herb Depp (ex-Polaris)	Stamford
Executive Chairman	Tony Ryan (ex-GPA)	Shannon
Marketing	Philip Bolger (ex-GPA)	Stamford
Portfolio Management	Bob O'Reilly	Stamford

Legal	Jim Caleshu	Stamford
Capital Markets	Howard Feinsand (ex-Polaris)	Stamford
Supplier Management	Hugo Flinn (ex-GPA)	Stamford
Used Aircraft etc.	John Flynn(ex-Polaris)	S. Francisco
Technical	Brian Hayden (ex-GPA)	Shannon
Sr Airline Liaison	Jim King (ex-GPA)	Shannon
Finance	Jim Walsh (ex-Polaris)	Stamford
Human Resources	Open	Stamford
Business Development	Open	Stamford

Out of 13 posts, only three are in Shannon, of which only one has any substance—Technical. Nine will be in Stamford. Only five are filled by GPA people and of those Tony is still expected to be a nonentity, despite the high ranking title on display to the outside world. Jim King has a 'cat that walks by himself' role to which he is ideally suited, but is outside the mainstream. The general belief is that Tony got him the job. Phil Bolger shares functions with John Flynn and it will be interesting to see how this works out, but Phil has been made head of Marketing, arguably the hottest seat of all. I am very pleased that Phil's longstanding quality has finally been properly recognised. Only Brian Hayden has remained unmoved with an uncomplicated outlook, as undisputed head of Technical in Shannon—another fine person, both professionally and personally.

The rumour is that Tony is waiting for the arbitrated outcome of his claim for a transfer fee, expected later this year, and will then leave. Certainly Tony does not seem to be part of the company insofar as it is now run from Stamford. I do not hear of Tony going over these days, whereas Phil and some of the others are there nearly every week.

Following the senior management choices, the reorganisation of us, the troopers, is to follow next within 14 days. Meetings are now going on in Stamford to make the selections.

Friday 1 April 1994

Maurice Foley has gone. He has left GPA Group plc in terms of full-time executive employment, though he remains a non-executive director on £50,000 a year.

There has been no announcement; no email; no party; no presentation. Nothing. Silence.

Monday 11 April 1994

At a presentation, supposedly to tell us our new postings and the new management set-up, Phil, who has now permanently relocated to Stamford, says Tony has resigned as executive chairman of GECAS Limited. He says it casually, almost in passing. Instead, Tony is to join an advisory committee which will perform that function in relation to the company. Nothing has been announced—is that it?

Jim King will be the MD of the Irish incorporation of GECAS. It is presented as being of no practical importance, merely a legality.

Monday 18 April 1994

Tony's position, or lack of one, is still something of a mystery. Although he has resigned as chairman, he is still apparently on the payroll.

Tony has still not sorted out his $35 million loan situation, although I hear there is a moratorium as regards payment. I think the period is two years. It is a huge amount of money when you haven't got it and presumably the default interest must be piling up. Apparently he offered the bank his Mexican house, but they turned him down. The feeling seems to be that he will turn to running Ryanair. Fair do's. He has pumped enough money into it over these last few years. It probably represents his best chance of making some money.

I also hear that Tony is pursuing his arbitration case against GPA Group plc—'his' company—for wrongful dismissal! He is saying his contract was due to run until 1996 and that he should be paid until its expiry date, plus he should be paid bonuses on top. There was a special GPA board meeting called for last Monday, held at Schroders, to discuss the matter. I believe this is the sorting out of Tony's compensation he was seeking earlier, around the time of the GECC rescue. The board has taken Leading Counsel's opinion. The arbitration is being held in England. The GPA Group board, consisting of Patrick, John Tierney, Brian McLoghlin and the newcomers, intends to fight. The defence appears to be that Tony was not unfairly dismissed and indeed that he actively courted a post with GECAS. Further, they will accuse him of having had a conflict of interest while he was still GPA's chairman, neglecting GPA's interests and behaving improperly. They will also say that bonuses are only earned out of profits, of which there were none.

I cannot believe that Tony would ever want this to come to arbitration. Maybe he feels that an earnestly fought arbitration will have a nuisance value and they will therefore settle, bringing him some funds. He used to talk a lot about loyalty to GPA, but he is the only person I can recall within the company who has ever effectively sued it. Ironic. I guess the loyalty he meant was to him, personally—when GPA *was* Tony.

Tony's office stays empty, except on the infrequent occasions when he is in. His spell remains such that no one feels able to use it. Strange in one way as the general culture is that since many executives are travelling, their offices can always be used by visiting executives. I did hear though that Bob O'Reilly has taken to using Tony's office on his visits from Stamford. Even I feel a real sense of wrongness about that. Bob is a hired hand. Only entrepreneurial leaders should merit the right to inherit Tony's beautiful pine-clad sanctum. Illogical, I know.

Thursday 28 April 1994

At a GECAS internal marketing conference in Kenmare, County Kerry. Lovely surroundings, if drizzly. The last speech of the two day session, which has been chaired by Phil—now executive vice president under Herb Depp and undisputed head of GECAS Marketing—is given by Jim King. The title of his contribution is 'Image', i.e. of GECAS, going forward. Jim is going back to his roots as a PR man.

Jim tells us how important image is to a company. He quotes the recent Joseph Jett setback for Kidder Peabody and GE Capital, where none of the media felt sympathy for GE. He also describes image as the sum of 'collections of characteristics which define a company's identity'. Harking back to GPA, he says the public had a 'perception of GPA as a product of failed arrogance'. He should know.

Jim goes on to describe an image boosting campaign, which he will mastermind, to visit and entertain airline top managements. He talks of top GECAS people having the MDS and chairmen of airlines over *en masse* in Shannon, giving them the full treatment. We, the marketeers, he says, will not be present at these occasions because if we are, people in the airlines 'at our level' will expect to come and their presence will detract from the exclusivity of the event. Most of us deal with MDS and chairmen of our customer airlines; most of us out-earn them; most of them will wonder why we are not there to look after them. But no. There is yet a higher plane—Jim's plane. That's what it sounds like. From where he and Tony still look down on us.

Back to reality. In the evening I see a hard copy of the incomplete management structure presented to us by Phil some weeks back. Some of it we have not seen before. One page has Tony's name in the middle in a box by itself, a member of the advisory committee, the other members of which are listed down the side of the page. Tony is shown as reporting to no one, with two people reporting to him—Anne Lee, his secretary, and his chauffeur, listed as 'Assistant'.

Colm's leaving party is mentioned. It was held a couple of weeks ago at Goosers in Killaloe, where they took the whole place over one Saturday night.

The party was well attended, especially by the ex-members of GPA Capital division which Colm had headed. During speeches, apologies for absence were read out. First on the list was Maurice. His name was met by a chorus from certain sections of 'Why was he born so beautiful? Why was he born at all? He's no fucking use to anyone. He's no fucking use at all.'

There is much resentment against Maurice for the collapse of GPA and the all round losses, even as against Tony. I think it stems from Maurice's role as executive in charge of the failed public flotation of GPA. I do not share this view. Granted, Maurice in particular, given his role as No. 2 in GPA and his role as intellectual counterweight to Tony's driving, must shoulder responsibility for allowing Tony's ill-judgments to prevail—as must all the old GPA board members in varying degrees. However, the crucial decisions to overbuy new and second-hand aircraft at the top of the market: to thereby place the company hostage to the international financial community and to the market; to misjudge the timing and share price of the IPO and to get everyone's back thoroughly up in the process—that was all Tony, supported unswervingly by Jim.

I still do not see how Jim and Tony can survive among us in any form.

Wednesday 18 May 1994

Tony is a loose cannon on our decks. Out of touch, he nevertheless insists on making tours of our customers. Unfortunately no one in Shannon can tell him to get lost, so he is able to disrupt our marketing activities, planning and executing these strange trips. As an example, he and Jim met East West Airlines earlier this month in London at the Ritz Hotel. This airline, based in Bombay, has mucked us about so much, not paying, not looking after the aircraft etc. that a firm decision had been taken by our in-house committee to repossess all our B737-200 aircraft they operate. The decision was announced and termed 'irrevocable' at a Monday morning meeting by Niall. The very next day Tony and Jim had their meeting with East West and signed a piece of paper promising support and looking at the further provision of Airbus A300 aircraft on lease. If any of us had done that, we would have been fired.

A small informal reception was held after all for Maurice on 13 May in the boardroom at 5 pm, organised by Patrick, 'in honour of [his] long and distinguished service'. The four and a half lines of Patrick's email represent the only written notice of Maurice's passing.

Wednesday 29 June 1994

During a meeting to discuss a current deal with a senior colleague, Jim's name suddenly crops up in the conversation. Unsolicited, he goes on to say that at a recent male bonding weekend given by Herb Depp for those who report directly to him, held at Ashford Castle in Ireland, Jim's conduct had been remarked upon.

Jim has apparently embarked upon the same pattern of behaviour with Herb that he used to employ with Tony—making sure he sat next to Herb at meals, moving his chair for him. All too familiar. He's even been out to Herb's ranch or whatever in Montana. Jim's rehabilitation programme is up and running. No one I have spoken to believes he should still be among us. You can guess our feelings hearing of his antics.

This colleague stated perceptively, harking back to the awful period when Jim was in charge of the Leasing division in GPA, that the problem was that Jim is personality, not merit, driven. Favourites prospered, others didn't, irrespective of their contribution. I just remember it as a period of terrible frustration with the way Jim ran, or rather didn't run, things, a crucial period, when we were holding the loaded gun of GPA's order book, with non-executive board members thinking we had the target well sighted, when in reality we had both barrels in our mouth and the safety catch off, each used aircraft deal increasing pressure on the trigger.

Friday 19 August 1994
Tony's arbitration action is due to start soon and is slated to last three weeks. He is rarely in Shannon.

Wednesday 24 August 1994
Herb Depp put out a notice to all GECAS staff yesterday, it reads:

> 'It is with great pleasure to [*sic*] announce two significant appointments.
>
> 'First, Jim King has been appointed Vice Chairman of GECAS Limited with the new and additional responsibility of heading our new aircraft purchase programme. This new programme to purchase on average over $1 billion of new aircraft each year is the most significant event in GECAS's future. It is essential we continue to upgrade our fleet for both competitive and income reasons and Jim with his vast experience and senior level contacts at all manufacturers is the obvious choice. He will continue his role as senior Airline Liaison and direct our PR campaign.'

Jim is back in the big time. 'The obvious choice', Herb said. This will be lost on Herb, and many others will have forgotten, but the last time Jim was promoted to vice chairman of GPA by Tony in late 1992, his new job then was to *reduce* our aircraft orders and assume PR duties. Hopefully the manufacturers have forgiven him.

Monday 5 September 1994

I am surprised to be told that Shannon Aerospace, the aircraft maintenance joint venture set up by Tony with Lufthansa and Swissair, is in 'deep shit' financially. With its very large modern facility across the runway from us and the number of aircraft coming and going, I had thought it a thriving business. It is a significant employer in the region for skilled personnel.

Friday 1 October 1994

Tony has apparently managed to settle his arbitration case without going to full hearing. I understand he got an acceptable percentage of his claim, what he was looking for in respect of pension (it must be considerable) and all his legal costs paid. I hear these are in the region of £1 million.

Garry Burke, ex-GPA Capital and now head of Capital Markets in GECAS, has been put in charge of deciding whether GE Capital should exercise its option to acquire the rest of GPA. I guess Garry should still have worthless shares in GPA, unless he had a loan which he could not pay and had to hand over shares as part of a settlement. It will be interesting to see which way the decision goes.

Sunday 9 October 1994

GPA is back in the papers. The lead story in today's *Sunday Telegraph* Business section is headlined: 'Banks Take Big Hits On GPA Staff Debts' and reads:

> 'Banks have written off tens of millions of pounds of loans to staff of GPA, the Irish aircraft lessor which collapsed from an abortive flotation into near bankruptcy. The money was lent to buy shares which were valued at $32.50 at their peak but plunged to virtually nothing.

GPA founder Tony Ryan has had the bulk of his $35 million loan from investment bank Merrill Lynch written off. The terms are covered by a confidentiality agreement but last night a GPA source said "It simply was not within Tony's capacity to pay. The bank has done no more that recognise that it would never get its money back."

GPA staff from top managers down to secretaries borrowed heavily to buy shares with the aim of cashing in on flotation. After the collapse many united and sought help from Richard Keatinge, head of Investment Bank of Ireland and James Osborne, the then senior partner of Dublin law firm Goodbodys.

The bulk of the banks' claims were settled at 12.5p in the pound but many people paid nothing. Some GPA directors such as Colm Barrington had firm non-recourse agreements with their banks, which secured their loans on GPA shares. Barrington successfully went to court to prevent Bank of Ireland taking money from his bank account.

GPA's one-time non-executive directors include former Chancellor Lord Lawson, former Imperial Chemical Industries chairman Sir John Harvey Jones, GATT Director General Peter Sutherland and former Taioseach Garret FitzGerald, who has just had heart bypass surgery, pledged his home to buy shares.

The collapse has been most dramatic for Ryan. Had the flotation been successful his stake would have been worth $250 million. He still lives at his country estate, Kilboy, and farms Limousin cattle.

But his staff have gone. The house and farm are thought to be held in a family trust. Ryan is also thought to have a villa in Ibiza and a house in Mexico near Sir James Goldsmith's home [he also has a place in Monaco they missed out]. He has been a patron of the arts and is on the board of governors of Ireland's National Gallery [he has probably the best collection of modern Irish art].

The terms of his departure from GPA have recently been agreed. These are confidential and the sums involved are sufficiently modest not to have influenced Merrill Lynch's write-off decision, banking sources say. The same sources said Merrill had to compensate other banks who participated in Ryan's loan.

The job of restructuring GPA, under its new majority owner, General Electric, has fallen to new chairman Dennis Stevenson and chief executive Patrick Blaney. They have made solid progress in the past year. A $980 million aircraft securitisation programme has been completed [not quite] and GPA has successfully participated in the rescue of America West from bankruptcy.

Debt remains at an awesome $5.4 billion but ratings agency Standard & Poors has upgraded GPA debt. Stevenson has called in investment bank Morgan Stanley [for] the next stage of the restructuring.'

Some loan that was. Talk about Teflon man. Tony appears to be in the clear. Settlement agreed, no litigation hanging over him personally. Apparent rank within GECAS.

Sunday 16 October 1994
The Sunday Times Business section has an article headlined 'Ryan's $1.3m payoff by GPA'.

Monday 17 October 1994
In an Aer Lingus B737-400 at Shannon, waiting at the gate to push back for the return to London, at the very last minute Tony comes on board, just like old times. Before taking seat 1C, his usual first row aisle, his gaze sweeps around business class. He twinkles briefly at Joe Clarkin sitting further back on the opposite side, doesn't see me further back again by a window and then comes face to face with Patrick, sitting immediately behind him. Tony's face remains immobile. Neither does Patrick give any indication that I could see of greeting. I guess having to shell out upwards of £2 million would wipe the smile off anyone's face.

Monday 7 November 1994
In Shannon. There are problems at the top management level in GECAS. Bob O'Reilly has already gone—for going over Herb's head, criticising his leadership to Gary Wendt, CEO of GE Capital. Herb is, I believe, not

destined to lead us for much longer. The head of Legal has gone; the head of Finance is very nervous. Phil has been switched to head of Underwriting (risk management) out of Sales, against his wishes. Herb and Tony are at loggerheads over Tony's unauthorisedly getting involved trying to cut deals in Mexico, where there is a near meltdown in aviation and we are owed over $20 million (shades of East West).

Sales/marketing people are leaving. Colin Hayes has recently gone to head up marketing at Orix, a Japanese competitor based in Dublin, at four times his GE package, they say. Rumours of other impending departures abound. Our eyes are outward. As the GE culture saps us, GECAS Shannon is not a happy place.

GPA securitisation chickens are coming home to roost too. Aircraft with unrealistically high book and insurance values are difficult to lease in the fragile market. Many securitisees have lost millions in their deals with GPA, buying aircraft at pre-recession prices and now having to come to terms with lease and value levels spectacularly below expectations. GPA, hence GECAS, has remarketing obligations for most of these aircraft, when they need to be re-leased. Usually the fees for doing this have been taken by GPA back in the good years, so now there is a feeling of doing it for nothing. Some of the investors are becoming very unhappy at what they see as unenthusiastic marketing of their aircraft by GECAS. They believe these outside owned units are taking second place to GPA and GE Capital-owned aircraft. For myself, I do not enquire too much as to ownership. I just try to give potential airline customers what they want, when they want it. 'Owner's consent' (to a new lease proposal) has now become a recurring issue. Owners lacking knowledge of the aviation market are pretty picky about wanting the best credit airlines and unrealistic sale prices. Most of the securitisees want to get out, sell their aircraft and draw a line under a past mistake. They were mostly in as a tax-saving scheme. Continuing onwards with their aircraft into the future via leasing is not always their preferred option. Unfortunately, there simply is not enough choice yet in the recovering market. You take what you can get and think yourself lucky.

More and more I feel like a broker, a dreaded intermediary. I cannot speak with certainty even about aircraft availability, in case an owner says no to a proposal. My airlines look at me in surprise, astonished that the great GE should have to pussyfoot around, its senior marketeers made to feel like office juniors out on their first trip. I hate it. With these elements and the various controls imposed internally by GECAS on the deal-making process, doing a deal now is like peeling an onion, one layer after another and each one makes you weep with frustration.

Sunday 20 November 1994

Today's *Sunday Times* Business section states that Patrick is seeking an extension of the banks' moratorium on the $5 billion plus debt for an extra year to 1997.

Elsewhere I hear the odds are against GECC exercising its option to acquire the equity in GPA. GPA may yet have to call it a day finally.

The article writes off Tony as having no further involvement except as an adviser to the GECC aviation committee.

GPA is taking some unusual decisions to conserve cash. Many of its aircraft have high book values, much higher than current market rates for a sale and too high for prevailing lease rates to cover. For example, one particular GPA-owned DC-10-30 has a book value of $27 million; it is presently parked having come off lease, costing money in parking, insurance and storage maintenance; it is deteriorating all the time as a machine. It needs a heavy maintenance check, cost around $4 million. Its sale value, needing the check, is about $10–12 million. A market lease rate might be around $200,000 a month. There is no way GPA can make a profit on this aircraft at these numbers. However, if it was to sell or lease at these market rates, that would crystallise the loss in GPA's books. It cannot afford to make that loss apparent at this time and so arrangements are being made to store the aircraft. It has to be a crazy decision, but there is an imperative crazy accounting logic to support it. There is another GPA DC-10-30 in the same position, off lease from LAP in Paraguay—remember that one? It needs $6.7 million to be spent just to restore it for passenger service. It will be stored and will degrade further.

Wednesday 7 December 1994

Herb Depp has got the heave-ho. He is leaving us to head up Marketing in GE Engines as from next Monday! He has lasted about nine months. The rumour is that there may be others going too. Our new head is to be Jim Johnson, ex-Boeing, ex-Pratt & Whitney. We do not know him.

I am in Shannon working on the sublease of a B767 from Britannia Airways to TACA in San Salvador and a lease of B737s to CSA in the Czech Republic.

Saturday 10 December 1994

It is the GECAS holiday (Herb decrees 'Christmas' is not politically correct, so we can't use it) party, being held at the Dromoland Castle Hotel, some miles up the road from Shannon. It is a very popular event with several hundred attending. The location is terrific, the drink free and the atmosphere festive. Tony is there. We are all in dinner jackets; he is in a light grey suit. He goes up to the microphone on stage to say a few words following an introduction by Niall to the occasion and an unnecessary but thankfully brief *au revoir* from Herb. Just walking up to the stage, unannounced, Tony gets an ovation from the assembly— mostly ex-GPA people now in GECAS. He looks as surprised as I am. Tony gives a short address of welcome. Thunderous applause follows. I cannot believe it. He in turn is being welcomed (back) by the majority of the company staff. They seem either not to have a clue about what he did to bring about the collapse of GPA, or care not. This is his first public outing in front of the entire Shannon staff of GECAS and he is being acclaimed. I feel very uncomfortable. Once again I have a very strong feeling of: is it me? Am I the one out of step here? I can imagine Tony is quite choked up by this reception. He smiles back, obviously enjoying the moment. Who wouldn't? He must feel he is forgiven and loved again by his people.

The evening is a huge success and proves that even if we are now an American subsidiary, the heart and soul and most of the people of GECAS are in Shannon, not Stamford or anywhere else.

At one time I found myself talking to Phil. He says nobody would believe the 'mountains of shite' he has had to put up with over the past nine months during Herb's reign.

I also hear elsewhere during the evening that soft loans that were given formerly to certain senior executives, for housing, for paying off share loans, are now being called in by Patrick. In at least one case he has threatened legal action against a former colleague, to recover money previously lent. I have no idea of the extent of this. Patrick as we know is seeking an extension of the moratorium. He must be under great pressure.

Monday 12 December 1994

I am in London. I have decided to forgo the inevitable scrum of the Monday morning meeting in Shannon, as everyone rubbernecks the new president of GECAS. I participate with my London colleagues over an unsatisfactory speaker system, along with our offices in Singapore and Hong Kong. Johnson says nothing I can hear. Later I learn he confessed to understanding very little of what went on at the quickfire meeting.

Friday 16 December 1994

Some revelations from last week. There is no love lost, professionally anyway, between Niall and Jim King, who appear to be competing for the top position of honour in Shannon. Niall is the senior commercial head of station as MD of GECAS Ireland (which he took over from Jim) and Jim has his position as vice chairman to give him apparent standing. Both of them were among select senior Shannon management invitees to a dinner given in Shannon for Jim Johnson. Requested by Johnson to give their opinion on the state of GECAS, Jim King as usual was first to reply. He told Johnson that GECAS was 'rudderless', with no sense of direction and no leadership etc. This went down badly with the others, who all disagreed with him. JK had a bad night of it and ended the evening, by an account, somewhat below par. I am very surprised if this lapse is true. It is not like Jim to show a hair out of place.

Also. At the end of the holiday party evening, those who were left repaired upstairs to a bar. Tony was there, as was Colm, having gatecrashed the party around midnight (he happened to be in the hotel on a shooting weekend), and was in his cups. Tony said words to the effect that GECAS was a failure, that it was a useless company and that the only people he had any respect for were those who had left to set up on their own or who had otherwise left GECAS to do something else— the implication being that those who had stayed in GECAS were not up to it.

Monday 19 December 1994

Our outstanding receivables now top $115 million. TAESA, Aeromexico and Mexicana, the three major Mexican carriers between them owe us $40 million. The Mexican financial accident has happened. The peso has lost 30 per cent of its value overnight. I hear Tony's Mexican house is on the market. That dream is over too.

For all the smart GECAS Stamford talk and meetings on Collective Action Plans etc. to cure the receivables, the number has just gone up and up.

GE is great at giving things snappy names and making them sound superficially effective, when in reality nothing much is going on. Who are we fooling? It all reminds me intensely of Catch-22. Everything has to look good and wonderful, even us. The turgid, insulting, puerile rubbish churned out by a patronising GECAS Human Resources as a guide to help us fill in our employee self-appraisal forms is beyond rational belief. The language and sentiments have us squirming. At this level it is impossible to disagree with Tony's assessment. However, inside the company, like well-drilled professional soldiers trying to fight in the way they have been trained in the midst of a battalion of raw recruits, the old GPA and Polaris hands are still doing the business. The deals are being brought back from the customers—the front line is working. From then on it is a shambles. More than 50 per cent of my email traffic is now internal stuff about procedures, endless shallow training courses, committee papers, on and on.

Tuesday 17 January 1995

The McDonnell Douglas litigation continues against GPA.

Marketeering in GECAS is like walking in treacle—slow, sticky, messy. Decisions are hard to come by; so is accountability. I have yet to feel the presence of the new boss in any form. Last week there was a meeting of senior GECC managers in Puerto Rico and this week all of GECAS congregates for an annual meeting for two days in Cancun, Mexico. Maybe at the end of it we will all have a better feel for things.

Tuesday 24 January 1995

The Cancun trip was a great success. Everyone enjoyed themselves and there was plenty of enthusiasm for the working sessions. I missed the first night, being delayed coming from Bulgaria, via Zurich, Madrid and Miami.

On arrival at conference reception I was given two items: one was a disclaimer to sign absolving GECAS from any responsibility from anything that might happen to me on any organised activity. It listed various eventualities—one was a change in surf conditions. The other was a thoughtful gift to mark my presence—on the bottom it bore a label, 'Of no commercial value'.

During proceedings Jim King was very subdued. He gave a short presentation which lacked any sort of flair and even bordered on lack of confidence. Later, wrapping up, our new president particularly disagreed with one of Jim's statements about our inability to beat ILFC's prices on new aircraft. I think I agree with Jim.

Amazingly, Tony was also at Cancun. He shuffled around, looking old, looking irrelevant. He kept out of things, making only one low-key point at one session about approval times for Letters of Intent. When he indicated his wish to speak briefly from the floor during the final question and answer session, Jim Johnson, who was running it, asked Tony why, amongst the tropical shirts and shorts we were all wearing *de rigueur*, he was wearing a black suit? Tony replied—to stunned, embarrassed silence—'Because the party's over.'

Wednesday February 15 1995

The current GECAS total receivables number has climbed to $133 million. This is money owed by airline customers to GPA, third party owners (mainly securitisees) and GE Capital, in respect of aircraft managed by GECAS.

Talking about it with colleagues, it seems that the future of GPA may be along these lines: Patrick achieves the moratorium extension, but has cash problems. These will force him to sell aircraft to stay alive. GE Capital buys a sufficient number of the best available at distress prices, having let GPA hang out on the line as long as possible. This process may be repeated, until GPA is bled dry of its usable aircraft assets. It is then abandoned, possibly to go bust. GECC never intends to exercise its purchase option. Why should it spend money when it can acquire the only assets worth having ultra cheaply? GPA is nothing now but debt, assets and potential liabilities.

GPA is presently acutely concerned about being sued by one, some or a class of third party owners of aircraft—the securitisees. These were GPA Capital deals struck back in the good days with aircraft investors with little or no aviation experience or expertise—income funds, realty companies, shipping companies, specialist aircraft portfolio (ALPS) companies. They are the Owners from Hell. They are mightily upset. The deals never realised their financial returns. Maybe there were misrepresentations. The owners are stuck with their expensive aircraft, which are also expensive to retain in flyable condition. They do not feel GPA or GECAS are doing their best to sort out the problems. I have mentioned this before. It is a real issue. They may not have a case, but the time and cost of international legal proceedings alone will be crippling. Some individuals may be sued too.

One owner, Qatar Investment Bank, has so far turned down three lease deals offered to it by GPA/GECAS on its B737-400 aircraft because it would not accept the credit risk of the airline lessees involved— frustrating for everyone: the marketeers who found the deals and have urgent unsatisfied customers; GECAS, expending money, resources and reputation on futilities; GPA, unable to discharge its remarketing obligations to the owner; QIB because it has the prospect of an aircraft with a value circa $30 million stuck on the ground, earning nothing, incurring daily cost and ageing.

I am told there have been quite a few letters of complaint about sexual harassment submitted following our return from Cancun. Apparently the first evening there, while I was still in transit from Sofia, was fairly exuberant—I remember hearing serial complaints of hangovers after my arrival the next day and the odd report of high jinks. There was also a fair amount of tut-tutting going on, about unseemly conduct, coming mainly from the US contingent. All I can say is—viva Señor Frogs, where we went on the second night. I had a great time at the dancing—unharassed and unharassing.

Monday 20 February 1995

In Shannon. At lunch Jim King joins our table. He is almost at the end of a large-scale exercise to place a huge new aircraft order from Boeing and Airbus, all powered, naturally, by GE or CFM (a joint venture between GE and SNECMA) engines. When the best manufacturer numbers are in, he and the team will be seeking the approval of Gary Wendt and Jack Welch to go ahead. Off again. The cycle. GPA Mark II. The ironies are so strong I find little to say, despite being interested.

Wednesday 22 February 1995

Today's *Travel Trade Gazette* reports that Tony has joined Ryanair, 'his sons' airline', as non-executive director and will become chairman at the year end when EU Commissioner Ray MacSharry's term comes to an end. It makes the point that this will be the first time he has held a position at the airline.

Tony may not have held a position at the airline before, but it was common knowledge back in the mid/late 80s that he was pulling strings. He would set up Ryanair to try to lease GPA aircraft at the keenest of prices, all the time castigating the then MD of Ryanair, Eugene O'Neill, and me or whoever else at GPA for not getting a better deal, while playing both sides of the game and able to see all of the cards—an impossible situation Eugene and I were mutually aware of.

Monday 27 February 1995

In Shannon. At the morning meeting, chaired by Niall, the receivables came up for their usual discussion at around $127 million outstanding.

GPA is now owed some $60 million by the Mexican carriers. TAESA's debt is rising by some $5 million a month. The Mexican problem, says Niall, 'is killing GPA.' The financial accident I predicted has well and truly happened. The GECC import in charge of GECAS Shannon Finance department adds that GPA's cashflow problems will start to adversely affect GECAS under the management agreement as GPA's ability to pay becomes an issue. I believe GECAS charges GPA some $30–40 million per year to manage the GPA fleet. I get a real feeling of crisis within GPA from these two.

In the *Sunday Tribune* newspaper yesterday, one of the lead stories in the Business section was Shannon Aerospace's (SAL) need for a $6 million cash injection from its three shareholders, GPA, Lufthansa and Swissair. SAL is not now expected to break even until at least 1997. Today I learn there are ructions because of course GPA cannot afford to pay its 33.3 per cent share of the injection. Lufthansa is already under German trade union pressure because it has closed one aircraft maintenance facility in East Germany; favouring the Irish company will not go down well, especially as it is a loss maker.

GPA's cash is dwindling. As this diary has recorded, GPA cash also includes amounts it is supposed to be holding representing maintenance reserve funds paid by GPA's airline lessees for future aircraft maintenance, though this is part of the dwindling. If GPA folds, there will be this huge hole, which should be full of cash to pay for the maintenance cost of hours already flown on engines and airframes, but isn't.

It is alarming. I get the feeling GPA is already in deep trouble and could go soon. If this happens I guess an administrator will probably allow the aircraft to stay under the management of GECAS, as will the various third party aircraft owners, *pro tem*. However, there would be plenty of vultures waiting to scavenge on any aircraft management contracts which may become available.

I hear GECAS has no appetite to buy any more of GPA's aircraft. However it may feel it has to. I guess it will depend on how much GPA needs and how well GECAS could progress without GPA in place. It is timing. GECAS only needs GPA until GECAS is up and running with its own ongoing fleet with which to make money.

Collapse is once more in the news. Baring Brothers Bank failed today, from apparently nowhere. If GPA follows suit there will be a difference—GPA has been on the slide since 1990. It has all been coming for a long time now.

Am I now entering the final phase of this diary?

Wednesday 22 March 1995

John Flynn has been made head of GECAS Marketing.

Outstanding receivables were $147 million last time I looked. This could be a mid-month peak.

For myself, I have just spent eight days in Harare trying to collect on a Government of Zimbabwe guarantee. No luck. After a few days the senior officials in the ministries involved simply hid from me. I want $2.6 million owed to GPA by Affretair. The Minister of Transport, no longer Dennis Norman, tells me the government has no money to pay. Four years ago on my first visit the exchange rate was six Zim dollars to the pound. Today it is 13. Aids too is ravaging the population. The transport ministry has already lost 40 of its civil service officers to the epidemic.

I had not been to Zimbabwe for nearly a year. It is much worse. Like Zambia next door, the people are defeated by rising prices. Wages are so low, they cannot keep pace. Everyone I meet is intensely dispirited. All the taxi drivers, always a country's litmus paper, tell me the same story—they wish Ian Smith was back in charge. How depressingly ironic. A senior female secretary in one of the ministries, prominently missing a front tooth, was telling me, highly embarrassed by her inadvertent whistle, during one of my interminable waits, that a replacement tooth would cost her nearly four months' salary. Free or even affordable healthcare for the average Zimbabwean has now disappeared. The usual African spiral down into destitution is well under way. What Afrikaners term 'the return to footpaths'. Soon the relatively prosperous Zimbabwe of 15 years ago—once the bread basket of Africa—will just be a distant memory for the older people. It makes me so sad. It is all so utterly unnecessary.

As soon as I returned from Harare, I left for Prague—from the heat of the veldt to three inches of snow, from wonderful summer days to leaden wintry skies.

Thursday 30 March 1995

I have the feeling GPA's position is touch and go. Probably only the reducing book value of the GPA fleet is keeping its head above water. Attempts in Mexico continue to halt GPA's leasing equivalent of the China Syndrome.

Jim King is quiet nowadays. He no longer seems like a presence. Head down.

I never see Tony except that his office and secretary are still there in GPA House, in the same place—the inner sanctum area.

Chapter 7

PROJECT ATLANTA
1995–1996

Monday 24 April 1995

In Shannon. Phil Bolger has resigned. He is going to join Mike Dolan's new company Pembroke Capital in Dublin.

Also gone is Garry Burke, head of GECAS Shannon Capital Markets, also to Pembroke.

A rumour has Jim Johnson already negotiating his exit package. A view is that GECAS is doing so poorly that Dennis Nayden, a minor god in Stamford and mainly responsible for getting GE into the GPA rescue and for GECAS, wants to start personally controlling GECAS to save his own reputation.

There is a feeling of instability everywhere in the organisation, from top to bottom. Will GECC keep GECAS? Will Pembroke and others entice more people away? Will the continuing loss of the old core GPA executives hasten the demise of Shannon and complete the Americanisation of GECAS? Will there be much in the way of bonuses next year at this rate?

The Mexican debt keeps rising. TAESA alone now owes GPA more than $35 million.

I talk to Liam Barrett, returned as GPA's temporary company secretary, standing in for John Redmond (away improving his qualification). Liam tells me the great escape plan for GPA is now for the company to turn itself into a giant ALPS. All its aircraft will be sold, with leases attached, to a special purpose company. The proceeds will be used to pay off the existing debt. Money for the purchase will come from the public sale of bonds. The new ALPS company will then have to manage its own administration and the fleet of aircraft for the bondholders. This latter may be done using GECAS or maybe even Pembroke might try for it. So many balls are in play. One thing is for sure: setting up an ALPS, with a fleet capitalisation of between $4–5 billion, will mean another bean feast for the professional advisers—the due diligences required, the legal advice, the valuations, the ratings, the prospectus, the public bond flotation across continents, the underwriting, and on and on. Millions and millions of dollars.

Clearly this is a last throw for GPA, to try to get out from under while it still has enough valuable assets left to make it feasible.

Liam does not convey desperation at GPA. Annual depreciation of fleet values is helping the situation. He sees a future. GPA is upset though at the GECAS performance, seeing all the changes, the inability to deal with the receivables (hardly GECAS's fault), the general instability and the removal of power to Stamford away from Shannon.

Graham Boyd is finding a new role in the UK rail privatisation. He is advising a bank on the leasing of rolling stock. We spoke today. He is up to date with happenings at GECAS and has been talking with Tony. Tony's reaction to Phil's departure was, how could any company let a person of Phil's calibre go? This, even though Tony has not really got along with Phil since the April 1993 coup, when Tony felt stabbed in the back by someone he had promoted through the company for ten years. According to Graham, Tony seems fine. He has sold his Mexican and Monte Carlo homes and has taken a flat in Cadogan Square in London. He is living off Ryanair profits, but is not running it. Why should he? The airline is doing well, he says.

Tuesday 2 May 1995

Jim Johnson and his direct reports (our senior management) had a three day strategy meeting last week. A missive has been put out. GECAS must make $250 million net income by 1998, $145 million in 1995, and will add $2 billion worth of aircraft each year to the GECAS fleet. Stamford will be the company HQ. Shannon will be the centre for European Marketing and Technical. Some additional support functions will continue to be located in Shannon (most presently are), full details in two weeks. Here we go again.

Thursday 4 May 1995

I return from Madrid to more 'alarums'. Trevor Henderson has resigned; so has another of the Shannon marketeers; and so has the No. 2 in Technical, Brian Hayden's deputy. All are going to Pembroke Capital.

Shannon is reeling, not only from news of the resignations, but also as the strategy missive takes effect. Yesterday the overall head of Finance told the Finance department, located in Shannon, that it was moving to Stamford. Twenty-four people are directly affected. Speaking to one of them, it seems maybe only four would actually be prepared to go to the US. Similarly with the Information Technology department and the Legal department etc. Similarly also with other parts of GECAS located in San Francisco and Dallas. Following these announcements the place is in a turmoil reminiscent of the final pre-rescue GPA throes.

To achieve his strategy, Johnson is disembowelling the organisation. Yet there is no flesh on the strategic frame (if there is one) and there is no certainty about Johnson's position. One might make the move to Stamford and within a fortnight be left high and dry.

There has been nothing either about relocation allowances, visa arrangements, redundancy packages. Human Resources seems no more than an Overseer's dept. They're no practical help at all.

My own position, like most other people's, is far from clear. I have been negotiating a move outside GECAS for about nine months now, but nothing is certain.

Trevor wrote a really inappropriate goodbye email—long, bouncy and upbeat, full of it. He even took a thinly veiled sarcastic poke at the GE culture. He obviously had much fun putting it together. It was hardly what the rest of us wanted to read. Marketing resignations make the rest of the staff, working away in the support backrooms, wonder what is going on. What do the marketeers right in the front line know that they do not? These departures are particularly unsettling.

Johnson's strategy message was itself gloriously mistimed, coming in at just before 6 pm at the beginning of a long Irish bank holiday weekend. Even Human Resources could not have done better.

Friday 5 May 1995

There has been a sea change in Shannon, such has been the adverse reaction to the requested moves. Direct report management seems to be backing down. Apparently Johnson took quite a beating when he came to Shannon last Tuesday to talk to all the staff about the new strategy and its implementation. There is to be another full staff meeting next Tuesday. Meanwhile, I hear that Shannon is getting a name for being bolshie and whingeing, not taking orders unquestioningly, which is the GE way. Good.

Criticisms are emerging about the quality of our senior management. If their organisational strategy they spent days last week discussing does not carry through, such criticism will be inevitable.

There is also a feeling that Gary Wendt has told Johnson what the total GECAS headcount should be and we are above it. So people will have to leave. This seems crazy; we are all already stretched and the organisation is supposed to be expanding. In US corporate culture you do not do your job—you do what your boss tells you. Like the US Army. Yessir.

Monday 8 May 1995

VE Day 50 years on today. I had planned to travel to Shannon tonight anyway, because of a visit by John Flynn, in the wake of the resignations, but Niall also rang me on Saturday to suggest I make the trip. He rang all the London-based executives to attend.

For the flight over, I had checked in early to be sure of a forward window seat, hopeful of good enough weather to see a pattern of beacons due to be lit across the UK as part of the VE Day celebrations. However, I boarded late and saw our so-said London office manager and his sidekick already on board. He was in another window seat with the adjacent aisle seat free. I had little choice and gave up my hope of beacon spotting. He told me he had heard that afternoon that the London office was to close. I spent the rest of the evening wondering whether I would have a job after tomorrow.

Tuesday 9 May 1995

What a day! How many times have I said that now? All the direct reports are in town. Each department is scheduled to have meetings with their direct report department head during the morning. Ours in Marketing is due at 10.30 am. John Flynn takes it. Somewhere in the middle he says the GECAS London office will close, but gives no other details. In the question and answer session he tells me I can continue with my present method, which as you know is to come to Shannon often on a Sunday and work the rest of the time at home, when not travelling. I relax a little. I am still in work. I feel like a small fish in a Spanish trawler's net. Today the mesh has been wide enough to wriggle through. Tomorrow may be different.

In the afternoon there is the full staff meeting in the Southern Hotel. Taking my seat I am very much reminded of the awful GPA briefing sessions we had here during 1992/3. I even end up sitting near the seat where I had endured one such with Nigel Wilson keeping his head down next to me.

The image is reinforced even more when the direct reports take up their places on the raised dais in front of us. From left to right we have Anders Johnson, head of Risk Management, having taken over from Phil; Brian Hayden; Jim Walsh, head of Finance and probably the most disliked person in Shannon at present; John Flynn; Jim King; Niall Greene; Richard Blume, newly appointed head of Legal; and finally Norman Liu, just appointed replacement for Howard Feinsand (previously resigned to go to Citibank) as head of Capital Markets & Structured Finance and reportedly Nayden's man. They are packed tightly together at the top table, whereas we sitting in the well of the room seem a depleted bunch compared to the GPA days.

Jim King makes the introductions. Niall speaks first. He begins by apologising on behalf of all the senior management for the events of last week. The Will Carling effect has come to Shannon. He then runs through the strategic aims and the headcount issue. There will be more redundancies.

Flynn comes next. He delivers his piece with a fixed grin on his face—this isn't his sort of do. Then Norm Liu, who announces that he has been with GECAS for one week. At one stage, talking about the $2 billion per year of GECAS's money we are to spend on aircraft assets, he tells us that we must realise that [GE] is 'the hugest chequebook on earth . . . unlimited money'. This seems at odds with the fixation on reducing headcount in a supposedly expanding company and in what Flynn has just told us is an expanding industry.

Brian Hayden comes next. His bit is easy. He has once again brought himself and his department through unscathed. He says he has been in the company more than a week but wonders whether he is any the wiser.

Jim Walsh walks to the podium at the side of the dais and gives us five minutes of corporate Americanese at its best.

Blume agrees that last week things were traumatic.

Anders wants to change the name of the Trading Floor, which he says is tainted by past associations, to 'Information Clearing House'—snappy.

Niall returns to give us an analogy in which theatre critics become 'intoxicated by denunciation'. So with us and we should all stop running GECAS down.

There are questions and answers. From the floor, Sean Jackson—our Mr Airbus Marketing—starts off by saying there is still a central feeling of instability which the meeting has done nothing to remove. He also says GECAS is losing vital production time by having its workforce so heavily distracted. He gets a round of applause. From us. Later I hear Sean was taken to one side in the days following and told by Niall that such responses are 'career limiting'.

There are few questions. Most revolve around redundancies. Jim King says that if anyone is made redundant, the company will discharge its responsibilities fairly and fully. Now where on earth have I heard that before?

Next, each of the panellists estimates when they expect to have their headcounts sorted out. It seems like the end of May or June.

It feels like a meeting at *Animal Farm*, where the pigs tell the other animals they are going to have to work even harder, with more misery. Gary Wendt would make a good Snowy.

After the meeting at the little reception which follows, in the same room, I find that my colleagues in the London office in Structured Finance have not been so fortunate as I. Norm Liu has told the office manager and one other that their jobs will go at the end of the month. The sidekick will be offered a Stamford transfer. The one other is looking shocked; the office manager has already departed for home, not waiting for the staff meeting. I heard at lunch that he had got himself a position at Citibank and was about to resign anyway.

No one is happy. I fly back to Heathrow on the evening flight. Liam Barrett is next to me. He is going to Hamburg to finalise GPA's extraction from Shannon Aerospace. They have struck a deal with the other two shareholders, because the cost of extraction was about the same as the cost of SAL collapsing—the other alternative—and the bad publicity which would have flowed from that, GPA could do without. More fallout from GPA as another flawed Tony initiative bites the dust. The road to hell is paved with good intentions.

By the way, the East West Airlines aircraft are still stuck on the ground in India with no money being paid, no maintenance being carried out and no immediate prospect of their being repatriated.

Wednesday 10 May 1995

Today I hear another experienced marketeer, this time female, is considering going to Pembroke Capital. The head of marketing in Asia, based in Hong Kong, has been asked to leave.

The firm feeling is that senior management is extremely worried about the haemorrhaging of talent, that the fabric of the company is walking out the door.

Friday 20 May 1995

Much is happening. It will take a remarkable turnaround to recover the lost ground. We understand a reduction of 75 people is being looked for out of a total of 250. A management meeting is going on now in White Plains which we believe is deciding fates. This meeting comprises more than just the direct reports and the Shannon office is denuded of managers. Not much work is being done is the message I got when I rang in from Prague yesterday. Everyone is waiting.

Two more have resigned from Capital Markets. One has refused a move to the US and is expected to join his old boss Colm Barrington, now at Nomura Babcock and Brown in Dublin. The other one is going to the US but to work for AIG, not GECC.

Norm Liu seems a tough character from reports on how he handled recent firings.

There is still no plan as to how the $250 million target will be reached in 1998. The indications this year are that we shall fail to reach the $145 million target by up to $50 million. That should set things alight.

From here it seems the company is being run with quite stunning incompetence. We are demoralised; all who can are looking elsewhere for jobs. The headcount issue has been applied with no planning, forethought or even courtesy.

By the way, while all this is going on in Shannon and London, the head of GECAS HR and her Shannon manager were away enjoying themselves on the so-called pinnacle trip—this year GECC has taken over two Cunard ships for ten days, cruising in the Mediterranean. The annual pinnacle trip is awarded to those people in GECC who have supposedly made the greatest contribution in the previous year. Quite how our HR representatives fit that description is beyond me.

There is no direction in the business, no leadership, no quality of management; just dictats. At this rate I doubt the business will be here in 12 months' time and it will have spent the intervening period falling to bits. So many people leaving, not being replaced, and redundancies occurring again.

Rereading earlier entries in this diary, I come across the reference to 'Neutron Bomb' Jack Welch. It is happening.

So far as I can see, none of the Cancun initiatives have come to anything.

I hear Pembroke is opening up a Shannon office. All the talk is they will be taking over the management of the GPA portfolio.

I am seriously thinking about getting a redundancy package for myself if I can and leaving anyway, even if the new opportunity I am hoping for fails to materialise. I just dislike being with GECAS so much.

I will never again work for an American company. This is not life; this is pure jungle. My work is suffering. I can never remember being so unproductive, so worthless. I feel so hamstrung by procedures. What a thing to say. Something has to happen.

Wednesday 14 June 1995

I returned from the Paris Air Show yesterday. Jim Johnson was in attendance. He had forgotten who I am. When we met in the GE chalet he had to look at my name badge. John Flynn was there. He seemed under pressure, looking after his boss.

Over dinner at the Café de la Paix with some ex-GPA colleagues, I was reminded that some of our executives are still paying off loans— really big ones—to banks due to the GPA share collapse. You would never know; they suffer in silence. Is it not incredible that these people so close to the GPA business were prepared to gamble away their net worth and far beyond on a venture I had been discouraging people from investing in for up to two years previously. Amazing how success and failure can look so similar to different eyes. I seem to recall hearing that before somewhere.

Yesterday the redundancy axe fell on some more people as part of the headcount reduction. On my return to London through the Docklands airport, I called Shannon just as the office was shutting at 9 pm to see who had been informed that day. I was given some names. The last one was Jim King.

Jim King is leaving—end of an era. He may well have wanted to in the end. GECAS is no place to stay. Apparently as a courtesy he is being allowed to leave after the others. His big new aircraft negotiations were never approved by the Stamford hierarchy.

Also going is Hugo Flinn and Michael Hayes, both good men. Also our key numbers man on the Trading Floor is off to Pembroke— another young man voting with his feet to join a new company with no business rather than stay in an established industry giant. Some indictment.

Having enjoyed her pinnacle cruise, and why not, marketeer Jane O'Callaghan has also decided to leave for Pembroke Capital.

The Shannon HR manager is being relocated back to the States. Last week Phil Bolger had a going away barbecue in Stamford. At it the Stamford-based GECAS HR manager gave out the names of people being made redundant before it was announced.

Monday 27 June 1995

Good news on the Affretair front. With Liam's help I have managed to get the Zimbabwean Government to cough up $2.6 million under the guarantee. We took them to the High Court in London and got judgment in our favour, after the Zimbabweans completely ignored the litigation, much to the judge's consternation. I duly went down to Harare politely waving the judgment and got the complete runaround, just as I had done waving the writ, some months earlier. At first I was invited to fictional meetings with government representatives in addresses which didn't exist—so childish, I could almost see the funny side. Unfortunately Dennis Norman's replacement is still zero help. Uninvited, I parked myself in the new Minister's outer office every day for a week, where I was about as welcome as a woodworm in a log cabin. I got nowhere apart from learning in detail about life in Zimbabwe—really grim—from his secretary, who seemed to have nothing better to do. I had to return empty-handed—not good. Finally it was only when the Court bailiff started physically removing items of furniture from the Zimbabwean High Commission in London that we got Harare's attention and funds transferred.

Wednesday 5 July 1995

Under the guise of improving the time it takes to do deals, the 'deal cycle improvement initiative', started at Cancun, has now published its team findings. It is a scheme of regulation which must now fall like a grid over each deal the moment the marketing executive feels he has one. The subtext is that GECC cannot stand a blank canvas on which a deal is painted to end up with the finished picture—this requires trust in one's employees. Anarchy. No, over the canvas is superimposed GECC's graph paper, each square numbered, each number a colour. I thought the whole point of being an experienced marketeer is that you know how to do deals, start to finish, but no. Now we have a rigid template to adhere to.

I feel like shouting 'I am not a prisoner, I am a free man'—Patrick McGoohan style.

In the *Daily Mail* today I saw two photographs of Nigel Lawson. Before and after. It said that he has been on a strict diet and has lost four stone, emphasising that the loss is not due to ill health. No wonder. He looks like a completely different person.

Latest rumour is that Jim King is to manage Baldonell Airport—a mainly military airfield near Dublin that Tony is trying to expand into a civil role for Ryanair.

There is a meeting for us marketeers on Friday in Shannon to officially inform us about Project Atlanta—the GPA refinancing, the Mega ALPS.

Tuesday 12 September 1995

Head of Finance Jim Walsh has been fired by Jim Johnson today. Just yesterday he gave a presentation in Stamford in the Marriott Hotel. I was there. Today he is gone by 8 am. After 22 years with GE. It's a tough place to work. I am in Chicago today with John Flynn. We are seeing Sir Freddie Laker. I am trying to push through a deal which will see Laker back on the Atlantic with three DC-10-30s we are utterly desperate to get out on lease. After everything I gained from Freddie, it would be wonderful to assist him back into transatlantic scheduled service with 'Skytrain' once more emblazoned on the side of the aircraft. It would also help the GECAS year end figures hugely, US general accounting rules wise, to get these deadweight ex-Mexicana aircraft, with their inflated book values, into service.

Monday 23 October 1995

Jim King wrote his 'retirement' email last Friday. No surprises.

GPA has now reached agreement with GECAS over the latter's contract to manage the fleet of the new Atlanta company, once it is set up. Apparently the advisers of Project Atlanta stated that GECAS's services were necessary to make the flotation of Atlanta a success—the magic and strength of the GE name. With this, GECAS and GE Capital embarked on a course of corporate screwing reminiscent of GRAPE. It has taken some months for a deal to be struck. More fees for GECAS, better GPA option deal for GECC. Anyway, Project Atlanta seems to be going ahead.

There was an article in *Commercial Aviation* a short time ago by one Scott Hamilton entitled 'Lifeboats out at GPA' or some such, against a famous graphic depiction of a stricken *Titanic*. The article was based on a recent SEC (US Securities Exchange Commission) form filed by GPA, together with connective material. It was a bleak read, listing the troubles piled up at GPA's door. They are many. It will be some feat if GPA gets Project Atlanta off the ground.

Monday 11 December 1995

In Shannon, I hear that John Flynn is leaving. No announcement has been made. It later transpires most people already know this news. Negotiations are going on to see if John can stay on as manager in charge of special projects.

It is a real blow to lose Flynn. He is very knowledgeable, a decision maker and good at his job. When I restarted the Laker deal this year, I brought the two of them together at the beginning, so that Laker realised that this time we meant business and for Flynn to get the measure of Laker. It worked a treat. The two of them got on like a house on fire. I guess neither of them accords others respect easily, so it was a mark of quality for both that they took to each other. Freddie Laker has actually asked Flynn to join his board of directors. This has been vetoed by GE Capital.

Sunday 7 January 1996

John Flynn is definitely leaving. He is just around in San Francisco whilst a replacement is being sought. I hear another bone of contention was John's exclusion from negotiations regarding the new aircraft order. This last subject has been rattling around for some time now. You will remember Herb Depp appointing Jim King to mastermind a new aircraft purchase. Well, that never got anywhere, although heavy negotiations with manufacturers did happen.

The breakthrough came last September when Jim Johnson obtained consent to go ahead from '260'—slang for Wendt and Nayden, deriving from GECC's address in Stamford—and purchase new aircraft. Since then a team has been working on the order, which is now nearing completion. It will be some 100 aircraft from Boeing and 40 from Airbus, almost all narrow bodied (single aisle), mainly new style Boeing B737-6/7/800s. Billions of dollars—GECC will finance. The story is that with our unbeatable aircraft prices and unbeatable funding costs, we will tear the balls off anyone foolish enough to compete with us. It all sounds horribly familiar. Whatever, the head of marketing has not been as closely involved as he would have liked and is fed up with it, to the point of it being part of the reason for his leaving. It is a real shame, because the organisation had been settling down—no major resignations for a couple of months, the market hardening in our favour.

What else has been happening? No Tony at the 1995 year end holiday party at the Dromoland Castle Hotel, nor Jim King.

At that do, JJ announced that GECAS would meet revised year end figures, as required by GECC. It is difficult to understate the importance of meeting expected annual figures in the GE culture. GE Capital being a conglomerate of businesses, its profit is built up from inputs from various parts of the whole. Each subsidiary or affiliate is expected to come up to individual profit forecasts. Too much profit seems to be nearly as bad as not enough—the point is that the forecast was not stuck to—i.e. management is not fully in control of its business, i.e. there is volatility, i.e. there could be uncertainty, financial shocks. This worries GE's institutional shareholders who look for safe and solid every time. The GE stock price and its rating are paramount. Adherence to annual figures appears to be the yardstick by which the heads of the GE empire judge managements. We made the figures folks, relax for a little bit. Forget the people. We made our figures.

There will be no Cancun this year. The question of a company conference anywhere simply has not come up.

Receivables are now fairly stable around the $100 million mark.

Behind the visible receivables curtain however the old lags, the airlines which have figured on these pages so often go on owing GPA vast amounts of money. Only now these are called restructurings.

The MD-11 based MDC litigation with GPA has recently been settled. It had to go to clear the decks for Project Atlanta.

During 1995, 211 aircraft transactions were closed by GECAS—that is better than one aircraft per working day. Considering the traumas of the year, this is a testament to the remaining marketing department and the recovering aircraft market as the world climbs out of recession.

Patrick is repeating with Project Atlanta his grand effort on Project Rebound. There are many similarities. Atlanta appears to be on track for its spring release to the public. Everything hangs on it for GPA. If Atlanta goes through, this diary will end, for GPA will settle back to being nothing more than the administrative function for the Atlanta vehicle. Patrick will have received his bonuses along with the rest of his senior management. If Project Atlanta fails, then GPA will collapse into administration, I would expect. I will, for the record, set it down. I have though had enough of this.

Tony is now never seen at Shannon, nor his presence felt, just Anne Lee plugging away outside his empty office.

Niall is on top in Shannon, but even he is finding it a testing time, shepherding the Shannon position.

Monday 22 January 1996

GPA's Atlanta project is getting to heart attack stage. *Air Finance Journal* for January gives a good rundown of the situation now prevailing and the structure. The Atlanta SPV is to be known as Airplanes Group. It will acquire 202 jets and 28 turboprops from GPA at an appraised value of $4.5 billion. Of these, 222 aircraft are out on lease to 82 airlines in 40 different countries. Funds to pay for the aircraft will come principally from stock certificates of different classes on public sale in denominations of $100,000, i.e. big time investors.

GPA is due to start marketing the stock about now, but first it has to get the go-ahead from its main bank creditors and shareholder 'creditors'—shareholders with much to lose.

The general feeling is that the refinancing is the only way to go. Without it GPA is doomed. The timing is becoming critical. It is starting to feel like the first IPO all over again, except this time I am removed from significant financial involvement. Patrick, John Tierney and Brian McLoghlin though must be feeling like cats on the proverbial hot tin roof.

Friday 9 February 1996

GPA has put out a press release dated 6 February. A spanner in the works has appeared—it is our old friends PSERS, the retired Pennsylvania schoolteachers. The Fund from Hell is back. *The Irish Times* headline on Wednesday, 7 February, runs: 'GPA faces fresh crisis on refusal of refinance package'. PSERS is refusing to go along with the terms Patrick needs to float Atlanta. PSERS has leverage, ergo it will use it.

Sunday 17 March 1996

Plenty to update. First, Project Atlanta is almost at the finishing tape. The PSERS obstacle has been overcome—again, it had to be. PSERS will be better off today or will have the promise of being so. Meanwhile Atlanta has successfully floated; the $4 billion worth of bonds were oversubscribed! It is the second largest corporate bond issue ever. There have been acres of press coverage, so no need to bore us all again here with the details.

I was in Stamford whilst the sale shenanigans were going on in New York. Patrick's mood was euphoric. I met one of his lieutenants in the Aer Lingus lounge on Thursday night, 14 March, returning to Ireland, tired but extremely happy.

Dennis Stevenson, GPA's chairman, is reported as saying: 'Whoever said this is one of the great Houdini escapes of all time is probably right. . . . This time last week we had $5.5 billion of debt. Now we have put $4 billion of that into a special company.' He also said about the PSERS problem: 'PSERS had a legitimate bargaining position. What we didn't expect was the sheer ferocity of the way they exploited it.'

The thinking is now that GPA, having freed itself from the immediate crush of its debt burden, is more susceptible to having itself bought out by GECC exercising its knockdown purchase option of $65 million—the price honed even more competitively and extended to 2001 as part of the negotiations between the companies which enabled GPA to go ahead with Project Atlanta.

Ironically, GPA now has a cash surplus in excess of $1 billion arising from the sale of the aircraft to Airplanes Group and an ongoing debt of $1.6 billion. It appears GPA is going to buy some aircraft to trade with, using the surplus funds. From the returns of this activity it intends to pay the debt as it falls due and make some profit.

One final thought. GPA must still finish all the novations of the relevant aircraft lease contracts, transferring over to Airplanes Group as lessor all the aircraft in their new portfolio, to complete the project. This needs to happen by month end. This alone has been a mighty task, with GPA hiring several ex-GPA people as consultants to assist. We're all involved making this happen with our customers.

Wednesday 27 March 1996

Norm Liu is the new GECAS head of Sales and Marketing. Structured Finance and Marketing have been merged. When I first heard this, my first thought was that I and my one other London colleague would probably get the push. Living away from Shannon, we now stick out like sore thumbs and the headcount issue presses—a no-brainer as we might once have said. Anyway, so far nothing.

John Flynn is now manager of Special Projects based in his home town—San Francisco.

Jim King is working for his long-time acquaintance and successful aircraft trader, Gunnar Bjorgenson. I am sure he will do well.

At the end of March, Tony severs all connection with GECAS and is leaving his office in GPA House. Anne Lee, his wonderful secretary (I can say that as she was once mine), is being made redundant. There have been no announcements that I could see. End of another era— well, not really. Tony's era ended in effect some time ago when it became clear he and Jim could not stage a comeback within GECAS. Tony is now the respected chairman of Ryanair.

Stamford is the seat of power in GECAS. Within the office there exists an inner *Gestalt* group—I call them the Stamford Mafia—who can make or break you. They come to group feelings about deals, people, whatever. They are arrogant, foul-mouthed and care nothing for the customer. Their god is '260'. I have not earned myself any points with my campaigning on behalf of Laker and Monarch Airlines in separate DC-10-30 deals. So what? Playing life their way could put you into a seriously long queue to get into heaven.

I suppose I ought to note that Fokker, based at Schiphol, has gone irretrievably down the tubes as a manufacturer in its own right. I cannot feel too sorry. It was a flawed management style. They built good aircraft though. Pity they had to bribe some people to take them.

I must be near the end of this saga now. I'm afraid the post November 1993 GPA happenings have not been so fully recorded here because I was in GECAS, but hopefully enough to preserve the chain of events until the final act. Except that it isn't finality. GPA will go on—managing Airplanes Group and now probably making a return to aircraft trading. Its problem is the GECC bargain basement purchase price option hanging over it for the next few years. If GPA becomes desirable, it will be bought by GECC. Patrick and his select band will earn another round of handsome bonuses—enough to retire on—if GE performs. Potential for conflict of interest exists here if GPA's shareholders would be better off with GPA standing alone. I would guess buy-off compromises could be the answer. Another so-called win win position for GECC.

Meanwhile, now that the last strands of Atlanta are coming together, Patrick and his small team already stand to make their hefty Project Atlanta bonuses for having steered GPA across the maelstrom—and good luck to them. The bonus pool is $12 million.

The task Patrick and Dennis Stevenson have just successfully completed looked absolutely insuperable at the end of 1993. But fate is amazing. As it turned out, Operation Rebound was without doubt the very best dress rehearsal Patrick and the team could have had for Project Atlanta.

No one expects the GPA ordinary or 'A' Preference Share value to return however. They went with the GPA IPO in June 1992.

Thursday 28 March 1996

GPA has today issued the following press release:

> 'GPA Group plc ("GPA"), the aircraft leasing company announced the successful closing of the sale of $4.05 billion of Pass Through Certificates by Airplanes Group ("Airplanes") and the repayment, from the proceeds of sale of 229 aircraft to Airplanes, of $2.9 billion of bank debt and certain other secured debt obligations.

> Patrick Blaney, chief executive officer of GPA, said:

> "With the closing of this offering and the quite enormous restructuring task of which this is the culmination, GPA's financial condition has been significantly strengthened, and its debt burden much reduced. This allows GPA to look forward with confidence to the future. GPA will continue to focus on its core business with the objective of maximising the value of its assets and satisfying its remaining debt obligations."'

We have all received the following email from Niall:

> 'I have just had separate calls from Patrick Blaney and John Tierney of GPA to confirm that this long drawn out transaction has definitely been closed this afternoon and especially to thank all those in GECAS who have contributed so much to the success of the project. On behalf of the GECAS Atlanta deal team, I would like to add my appreciation also.'

There can be no doubt that the saving of GPA as a corporation represents a staggering achievement. This time it is a true triumph—for Patrick mainly. Like the *Memphis Belle*, what's left of to hell and back GPA has landed safely, courtesy of a miracle.

Wednesday 3 April

Today I got the push. I am to resign tomorrow. It has not taken Norm

Liu long to sort the two remaining London staff out, as I knew he would—we had become oddballs.

With Tony cutting his last connections with GPA at the end of March and the preservation of GPA completing at the end of March, the reason for this diary had also come to an end. It is as if, like a dying man, I have managed to hold out just long enough to finish my task before expiring. However, as the expiration was not under my control, one really has to wonder at the quite perfect timing of my going.

Thursday 4 April 1996

My telephone has started to ring as long-term colleagues and friends in GPA and GECAS begin to call. Suddenly the world is an even more exciting place. My senses are alive. I am elated to be out of GE, whatever. The next chapter of my life is about to begin. Whatever rewards the future may bring, I will never repeat the profligacy of the GPA money factory years, a lesson like most hard learned. But hey, nice to have experienced some real cash and for that, Tony, thank you, thank you. For the rest, what a terrible shame. I have lived through interesting times. I can see why the Chinese might use the expression as a curse.

Patrick has replied today to a brief note of congratulation I sent him. He says: 'I think that the completion of Project Atlanta in the way in which it was done has proven for once and for all that GPA was a real viable strong business, and that its people, wherever they now reside, are among the very best in the business.'

Chapter 8 ∾

| EPILOGUE

This diary started out as an exercise to capture on paper events leading up to what I believed would be the demise of GPA. I didn't think anyone else would be doing it, and equally it seemed to me that someone ought to. GPA and Tony Ryan were so well thought of throughout Ireland, I knew the general fallout and public interest following on from a collapse could be considerable. The diary might have to chart the fall of a people's hero and 'his' iconic company, if my fears were correct. Well, the worst happened. What I hadn't banked on was the emergence of arguably an even greater hero, to save the day—largely.

The willingness of corporations, institutions and individuals to bind together in complex structures, driven by an inspirational leader to take risks and make profits is well known. What this book illustrates is the corresponding valuable lesson that there is an even greater willingness, when stakes are sufficiently high, to confront, unravel and compromise seemingly insurmountable problems to avoid common disaster—given an inspirational leader. Patrick Blaney, who emerges more or less from nowhere is the real hero of this book and effectively saves GPA twice over by his undoubted corporate heroics. The embodiment of 'cometh the hour, cometh the man', he turned out to be GPA's real Paddy Factor.

Patrick will be the first to say it was teamwork and of course he is right, but exceptional teams need an exceptional leader, and he was it.

In the end, Tony was eclipsed, and his manoeuvrings to slide out of any culpability and ensure his continuity at the highest level were less than edifying to witness. Ultimately, and I suppose happily, he was able to escape across into his personal lifeboat, Ryanair, with his reputation, though battered, ironically kept aloft by the achievements of a subordinate he had once called a traitor.

Further back, on the previous page, I used the word 'largely'. What I mean by this is that for the bulk of the staff of GPA, the saving of GPA in 1996, via Project Atlanta, was almost an irrelevance, although from a sentimental point of view it was of course pleasurable. Why? Because the heart and soul of GPA was its people—that dedicated, intelligent body of men and women that GE found so difficult to handle in the early days of GECAS, such was their loyalty to the ideal of what GPA had been. The key to GPA, from a staff point of view, was the ability and freedom to participate in the success of the company in real, significant ways—via shares and by feeling part of it all. Here was a company in a glamorous, high earning industry, passing on to its employees tangible returns and self-esteem in exchange for superior performance. It was a bargain which suited both sides—board and staff. Everyone benefited. The board, mainly Tony himself in reality, was held in the highest regard for what had already been achieved and for the generous profit-sharing mentality—so rarely found. He may not have been the easiest person to work for, but it was worth it. In GPA, if you observed the pact, staff were set very well for life—financially, socially. It was a career—for most in their own backyard in western Ireland. Sure, there would be downturns, but an expanding GPA was here to stay. What was never in the equation was that the board would be so foolhardy as to risk everything with no contingency plan, just when things were going so well, and then compound a potentially fatal error with poor management. Patrick, superbright, financially talented, forced himself into the breach just in time and, incredibly, saved GPA, but not the staff. He saved the banks, he saved the institutional shareholders, the bondholders, but not staff. True, most went over into GECAS, but it was never the same. The value of our shareholdings had gone, even if the shares themselves had not been repossessed by the banks. Also, GE and GPA were at opposite ends of the corporate spectrum. What we had, in every sense, was lost.

As an employee and shareholder of GPA, I shared in the pain and my dreams were broken too. Employment opportunities such as GPA do not come around too often.

I have not enjoyed being critical, but as it turned out there was at times much to criticise. I have tried to tell it as it seemed to me, at the time it was happening. That contemporaneity must be the value of this account.

Unfortunately, for a while I seemed to become more bitter on paper as the story unfolded. I apologise. I can only ascribe this to my growing feelings that an accurate subtitle to this tale could be 'The Great Escape'. Over a billion dollars lost; many millions more unnecessarily spent; share values wiped out; debts accumulated; careers lost; heartaches caused. No one, it seems, was responsible for anything.

At least nobody can accuse me of hindsight.

POSTSCRIPT

In 2000, after further restructuring and negotiations with GE over the purchase option, Patrick Blaney sold GPA, by this time renamed AerFi, to Amsterdam-based Debis AirFinance, part of the Daimler Chrysler Group. As a result there was a final payout to those who still retained shares in GPA.

It was reported that Tony Ryan made approximately $50 million from the sale.

GLOSSARY OF TERMS

Aerocitra: A GPA Group joint venture set up with Garuda, the State airline of Indonesia, to buy MD-11s, some for operation by Garuda.

Aircraft types (prices, values and descriptions as at 1994)
Airbus
A320 – midsize, 150 seats, twin engine, narrow body, new technology. New $40 million plus.
A310-300 – small widebody, 230 seats, twin engine, medium/long range, new technology. Present value $30 million.
A300 – the first Airbus, medium range, twin, widebody, 300 seats, new technology but ageing. Present value $10 million.
A300-600 – the longer range, larger, newer version.

British Aircraft Corporation
BAC1-11-200/400/500 – obsolete, 70–100 seat, short range, twin.

Boeing
B737-200 – old technology, short/medium range, twin, narrow body, 100–120 seat. Almost as common as a $1 note and just as exchangeable worldwide. A good one $4.5 million.
B737-300/400/500 – new technology, derivatives of the -200, in varying sizes from 100–150 seats. Cost new $30 million plus.
B767-200/300 – medium/long range (long range with ER suffix), widebody, twin, 200–250 seats, new technology.
B747-100/200/300/400 – the original Jumbo jet, 300/400 has extended upper deck, 400 has very long range. Prices vary from under $10 million for a good 100 through $160 million for a new 400.

De Havilland

Dash 8-300 – 50 seat, turboprop, new technology. $12 million.

Fokker

F100 – short/medium range, twin, 100 seats, new technology. $22 million.

Lockheed

L-1011-1/15/100/200/500 Tristar – 3 engine, 300 seat, short/medium/ long range, obsolete. Value of good -500 $17 million, value of good -1 scrap only (Americanese—parting out).

McDonnell Douglas Corporation

DC-8-71 – stretched and re-engined version of original DC-8, 4 engines, longish range, 200 plus seats, bought for conversion to freighter, obsolete except for CFM-56 engines.

DC-9-10/15/30/40 – short/medium range, twin, 80–140 seats, mainly in US domestic use, obsolete. Best value for a good DC-9-30 $3.5m.

MD-80/82/83/87 – midsize, medium range, twin, narrow body, just about Stage III noise compliant, but obsolete in reality. For a good MD-83 $12 million.

DC-10-10/15/30 – widebody, 3 engine, medium and long range, 300 seat, obsolete. A good one $17 million.

MD-11 – longer, newer than DC-10-30, with sexy winglets, otherwise indistinguishable. New $110 million plus.

ALPS: Aircraft Linked Portfolio Securitisation. A picked group of aircraft with leases attached is sold to a group of investors, to realise for the seller the capital value of the aircraft initially and to provide management fees thereafter for looking after the whole set-up for the duration.

AMR: American Airlines's holding company.

AOC: Air Operators Certificate. The licence to fly commercially.

AOG: Aircraft On Ground. Anathema. An aircraft not earning money for a lessor. Also in airline parlance an aircraft with a technical problem, sufficient to stop it being flown.

Air Tara: The technical, AOC holding arm of GPA Group. Responsible for GPA fleet maintenance, engineering and lessee technical monitoring.

CATIC: Chinese aviation construction company.

CCF: Corporate Credit Facility (previously CDF). The main source of finance for GPA's aircraft acquisitions. Funds came from a consortium of 138 banks.

Chapter 11: Section of the US Bankruptcy Code. Enables bankrupt companies to stop paying debts and continue in business. A good scheme for the bankrupt, much abused by US airlines.

GECC: General Electric Capital Corporation. The financial services arm of the world's largest corporation.

GECAS: The company set up by GECC in 1993 to run the combined operations of GECC's existing aviation business together with aircraft previously managed by GPA.

GPAA: GPA Airbus. The GPA /Airbus/PWA/Banque Paribas JV set up in 1987 to buy and lease out new Airbus aircraft, mainly A320s. Originally headed by Peter Swift.

GPA Capital: An internal division of GPA Group responsible for financial services, securitisations, ALPS, *ad hoc* financings etc. Its sales of GPA aircraft were essential to GPA's profits.

GPAF: GPA Fokker 100. The GPA /Fokker/Mitsubishi JV set up in 1986 to buy and lease out up to 100 new F100 aircraft. Originally headed by the author.

GPA Jetprop: The internal GPA turboprop marketing department. Initially a JV, GPAJ bought new Dash 8 and ATR aircraft for leasing out. Originally headed by Niall Greene.

GPA Leasing: An internal division of GPA Group. Responsible for the operating leasing and marketing of GPA's aircraft and contracted third party owners.

IPO: Initial Public Offering. The ill-fated GPA Group share flotation, called initial because there were to have been more.

IAL: Irish Aerospace. The GPA/MDC/Mitsui JV set up to buy and lease out MDC aircraft, mainly MD-83s. The first GPA new aircraft JV. Originally headed by Jim King.

IATA: International Air Transport Association. The principal airline trade association.

ILFC: International Lease Finance Corporation. GPA's principal competitor, based in Century City, Los Angeles.

Lessee: In GPA terms, an airline leasing an aircraft.

Lessor: The person from whom an aircraft is leased.

Letter of Intent: A non-legally binding agreement setting out the principal commercial terms of a lease contract to be signed within one month. Signing an LOI plus payment of a refundable initial deposit takes an aircraft off the market for that time.

MAS: Malaysian Airlines System. The national airline of Malaysia.

Maintenance Reserves: Money paid monthly by lessees, based on hours flown in the previous month, to pay for future maintenance for or replacement of specific items—airframe, engines, undercarriage, auxiliary power unit—accumulated to guard against lessee insolvency.

Mezzanine: A euphemistic term of art. It represents that layer of debt between theoretically safe senior debt carrying a lower rate of return and high-risk junk debt at the other end of the scale.

Operating Lease: Basically an aircraft rental, where the period of rental does not constitute the entire life of the aircraft, so that there may be successive operating leases in the life of an aircraft. Typically when a lease expires the aircraft is returned to the lessor for immediate re-leasing.

Operation Rebound: GPA's corporate effort to rescue itself from bankruptcy in the aftermath of the failed IPO.

Operation Rebound 2: The continuation of Operation Rebound after Patrick Blaney was put in charge of it.

Project Atlanta: GPA's scheme for final salvation, led by Patrick Blaney and Dennis (now Lord) Stevenson.

The Paddy Factor: Tony's expression post-IPO to explain possible reticence on the part of the outside world towards investing in an Irish company—his point being that GPA was light years away from traditional Irish caricatures.

Trading Floor: GPA Marketing's control room in Shannon, where all the information from the field is sent and from where day to day information, guidance and instruction is given to support the travelling executives.

INDEX